P9-CAE-602

MORE PRAISE FOR *WHERE STUFF COMES FROM*

"Penetrating insights and details abound ... Highly recommended."
—*Choice*

"Manages to answer questions that have puzzled me for a lifetime."
—Spider Robinson, *Science*

"Could work to end blame-the-consumer guilt-mongering in the popular discourse."
—*Publishers Weekly*

"A witty and surprising voyage."
—Minnesota Public Radio

"*Where Stuff Comes From* is MUST reading for anyone interested in the power of the manufactured world."
—James B. Twitchell, author of *Living It Up: Our Love Affair with Luxury*

"Superb, a witty and verbally pyrotechnical book. *Where Stuff Comes From* is deeply subversive and revolutionizes our thinking about consumerism. Molotch criticizes the shallow puritanism of anti-consumerist orthodoxy from Veblen to Jameson for its 'bias against exuberance.'"
—Jules Lubbock, author of *The Tyranny of Taste*

"Molotch's spicy and incisive anthropology of design brilliantly illuminates the social, aesthetic and material dynamics that give us new consumer goods...He shows that social theorists and activists need to better understand how design works, because this is the stage where pressures for more environmentally sound and socially equitable production and distribution can work most effectively."
—Francesca Bray, Professor of Social Anthropology, University of Edinburgh

WHERE STUFF COMES FROM

How Toasters, Toilets, Cars, Computers,
and Many Other Things
Come to Be as They Are

HARVEY MOLOTCH

q + a : 65,

Routledge
NEW YORK AND LONDON

First Routledge hardback edition, 2003
First Routledge paperback edition, 2005

Published in 2005 by
CRC Press
Routledge
Taylor & Francis Group
6000 Broken Sound Parkway NW, Suite 300
Boca Raton, FL 33487-2742
270 Madison Avenue
New York, NY 10016

Published in Great Britain by
Routledge
Taylor & Francis Group
2 Park Square
Milton Park, Abingdon
Oxon OX14 4RN

© 2005 by Taylor & Francis Group, LLC
Routledge CRC Press is an imprint of Taylor & Francis Group

No claim to original U.S. Government works
Printed in the United States of America on acid-free paper
10 9 8 7 6 5 4 3 2 1

International Standard Book Number-10: 0-415-95042-2 (Softcover)
International Standard Book Number-13: 978-0-41595-042-8 (Softcover)
Library of Congress Card Number 2003001191

This book contains information obtained from authentic and highly regarded sources. Reprinted material is quoted with permission, and sources are indicated. A wide variety of references are listed. Reasonable efforts have been made to publish reliable data and information, but the author and the publisher cannot assume responsibility for the validity of all materials or for the consequences of their use.

No part of this book may be reprinted, reproduced, transmitted, or utilized in any form by any electronic, mechanical, or other means, now known or hereafter invented, including photocopying, microfilming, and recording, or in any information storage or retrieval system, without written permission from the publishers.

For permission to photocopy or use material electronically from this work, please access www.copyright.com (http://www.copyright.com/) or contact the Copyright Clearance Center, Inc. (CCC) 222 Rosewood Drive, Danvers, MA 01923, 978-750-8400. CCC is a not-for-profit organization that provides licenses and registration for a variety of users. For organizations that have been granted a photocopy license by the CCC, a separate system of payment has been arranged.

Trademark Notice: Product or corporate names may be trademarks or registered trademarks, and are used only for identification and explanation without intent to infringe.

Library of Congress Cataloging-in-Publication Data

Molotch, Harvey Luskin.
    Where stuff comes from : how toasters, toilets, cars, computers, and many other things come to be as they are / by Harvey Molotch.
        p. cm.
Includes bibliographical references and index.
    ISBN 0-415-94400-7 (hbk.) – ISBN 0-415-95042-2 (pbk.)
1. Engineering—Popular works. I. Title.

TA148.M65 2003
    620—dc21   2003001191

Taylor & Francis Group
is the Academic Division of T&F Informa plc.

Visit the Taylor & Francis Web site at
http://www.taylorandfrancis.com

and the CRC Press Routledge Web site at
http://www.crcpressroutledge-ny.com

To Jack and the memory of Joe.
They saved me more than dough.

CONTENTS

CHAPTER 5

Venues and Middlemen

CHAPTER 6

Place in Product

CHAPTER 7

Corporate Organization and the Design Big Thing

CHAPTER 8

Moral Rules

PREFACE

Where I Come From

I was born into the retail car business on one side and the home appliance world on the other, strategically placed to enjoy each new feature of the post–World War II prosperity. I caressed the taillights of my mother's Oldsmobile "88" and experimented endlessly with the Webcor stereo in my room. I used both to win friends and influence people. In late adolescence, caught by the winds blowing what would later be called "the sixties," I rebelled with a small foreign car and a better high-fidelity system. I used my mouth as well as my brain to bite some of the hands that fed me. Active in the New Left, I critiqued American materialism and denounced what I took to be its foreign policy reflection in the immorality of the Vietnam War.

Right about the war, I was less right about the goods. I now think the zeal to condemn people's products was and remains both bad political strategy as well as intellectually naïve. This book tries to work it all out, and I hope it does so in a way that sheds light beyond the vagaries of my own biographical tensions. One may not be able to go home again—Webcor, Oldsmobile, and much else are gone—but the wandering can turn up some things that are new and perhaps, even for others, interesting.

How we desire, produce, and discard the durables of existence helps form who we are, how we connect to one another, and what we do to the earth. In addition to ordering intimacies, these urges and actions influence the way peoples across large stretches of time, cultures, and geographies align, exchange, and conflict. I put aside both critics' simple denunciations and merchandisers' unyielding boasts to learn where, in both the large sense and in the small details, modern products come from. A good scan may even help make for better goods and more worthwhile lives.

Acknowledgments

I thank Howard Becker and Mitchell Duneier for making my problems their problems; they gave me all. Sharon Zukin provided detailed critique that greatly strengthened the project as did Donald Lamm and William Twining. Francesca Bray, Gilles Fauconnier, Samantha MacBride, Daniel Miller, Linda Nochlin, and Naomi Schneider read individual chapters (or more) and responded with indispensable advice. Jonathan Ritter was my generous and proficient photographer, fact checker and all-round support system. Curtis Sarles ably combed the entire manuscript for last troubles and taught me website miracles. Among friends and colleagues providing important details, good cheer, and funny stories, I point fingers at Eva Cantarella, Ruth Cohen, Stan Cohen, Tony Giddens, Debra Friedland, Roger Friedland, Philip Haddock, Dianne Hagaman, Natalie Jeremijenko, Guido Martinotti, Susie Orbach, Joe Schwartz, Serena Vicari, Nina Wakeford, and Arlene Zurcher. Karen Shapiro did my toasters; Ilene Kalish was my bright light at Routledge, ever at the intelligent ready. The late Deirdre Boden was a comrade who talked to me about everything.

I appreciate financial and logistical aid from the William and Flora Hewlett Foundation "Hewlett Fellows" grant #98-2124 to the Center for Advanced Study in the Behavioral Sciences; the Rockefeller Foundation Bellagio Residency Program, and a London School of Economics Centennial Professorship. I will always be grateful for a career's worth of support from my esteemed colleagues at the University of California, Santa Barbara; I also owe a debt to new associates at New York University. The patience of so many informants from within the design profession generated both information and pleasure.

I pay special homage to my life partner, Glenn Wharton, who put me on to bibliographic sources, fresh ideas, and the presence of art, crumbling and otherwise, in all that we do.

CHAPTER 1

Lash-Ups: Goods and Bads

Where does it come from, this vast blanket of things—coffeepots and laptops, window fittings, lamps and fence finials, cars, hat pins, and hand trucks—that make up economies, mobilize desire, and so stir up controversy? The question leads to others because nothing stands alone—to understand any one thing you have to learn how it fits into larger arrays of physical objects, social sentiments, and ways of being. In the world of goods, as in worlds of any other sort, each element is just one interdependent fragment of a larger whole.[1]

Like a toaster. It does not just sear bread, but presupposes a pricing mechanism for home amperage, government standards for electric devices, producers and shopkeepers who smell a profit, and people's various sentiments about the safety of electrical current and what a breakfast, nutritionally and socially, ought to be. Any particular toaster also contains the trends in fine and popular art that give it a particular look and texture of operation, including—in many models—a human satisfaction in the sound and sight of the pop-up moment. There are merchandise critics, trade associations, advertising media as well as the prior range of goods and hardware within which it must fit—wall outlets for its plugs, bread slicers calibrated for a certain width, and jams that need a crusty base. There is a global system that yields a toaster's raw materials, governments that protect its patents, a labor force to work at the right price, and a dump ready to absorb it in the end.

Somehow all the elements come together more or less at the same time and in a given geographic place that operates not just as a container, but as a crucible that yields up one particular product and not another. Miami has produced no toasters at all, but Mt. Airy, North Carolina, became, during its day in the sun, the "officially designated Toaster Capital of the World."[2] Toasters are indispensable in U.S. and British households; almost no Italians have them. In terms of timing, it will not do for one needed element (like jam) to be accessible in say, the mid-nineteenth century, but then to disappear just when another element, say electric outlets, are in place. So with other products: it may not work out if the trim of a dress arrives even a moment after the designer has left the room; a computer program fragment absent at the wrong moment is death to the new software.

Somehow, everything must—and this is the crucial idea—"lash-up"[3] such that the otherwise loose elements adhere; only then can there be a new thing in the world. Like a plant variety in the forest or a microbe among the animal species, a product comes about and stays around—sometimes for a relatively short time and sometimes for epochs—to the degree that the diverse elements that make it up continue to be. Electrical outlets in the kitchen make the toaster appliance useful just as the reality of the appliance incites builders to put in outlets near the kitchen table. The Anglo-Saxon support for toast continuously reinforces the existence of toasters just as such an eating-appliance habit helps mark off a particular people as distinctive. Not just having a taste for toast, people *enroll*, as sociologist Bruno Latour would say,[4] in the toaster project. Their commitment becomes evident when something goes wrong (no bread? no outlet?), yielding immediate acts of restoration.

Individuals enroll, organizations enroll, and even—in a sense—objects enroll. Objects too have a life in them, maybe not as in a "Toy Story" movie when dolls and action figures leap off shelves and discuss their fates, but in the way they sustain social practices just as those practices sustain them. Any search for the source of stuff must therefore look for this continuous mutual stroking between object and action that makes a thing "interactively stabilized."[5] It also means a hunt for breakdown—for how elements stop working together, prompting at least a tweak in the new model if not the disappearance of a product altogether. Change too is normal, maybe even inevitable. Tracing the connections in products can show how the social and the material combine to make, depending on circumstance, both change and stability happen in the world.

There have been other approaches toward figuring out where stuff comes from. Teachers instruct schoolchildren that stuff was "invented"—usually by means of a genius like Thomas Edison. The great man, through inspiration and perspiration, just does it. But even Edison depended on others' work; he was part of a 14–person team when he "did" the lightbulb. More profoundly, he was always dependent on the surrounding web of political and cultural practices that made each of his innovations possible.

Less oriented toward a genius or even individuals at all, some see new stuff evolving through a great march of ever-improving artifacts, more or less driven by their own internal logic. One good gadget begets the next in just the way science knowledge is supposed to gather up. Engineer Henry Petroski—the rightly esteemed expert on "the evolution of useful things"—holds to this model.[6] In economists' view of the world, Petroski's formulation makes sense. Markets "demand" stuff and that is what companies produce—optimal stuff, in fact. New stuff comes into being precisely because better ways are continuously being found to satisfy bidders' tastes. Sovereign consumers place their orders and the output is what we see in the stores. But tastes and improvements cannot be taken as self-evident, and neither can their origins. What is or is not "useful" and what is or is not a "taste" also arise from the complex mixtures of enrollments and intersections always behind everything.

There are critical scholars who complain about goods as nothing but bads. Sympathetic as I am with such grumbling, blanket denunciations are as overly simplistic as the product boosters' ceaseless cheers. They too efface the production system's actual operations. The book titles of Vance Packard's best-selling trilogy summarize the complaining quite well. *The Hidden Persuaders* (1957) focused on corporate capture of consumer minds; *The Status Seekers* (1959) illustrated how ordinary people were made vulnerable to the manipulations, and *The Waste Makers* (1960) used the car industry to portray the needless destruction that resulted. These popular books echoed more sophisti-cated analyses by the Frankfurt School of Marxian critical theorists founded in Germany between the world wars. Such thinkers were responding to the fact that labor did not revolt or even support trade unions with any consistency. Instead, workers wanted to consume material goods and experience commercial amusement. Through capi-talist capacity to enthrall with mostly useless and shoddy artifacts, the theory went, people sublimated their more rational socialist urge into consumption and the dream of goods. Consumption thus signals alien-ation, as people substitute dead material for control over their working conditions and the goal of more meaningful social lives.[7] To bring all this about, producers must use gimmickry like planned obsolescence, clever advertising, and other seductions to deliberately foster dissatis-factions and build markets for still more superfluous outputs. For their part in this dreary, self-mortifying pursuit, consumers compete against one another in a game, as Thorstein Veblen put it, of "conspicuous con-sumption."[8] Once others gain access to what you have, new stuff has to be acquired in an endless cycle of unhappy waste.[9]

The bad news runs on. Each of the world's religions sponsors its own version of asceticism, reflected in the lives attributed to its priests as well as in doctrine and ceremony. These merge, sometimes in explicit ways into contemporary environmentalist thought, with the defense of nature intrinsic to doctrines of morality and transcendental responsibility. The "throwaway society" endangers God's plan and the natural eco-system. Corporations tend to create goods using the most esoteric chemical compounds because they are the easiest to patent. They also do not break down in nature and have unknown effects on natural systems.[10] Product development thus has "a logic of diges-tion"[11] that is neither righteous nor healthy. In a feminist variation, exemplified by the traveling gallery show of home appliances called "Mechanical Brides," merchandise "improvements" strengthen the chains that bind women to housework—with artiness (like the pastel washer) as part of the trickery.[12]

One way or the other, stuff produced and consumed by most peo-ple has been interesting to social thinkers as demonstrating a danger-ous means of production and a system that misleads or dupes. A poisonous vine, the critiques imply, can produce only noxious fruit, and, thinking in the other direction, such terrible stuff can come only from a pernicious system.

Ironically enough, a good deal of the basis for such critique comes from the mouths of producers themselves. The term "planned obsolescence" was coined not by a Marxist critic, but by the industrial design pioneer Brooks Stevens, who thought it a virtue to implant "the desire to own something a little newer, a little better, a little sooner than is necessary."[13] Norman Bel Geddes, another important product developer, said he wanted to stir up a "cupidity and longing to possess the goods."[14] In a 1937 reflection, a New York ad agency executive urged his colleagues to inject "a little fear in advertising . . . fear in women of being frumps, fear in men of being duds."[15] A prominent business leader urged his colleagues forward with a call for "creative waste."[16] The adulatory business press repeats corporations' visions of themselves as intelligent, effective, and powerful, with richly persuasive techniques to manipulate consumers and build demand.

The specter of a manipulative corporate hold over needs and desires is thus not a fantasy coming from nowhere. But among any group of people, there will be many voices saying all sorts of things, however inconsistent with one another. And even when they all do speak alike, that does not mean they know what they are talking about. Even right before the Great Depression as well as before the more recent collapse of the Internet boom, industrialists were still talking bullish. Businesspeople's wishful thinking or bravado should not be mistaken for empirical reality. It just is not that easy for the corporate apparatus to fool all of the people all of the time. It takes some real effort, as I will try to show, to beat out one's competitors and develop a commodity that will not soon end up in the dustbin of business history.

Critics do accept, even celebrate certain kinds of goods—things that apparently do not arise from corporate cunning. Handcrafted material, especially when thought to emanate from indigenous peoples' spiritual urges, transcends evils of conspicuous consumption, planned obsolescence, and techniques of domination. Also prized are goods touched by art-historical and intellectual pedigree, like products linked to the Bauhaus school of art and design—goods consecrated for enduring functional beauty. More recently, there has been appreciation for merchandise modified by the less powerful, like low-rider cars among Chicano youth who "create the car as a site of resistance" or goods inverted in use, as when teens wear oversize pants or decrepit U.S. military garb.[17]

Rather than exceptions to the goods systems, I think, handmade creations, "aftermarket" customizing, and making things useful are all part of it. Handicrafts shift in and out of popularity much as machine-made goods. Diverse "outside" forces influence indigenous artifacts even in remote places. Bauhaus stuff represents, in my view, just another style—a judgment in no way intended to belittle the talent that created it. Similarly, when those from below alter goods after purchase they act in ways quite like the affluent. Wearing underpants as outerwear is more like stretching a limo than meets the eye. Besides marking difference for their respective users, such aftermarket adaptations become immediate stimuli for new products, tailored to the newly evident tastes. With a sharp eye toward innovators, deviants, and first-adopters, companies respond to what folks do.

I hold off on judging what is a good or bad product and certainly offer no expert opinion of what is good design. But I will be trying to show just how one product possibility takes hold compared to another, opening the opportunity perhaps to then know how it really could have been different. What I hope to avoid throughout is making common cause with those who condemn the lack of quality and individuation in what people seem to want. Though not oblivious to the dangers of goods, I bracket the specifically destructive tendencies of modern markets. Too much judgmental artillery has made it hard to see the artifacts through the smoke, much less touch them, turn them over, look inside, and ask questions about how they came to be and how they fit in to lives and economies. "The materialists are not interested in the material," anthropologist Francesca Bray succinctly remarks about so many past analyses of goods.[18]

Related to my agnostic strategy, I interchangeably use terms like "stuff," "commodities," "artifacts," "things," "products," "merchandise," and "goods" despite their differing ideological and intellectual nuances. Among the multiple forces at work in determining stuff are elements that can be found in almost any economic or social system. Figuring out what those might be, including the search for thrills, distinction, and solidarity, may help us disentangle the predicaments of our own time.

The Anthropology of Consumption

Whatever its antiquarian flaws, classical anthropology still has much to teach. It may be that prior generations of ethnographers were guilty of uncritically using their own cultures' assumptions as a basis for understanding and judging those who were unfamiliar—"othering" them, as we now can say. But the visitors to exotic places did treat material and nonmaterial aspects of life as together making up their subject matter. A culture, anthropologist Robert Redfield said, consists of "shared understandings made manifest in act and artifact."[19] As a matter of routine, such notions motivated ethnographers to study goods as a route into the whole social world. The spirit was empirical and, at least compared to those doing goods analysis among modern peoples, often conducted with a lighter load of theoretical baggage. At their best, scholars examined the actual procedures—the "deeply embedded operational sequences"[20]—including the technical, functional, spiritual, and artistic elements that enter in at each phase of history of a people and in the making of a single artifact.

We can advance an understanding of the analogous contemporary process by working through the details of goods, thinking of them as playing a more or less similar role in lives today as they did in pre-capitalist eras. Douglas and Isherwood's original—and largely unheeded—call for a contemporary "anthropology of consumption" rests upon such presumed continuities with pre-modern settings. "Consumption," then as now they cogently argue, "is the very arena in which culture is fought over and licked into shape."[21] "Consumption uses goods to make firm and visible a particular set of judgments in the fluid process of classifying persons and events," with goods acting as "markers" of social location and collective pasts and futures.[22] Decisions about what precisely to make and acquire, and when, where, and how to do it involve "moral judgments about what a man is, what a woman is, how a man ought to treat his aged parents . . . how he himself should grow old, gracefully or disgracefully, and so on."[23]

In her analysis of some home furnishings in late imperial China (seventeenth through nineteenth centuries), Bray points to such things as the marital bed, the chair (an idea imported from foreigners), woven fabrics, and most especially the household stove as each embodying relations of gender, nation, and kinship. "The Stove God was as much a symbol of family unity as the ancestral tablets" (there were also "stove scriptures").[24] Even among the poor and under conditions in which extended kin shared other aspects of dwelling space, every family (even when headed by brothers) had its own stove, imperative given the larger role the appliance played in situating individuals within the cosmos.[25] The orientation to home furnishings as embedded in larger meanings parallels attitudes toward the house itself, including its major elements of architectural form, dimensions, and siting. Chinese houses have, in Bray's phrase, an "invisible architecture" that was made explicit in imperial China but that remains—and here I move toward my modern application—as an implicit feature of design and consumption routines more generally. There are tacit "rules," or at least sensibilities, in contemporary life that determine the social meanings that surround a thing's acquisition and use—who has rights to sit where and on what occasion, or to adopt which posture on what kind of goods. People work their physicality and "furnishings" as a cultural ensemble of their time and setting. In the extreme, they deliberately deform their bodies to meld with their merchandise. Kayapo men of Brazil install large ornamental wooden plates in their mouths to hugely stretch their lips; the Ndebele women of South Africa elongate their necks with braces that gradually push their shoulder bones down several inches. Ear piercing, foot binding, diaphragm constricting, and breast cinching are other examples of reworking bodies—women's bodies in most cases—into larger ensembles of goods using makeup, jewelry, tools, and clothes.

The "identity work" of goods does not occur in a single instance of consumption, nor even at particularly important rites of passage, although some happenings and acquisition events may carry special significance. Instead, identities and consumption constitute one another through routines of daily acquisition and continuous use.

George Rodger, Young Masai N'dito in Ceremonial Dress, *1979.*
©*Estate of George Rodger.*

"The bulk of provisioning," Daniel Miller writes of buying goods at a shopping center, is connected to "an ongoing relationship, an underlying constancy complemented by a mood, a compromise, a smile, a punishment gesture, a comfort, all the minutiae that make up the constantly changing nuances of a social relationship."[26] Put more succinctly, "Objects are social relations made durable."[27]

In displaying their consumption aspirations and accomplishments, individuals exhibit to one another and confirm for themselves that they belong to particular groups. For gay men according to ethnographer Frank Mort, specific consumption habits—"clone" clothing and home decorating materials—were intrinsic to the formation of a distinctive community. For gay men, "consumption goods guaranteed effective participation in a new society. They also provided the conditions of freedom to 'be oneself.' . . . Consumer rituals and a contemporary sexual lifestyle were understood to be inextricably linked."[28] Mundane heterosexual toaster choice can also help realize a particular consumption tribe—based on ethnicity (bagel-wide slot), economic class (the Dual-it CPB-2, which sells for more than $200), or some more subtle aspect of subcommunity (like the retro models now favored by "fashion-forward" consumers).

The specific "feeling" an object gives off helps to constitute what indeed it *is* in social terms. Objects gain sentiment from accumulated social and physical use, worn surfaces in certain places and sedimented odors of specific peoples and their routines. Among the Trobriand Islanders, continuous exchange of beads and other decorative objects created physical wear that made palpable the large number of hands through which they had circulated, thus binding peoples together across large distances and over long stretches of time.[29] So it is with contemporary goods. People wash their jeans, buff their cars. Through physical handling as well as mental manipulation, "usage develops the physiognomy of an object; contact with its possessor puts into it resources of expressiveness."

Marcel Proust was not the only modern observer to find redolent "information" in his mother's perfume, the cakes served to him or the wallpaper of his room. The objects of his life could never be adequately represented as particular brands or commercial design patterns.

Instead they had meaning through the mutually reinforcing details that he—and, to a degree, he alone—could sense. So it is that every object, and each aspect of every object, is rich with meaning and affect, however demeaned as "fetish" for both tribal and modern peoples.[30] Sometimes, and in ways inexplicable to those who experience it, the "charge" can be especially strong, calling forth social-psychological associations that move the observer. The strength of the charge also depends, of course, on life stage and other circumstances. A teenager's first car carries more magic than a professor's final Volvo. A gown for the ball means something different than pants for work. But even ordinary things can take on elements of the "secular sublime"[31] in their ability to order social arrangements and one's place within them. By drawing on these meanings artists can excite passions by putting mundane objects to work in still life, collage, or as theatrical stage prop. The urinal that Duchamp installed in an art gallery could shock not just because it was a common manufactured item, but also because he was juxtaposing that appliance's polluting connotations with a high culture setting.

At the most profound level, artifacts do not just give off social significations but make meanings of any sort possible. That a urinal can be assumed to be for peeing, full stop, is a bedrock social agreement that Duchamp trades on to do his mischief. Given the inherent ambiguity of all reality and the nagging suspicion that we always exist on the edge of existential chaos, objects work to hold meanings more or less still, solid, and accessible to others as well as to one's self. They form the tangible basis of a world that people can take to be a world in common, things to be taken as "real" in an agreed-upon working consensus. The presence of goods helps anchor consciousness against the social vertigo of living in a world of random and dreadfully unsteady meanings.[32] Having a toaster, we all implicitly agree, is a reasonable way to make breakfast, not a pillow or an artwork or merely a constellation of meaningless sensory inputs. Treating a toaster as a breakfast appliance and acting toward it as such helps suspend the potential for chaotic doubt. The physical existence of the toaster and the circumscribed technique of operating it help make our world possible. We can ignore that the toaster can come in a variety of different styles, shapes, modes of oper-

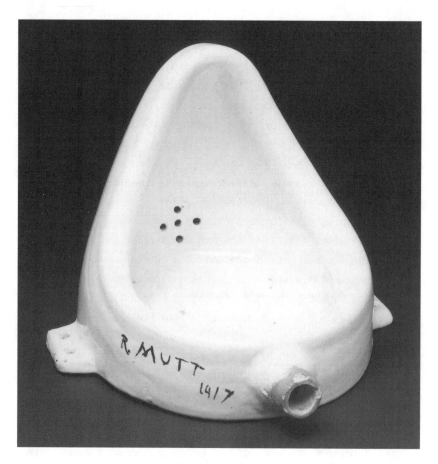

"The Fountain" 1917
Marcel Duchamp, Fountain (Second Version), 1950. ©Philadelphia Museum of Art:
Gift (by exchange) of Mrs. Herbert Cameron Morris; ©Artists Rights Society (ARS),
New York/ADAGP, Paris/Estate of Marcel Duchamp.

ation, and depends on so many other social and technical elements that
maybe it does not so clearly exist as a clear and separate thing at all. We
can bracket the fact that toasters are used for things like pizza or waf-
fles, or exist on the arbitrary judgment that toast is something that is
worthwhile enough to keep in our world, even though it is irrelevant to
other worlds (like that of the Italians). By treating the toaster as "simply so," we reassure one another that we see the world in a similar way,
that we are sane and that there is a stable reality "out there."

Now we have a first and fundamental answer to our question of where stuff comes from. Goods provide a basis, in a number of different ways including their use, for there to be a sense of social reality. They help us be sane.

In addition to the intrinsic connection it makes between the social and the artifact, classical anthropology has another idea worth taking on board in the modern context. Art and spirituality are endemic to economic activity, rather than superfluous or in opposition to it. In anthropological treatments, artistic expressions of all sorts, including various aesthetic motifs, simultaneously reflect and constitute the very nature of the culture, including how it comes to be productive. Scholars take the "decorative life" very seriously indeed. Speaking of Iatmul (New Guinea) people's relation to their domestic equipment, Gell says "the decoration, which is distinctive, binds the lime-container to its owner in a most intimate fashion; it is less a possession than a prosthesis, a bodily organ acquired via manufacture and exchange rather than by biological growth."[33] People work to decorate but also decorate to work. That is, in expressing themselves artistically, they find a motivation to make things happen and in that same way tools become more usable. From this comes food and other means of sustenance.

To be sure, one can go too far with art, treating it as about the only thing one needs to understand a culture. Some have complained of archaeologists who, in too facile a way, use motifs, colors, and forms of pots and baskets to deduce the underlying meanings, structures, and processes of the culture. Dubbed "ceramic sociology" by detractors, this approach substitutes access to decoration for real ethnographic evidence.[34] Though it makes some sense when other kinds of evidence are lost to history,[35] this approach surely is not viable for a contemporary anthropology of consumption. No matter what the circumstance, there is only a loose coupling between any aspect of a given artifact and the rest of a culture. One needs to know, for any given piece, just how it came to be, in material and social terms, over the life of a craftsperson and over the life of the people in which the maker lived. In other words, we need to know its social and material linkages, or *chaines operatoires* as one school of French archaeologists call it.[36] One must go beyond the surface of a piece to examine the decisions that went into making it,

13

including the constraints imposed by available technologies, gender relations, and other aspects of social organization.[37] Too much of the analysis of contemporary production and consumption resembles ceramic sociology. Reflecting a tendency inherited from the Frankfurt School of an earlier era, but much elaborated in postmodern theory, analysts grab the surface features of an appliance, a Disney attraction, a video game, or a hotel lobby and declare it a "text." Scholars then "read" the larger patterns beneath. From the motif of Mickey Mouse at Times Square one can deduce a shallowness to urban life; by looking at a fantastical piece of postmodern hotel architecture one understands how society has become mired in illusion; by watching people's zeal for goods with designer labels, we can read people's insecurity with their own identities. Such analytical gossiping cannot substitute for searching out the social evolution and detailed practices that stand behind the tangible outcomes.

Apart from methodological problems, the mistakes in such readings arise, I think, from a bias against exuberance and other human activity that is not practical in a narrow sense. The critics always seem so dour, upset that people under capitalism are having fun or are otherwise behaving in an "irrational" way. So much scholarship, indeed the very heart of classic sociological theory, treats post-tribal and post-medieval societies as virtually defined by the break with spiritual motivation, communal sentiment, and sensuality. Indeed, this sundering with a romantic, undisciplined, or mystic-inclined past, so the big story goes, is the reason there could be modernization at all. In explaining the rise of capitalism through Protestant religiosity, Max Weber invoked the Calvinist version of rational and individualistic striving. Capitalism could happen because there finally came a religion whose God moved off stage so people could, with rational single-mindedness, devote themselves to material achievement. It is a religion that works because it gets spirituality (and sensuality) out of the way, substituting the denatured spirit of capitalism for transcendental glory. Even critics of capitalism, Marx most famously, seem to accept the goodness of the rationality it claimed for itself.

One way or the other, modernism is set up as an inversion of all that has come before. Whether in studies of development dynamics in poor countries or anxiety about school behavior or the factory floor, evidence of the aesthetic or the spiritual (or the frivolous or the intoxicating) is noticed as a production distraction, ephemeral to the serious matters of life. The value of sensuality or fun at work, and the idea that real goods can come from them, have thus been a hard sell, both on the left and right. Social theorist Daniel Bell, reflecting a common view, juxtaposes "play, fun, display, and pleasure" as antithetical to "virtue of achievement, defined as doing and making."[38] For those on the left, omnipresent alienation is supposed to be a growing scourge helping to ready the workforce for revolt. The idea that work contains sensual pleasures is counter-intuitive and hence unrecognized. On the right, too, work is drudgery, which is why it becomes necessary to motivate dutiful labor with money or by promising eventual leisure—if not on earth, then at least in heaven. Although gestures toward creativity on the shop floor and even allowance for a little fun now creeps into management talk,[39] behavior not clearly relevant to the bottom line mostly meets with skeptical anxiety.

Just how, in the contemporary world, can we imagine aesthetics, fun and spirituality as entering into goods given all the resistance to seeing it there? Again, we need to look carefully, with a wide enough scan to consider amusement along with the other inputs into production processes—including, of course, the pain and suffering that many do indeed experience.

THE DYNAMICS OF CHANGE AND STABILITY

Allowing fun and expressivity into the production picture delivers, as one of the first payoffs, some insight into the problem of how and why goods change compared with how and why they do not. Besides growing anthropological evidence that there has always been more change than meets the contemporary eye, a theme for a later chapter, there are basic features of human cognition and spirit that both limit and encourage changes in the material world. Tendencies toward both constancy and change have profound roots; the specific kinds of goods that come to be derive from how these tendencies are dealt with at a particular time or place.

Let's look first at the fact that things seem to always keep changing. Too easily dismissed as superfluous "fashion," change is driven by built-in social motors and need not be prompted by outside marketeers. In some realms of changing goods, there are no marketing mechanisms at all. One is the illicit drug industry, a huge part of the world economy as well as a major source of opposition from authorities. Drug use seems to have its own fashion dynamic as various substances gain and lose popularity. Although government efforts do have an effect on price and availability, there seems to be an internal autonomy that determines, for example, that a hallucinogenic like LSD should lose out to Ecstasy among the comparable population segment of a later generation. Similarly, among a different group, the appeal of heroin in the 1950s and '60s gave way to crack in the late 1980s and '90s. All advertising—"just say no" campaigns—runs against these substances, yet they rise and fall with little reference to the anti-merchandising efforts, even "war," waged against them.[40] Similar fads and fashions arise in linguistic patterns, especially among youth, who pick up, disseminate, and then abandon phrases, styles of intonation, and body kinetics in ways that cannot be explained either by commercial exploitation or government activity. Fashion comes from somewhere deep.

Sociologist Stanley Lieberson documents the autonomy of fashion in choice of baby names. At least in the United States, children's first names come in waves and then, with few exceptions, decline in popularity, sometimes disappearing almost completely. "Jennifer" emerged from virtual non-use at the end of the nineteenth century to become the most popular girl's name in the United States from 1970 to 1985, then to abate. But there was no "Jennifer" marketing apparatus, Jennifer lobby, or Jennifer NGO. To start explaining change, we need to suppose something like a human proclivity for something a bit different, new, or inventive. The use of Jennifer did not start all at once, but through leaders, "first-adopters," as they say in merchandising and anthropology. Within any group there are individuals who are stronger in this tendency to start the change ball rolling. Some people desire an unusual name for their child and as they act on the desire, they bring something new into being. But because the pioneers make their choices without knowing what others are simultaneously doing, the result can be that a name chosen for being unusual turns out not to be so unusual. If innovators are responding to common cues in the social environment there can end up being a whole gaggle of "Jennifers," where there were once very few. Then, when innovative parents start discovering how common "Jennifer" has become, it falls from favor among those with the name-pioneering inclinations. They move on to a newer model—"Jocelyn," perhaps. Meanwhile, Jennifer becomes an appropriate name for parents wanting to conform. Eventually, the name can become so common that even conformers avoid it. U.S. birth records are littered with once highly popular names that are now in almost total disuse—"Ethel," for example. There is thus a dynamic for fashion: names rise and fall together because people are responsive to what they think others are doing but are not aware of just what that is.

Choosing merchandise has some of the same qualities as choosing first names. Economists now regard some types of merchandise as "positional goods," meaning that people want or do not want them because others have them. They do not want the product for its intrinsic merit, but because having it will position them better relative to other people. In my view, all goods have a positional aspect, and this sets up the same kind of internal dynamic for merchandise change that Lieberson finds for names. Those most disposed toward innovative products respond to cues available to others as well. Hence what might seem a distinctive choice becomes a collective one, with mass consequence. Sizable numbers of pioneers choosing, say, a Bauhaus-like rectilinear toaster (dominant in the '80s), begin the process that takes that style of toaster toward a still larger constituency and then abandonment. It becomes too common.

Some people wanting to be distinctive may have selected Early American colonial furniture, say, in the 1940s—when styles like English Chippendale were more popular—only to later learn that too many others were moving in the same direction. Early American became a mass fashion and spawned one of the largest furniture manufacturers and retail chains in the United States, "Ethan Allen," named for the U.S. Revolutionary War hero from Vermont. But Ethan Allen the company was headed for trouble when so many enrolled into the style that not even conformers wanted it anymore. Ethan Allen then adapted by moving into a version of American craftsman style that took hold in the late

'80s and it struggled to market a French country look, however incongruous with its name. For Early American as for any other style, "overpopularity becomes the seed for the fashion's destruction."[41] Like those who choose the last Ethel, consumers who select the last Early American dining set sit alone, at risk of the stigma that comes with deviance. As Lieberson remarks about the overall dynamic, "a certain instability is thus inherent in fashion because of the 'errors' this collective process generates." These kinds of internal mechanisms are, he says, "the building blocks underlying virtually all changes in taste."[42]

External events also do matter, in names as in merchandise. The stardom of Gary Cooper helped keep "Gary" among the top 20 boys' names in the United States from 1935 to 1959 (although Bogart did nothing for "Humphrey"), just as big Hollywood movies often, although not always, influence fashions in clothes and hard goods. The rise of Hitler ended "Adolph," just as World War II made for simpler furniture and clothing designs. Monica Lewinsky's White House service may well have decreased the number of girls named "Monica" after 1998 (this is my surmise), while the Queen of England moves British taste in women's clothing and artifacts toward the dowdy and traditional. Assimilation-oriented American Jews, responding to the prevalence among Anglo-Saxons of names like Stanley, Seymour, Sheldon, and Morton, so conformed that these names became "Jewish names," around the 1920s, which meant that WASPS stopped using them and then, with their emulation function lost, Jews spurned them as well.[43] So too in the product world, consumers in the pursuit of innovation or conformity draw on prevalent social distinctions and mimic the esteemed, in ways consistent with the ideas of analysts like Veblen. But even in these examples, emulation is never the only thing going on; we return to the idea of wider forces at work. There are the "bedrock" internal mechanisms, changing cultural meaning, along with variations in personality, spirit, and, as I earlier intimated, the very mechanisms through which the mind works. And, yes, also the proclivities of corporations after money through the sweat of other people's brows.

The other side of built-in change is built-in stability. Even in twentieth-century America, Lieberson finds, people do not name their children any old thing, not even the pioneers. Instead, new names are typically built on old names, as when a name like "Marilyn" comes around, at least partly through a rising fashion of adding a newly popular "lyn" sound to prior names entering decline, like "Mary" (additional examples from the same era include "Carolyn," "Jocelyn," and "Rosalyn").[44] There are other people who wish to conform more completely, hence generating perennial popularity for "John," "James," and "Robert"—all on the U.S. top 20 boys' name list since 1906. There are also family traditions in which some names persist in the lineage over generations.

As I will try to show, people also stick with certain kinds of goods—Scotch Tape, both the product and the brand, has had a very long run. But as with the adjustment of "Mary" with a "lyn" update, so new goods accommodate to old patterns, typically changing only incrementally. There have been changes in Scotch tape over the years, but gradual ones. When in 1960 the 3M company introduced a variant that would not yellow over time, it called its product "Scotch magic tape" (holding on to the "Scotch") and also kept the tartan plaid packaging, although switching from red as the dominant color to green. The company kept the dispenser, for a time, as it was. Change and conformity are thus not only both on the scene at once, and existing in the development of a single product, but exist through one another. Allowing some conformity with the past enables people to accept something new, while the innovation helps keep the old product going into the future.

The social dynamics at work, conformity and change, also are tied in with one another. Emulators have two challenges, one involving timing and the other arising from the vast range of details they need to get right. In terms of timing, if what you want to conform with is also changing, you must keep up or, quite ironically, end up as different—the "last Ethel" problem. To avoid deviance or, in a more benign label, being called "eccentric," people have to move along with the group. They must know when to change in order to conform or they will stand as an example to others of what happens when you are just "out of it."

To emulate, conformers are plagued by being able to see only a portion of what is going on around them at any given moment—including the kinds of stuff people they wish to imitate are buying and using.

Folks pick up on the surrounding cultures in at least somewhat idiosyncratic ways—they may see only the living room, but not the bedroom, or see a retro piece as deco when it is "actually" postmodern. Even within a world of conformers, each conformer thus acts differently. With each striving to emulate the other, there will be a never-ending chain of adoptions and adaptations that, as they move through the network, change the substance. Like rumors that spread from one person to the next, replication is never exact and the "errors" cumulate to qualitatively different kinds of outcomes. In this daisy chain of imperfect emulation, change becomes incessant.

Better understanding of the stuff system, including its "deep" mechanisms of change and stability, can be helpful to the world. My bet is that we can improve goods—both socially and ecologically—and comprehend more about the society that produces them if we understand how and why they come to be as they are.

THE ROUTE

How to do it? My first step was to go where I thought the action was, to those whose job it is to turn cultural currents into economic goods: the so-called product designers (or industrial designers, a synonym in my usage). My hunch was that by investigating the concrete practices of the design workplace, I could wend my way to the larger issues of culture and economy. Since these are the people most directly responsible for the way products present themselves, they would be central to the process that creates, in whatever combination, seduction, obsolescence, utility, or aesthetic satisfaction. By discovering what affects how designers do their work—what they consider and put up with as they move through their routines—one can trace the forces that shape things.

In the chapter following this one, I report my findings on the designers' goals and routines—the way the profession operates. In successive chapters, I take up issues beyond the design workplaces, many involving conditions in other business settings as well as across historic and geographic circumstances. In chapter 3, I investigate how, in past eras and among different cultures, efforts to make goods both attractive and useful were carried out. This is my chance to consider the arts and to address the perennial debate: What does or should count more—utility and function or aesthetics and form? Through the history of specific goods and production systems as well as analysis of contemporary products, I try to show how—more than meets the hand or the eye—function and form both enter into making effective artifacts.

In chapter 4, I take up the problem of change and stability by showing how, once again, form and function, aesthetics and utility, work in tandem. Within any product and across the range of a people's goods, style and fashion make things new and different while other forces encourage continuity. In chapter 5, I show that those in the distribution systems—people like store owners, but also some less likely suspects—influence what stuff can be. They provide not just settings for products, but shape what they sell. In chapter 6, I deal with the fact, sometimes taken for granted, that all stuff must come from some geographic place. There must be the right somewhere for there to be the right stuff. The way cities and regions operate, including their local character and traditions, shapes the nature of things.

Chapter 7 investigates how arrangements in economic organization work into the goods; merger movements, outsourcing, and other currents in business life, particularly those of recent vintage, have consequence for what is out there to buy and use. The development of brands represents a corporate redefinition of stuff and changes the particulars of products. Stories among investors including growing appreciation of the very idea of design further shapes goods. Government actions, like setting standards, involve conflicts among corporations, non-governmental organizations, and nations; the way they are settled also ends up in our stuff.

I finish with a return to the old problems that have so consumed critical scholars, problems that they were right to address but that can now be treated in a more straightforward, or at least different, way. So in chapter 8, I shed whatever degree of moral neutrality I have been able to simulate and take my stab at making things better. There are ways, taking into account how goods really happen, to make some strategic improvements.

Now, on to the world of design practice. I report on my visits to some creative people who must somehow accommodate it all—technology and engineering, form and function, change and stability, shop-keepers and wholesalers, individual tastes, corporate organization and even some moral notions held by themselves and others. Their route to doing a job is our route to better understanding where stuff comes from.

CHAPTER 2
Inside Stuff: How Professionals Do It

Every artifact has a designer, whether amateur or self-consciously professional. Nowadays, the work of design—the intentional use of cultural
and material resources to create a worthwhile artifact[1]—is where the
cultural rubber hits the commercial road. Designers' backgrounds,
their mode of operation, and the way they organize their work all affect
what stuff ends up being. Although acutely aware of the going trends
and business requisites, designers also bring their own professional values and experience to the work. In a realm where there is so much
uncertainty as to what will succeed, specifics like designers' own biographies and individual tastes have opportunity to weigh in. But as with
their stuff, designers occupy a niche, a spot in an ecological web of
institutions, inducements, and impediments; they cannot just do what
they want. In talking to many dozens of designers (at least a hundred),
observing them in their offices and at their conventions and meetings,[2]
I tried to learn just how their mode of operations, including the impediments they face, shapes the stuff we know and use. Almost all of "my"
designers are product designers as opposed to fashion, textile, graphic,
or software creators. I also slighted design engineers, a closely allied
tribe whose members often work directly with my core group of product designers. Most of the designers I know work as consultants rather
than (as is common in the auto industry, for example) as employees of
the businesses they design for. Reflecting common language in the

trade, I refer to these outside businesses as "offices" or "consultancies," to distinguish them from the "firms," "companies," and "corporations" that are their clients. Although there is no way to know the relative proportion of goods that come from these consultancies compared to in-house designers, in terms of innovation, technique, and product leadership—automobiles excepted—these outside offices are where the action is.

Professional Challenges

Intrinsic to design practice are the challenges designers face from their clients and the larger worlds in which they operate. Every profession has its "story," one needed to build image in the outside world as well as provide some motivation to do one's work, even just to get up in the morning. The story—and certainly the conditions that lead to it—affect the content of the work output. Designers hold the vision that they both increase clients' profits and are good for life. They mount this story in the face of intellectual critiques of the stuff their labors create, but also—and as a more pressing matter—the suspicion within the business world that they are not really essential in the "hard" realm of technology and money-making.

As a profession, design is a newcomer; prior to about the 1930s, producers used artists, craftspeople, engineers, and draftsmen to specify what an artifact would be. Only later did corporations, most notably Bell Telephone and Pennsylvania Railroad in the United States, hire individuals specifically to design their products. In Europe, especially at the Bauhaus in Germany and companies working directly with it, and in Italy at Olivetti, professional design work came to be built into production routine in a more thoroughgoing way. Some companies, especially in the United States, continued well after World War II to turn out goods without the benefit of professional design—some still do. It does matter. Look at the pictures on the next few pages to compare Heimstra Design's reconfiguration of a device for open-heart surgery with the first engineered version—one that also, in a sense, can do the job (although never put into clinical application). These are two different things with different consequences for product profitability and ease of use.

design = user-friendly products

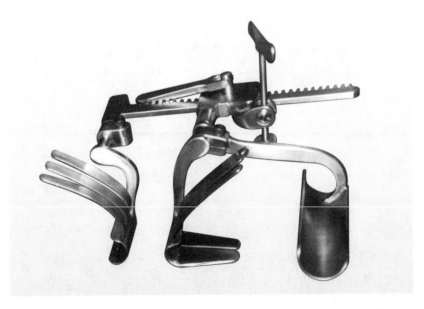

Heart surgery appliance (before design). Minimally Invasive Coronary Bypass Device.
Photograph ©Hiemstra Product Development, LLC.

Heart surgery appliance (after design). Minimally Invasive Coronary Bypass Device.
Photograph ©Hiemstra Product Development, LLC.

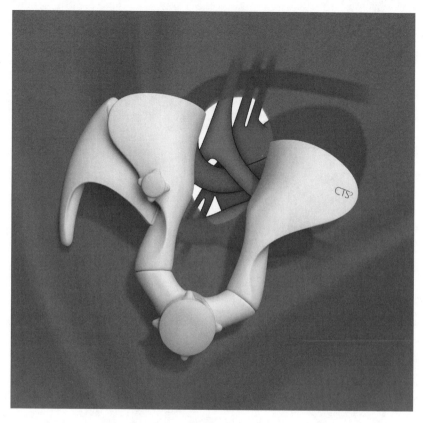

Simulated application, Minimally Invasive Coronary Bypass Device.
Photograph ©Hiemstra Product Development, LLC.

The low pay and power of designers, relative to others in the business world, provides some concrete evidence of marginal status. Average entry-level designer salaries, according to a 1996 survey, ranged from $28,000 in consulting offices to $35,000 in corporations.[3] A 1991 *Fortune* magazine survey reported typical salaries to be about $35,000, with a large corporation's design chief making $100,000—"much less," said *Fortune*, "than [a] counterpart in engineering and marketing."[4] Heads of large companies rarely come from design backgrounds, but instead from finance, marketing or (at least in the past) mechanics and engineering.[5] Design consultancies are not in prestigious office buildings. In New York, for example, they will be found downtown in gentri-

fying areas rather than midtown; in LA, they are not in Beverly Hills—
but they are also not found in slums, either.

Designers' small population size augurs weakness, at least in terms
of organizational clout. There are far fewer designers than the hundreds of thousands of engineers, marketers, and advertising people
who populate production systems. Of the twelve thousand or so industrial designers in the United States about a fourth were, in 1997, members of the Industrial Design Society of America (IDSA). Not an
indicator of strong professional development, three-fourths of practi-
tioners think it not worth the price of their dues to have the IDSA designation behind their names. Attendance at annual IDSA conventions
runs not much more than five hundred.[6] Even within large corporations, design staffs tend to be small, perhaps 30 people. A handful—
maybe six in the United States—have reached the size of several
hundred. Some offices comprise only a single person, perhaps operating at miscellaneous jobs for marginal firms but also on occasion having one or two major clients that keep them busy. For example, when
he was still a solo practitioner, California designer Richard Holbrook
had Casablanca ceiling fans and Thermador kitchen appliances as his
primary clients. Larger offices may also have clerical personnel, model
builders, computer support specialists, and engineers.

Government—at least in the United States—does not license or otherwise provide recognition. No state or national boards certify someone
as an industrial designer; neither degrees nor membership in the IDSA
carries legal weight in terms of access to work or meeting any product
regulatory requirements—such as for safety or recyclability. The U.S.
Census established an industrial design job category (an SIC Code)
only in 1995.

Evidence of inattention to design (and designers) in the United
States starts with school. Children have to memorize the names of
explorers, inventors, and artists but not of designers. Although sometimes included in school curricula in other countries (Australia, The
Netherlands, and the United Kingdom), design is rarely acknowledged
as a skill or designers as a profession in the U.S. Teachers do not give
much positive notice to young people's self-motivated sketching of
dresses and cars, their building of models, or their constructing of

Rube-Goldberg contraptions. Art teachers admire technical precision or self-expression while so-called industrial arts emphasize technology, not its merging with art. Official school culture does not prize—indeed it more likely disdains—consumption artifacts or kids' efforts to modify them.

At the college and university level there are only about 45 design degree programs in the United States; unlike most fields, design is taught primarily at specialized schools, such as the Art Center in Pasadena, Pratt in New York, the Rhode Island School of Design, and Detroit's Cranbrook. Approximately 20 institutions provide some form of graduate training,[7] but only one, the Illinois Institute of Technology, offers a Ph.D. Some universities run their design programs out of engineering schools, others out of art departments.

Although change is afoot, designers (including design engineers)[8]— still worry that corporate bosses and clients see them as merely "making things pretty";[9] never mind that their work is "denigrated" in the circles of real art.[10] The dual suspicions, from business and art, go back a long way. "A large number of artists," Gottfried Semper wrote in 1878, "many of them gifted, are working in steady employment for the French and English industries, in a kind of dual subservience." Making up their "degrading situation" is that "their employer thinks of them, on the one hand, as burdensome taste-makers and form-beautifiers, whom he does not consider his equals, seldom paying them well," along with "the hierarchy of the academic art world, which puts him down."[11]

They can do without the art world, but to have a livelihood, designers have to show they mean business. They have strategies. In working against stereotype they may propose that they know materials, markets, factories, and technologies, although the range of claims will vary with the size of office and audacity of its owners. To demonstrate practical competence, a designer may, without fee, take the client's product apart and reconfigure its elements to show how it can be made more cheaply and more functional, as well as be better looking.

Most tell of past success in developing profitable goods, sometimes involving vast profit. When they are given maximum responsibility and autonomy, designers argue, such outcomes are more likely. LA's Spencer Mackay takes credit for a non-invasive body thermometer

(Thermo-Scan) that turned the client's $6 million investment into a company that soon after sold for $140 million. Heimstra's surgery appliance redesign (fig. 2.2) turned an initial $6 million investment into a prototype that leveraged $300 million in investment capital. Boston-based Fitch Design's transformation of the Bernoulli computer file back-up system into the Zip drive saved Iomega corporation from its demise and propelled the single largest stock market run-up for any listed company in 1994; Iomega's CEO praised Fitch's accomplishment as "reinventing a company through design."[12] These tales circulate within design media; the consultancies put them up on their walls and feature them in presentations to clients.

More than any other actors, designers are in a position, they say, to know how specific variants will influence the product's success and thus how to judge among options, including how to fabricate the artifact. From experience on varied goods for different clients, they know modes of fabrication, materials, suppliers, consultants, and markets. They may, on occasion, manipulate tooling and processes on the factory floor, developing techniques to make a specific product possible. They may also have access to prior market research from other products, including the competition's stuff, which they may have themselves previously worked on. They have the resources, in other words, to do more than many clients might suppose.

Designers have to think about patents. Coming up with something new means not just new in style and functionality, but "legally new." This requires an approach the authorities will consider authentically different from what in patent terms is called the "prior art." If not itself patentable, the designer looks for ways to make sure the new product at least does not infringe on someone else's patents—including those put in the way just to frustrate new entrants. A product's specific configuration may have to be guided by the precisely detailed conventions of just what is or is not a patentable variation of patented versions. In creating the Verse microphone, the designers wanted to avoid making royalty payments on prior versions, payments that would have exceeded the product's manufacturing cost.[13] Instead of the conventional (and patented) arrangement of circular base, pivot, and strawlike extension with a microphone bud on the end, the design firm of Fiori (of

Verse microphones gained their form from the need to escape licensing fees. Labtec ® Verse™ microphone. ©2002 Labtec. All rights reserved. Labtec, the Labtec logo and other Labtec marks are owned by Labtec and may be registered. Used with permission from Labtec.

Portland, Oregon) made it as a simple base and stalk. The new microphones have a unique form that includes a bypass of existing patents.

Rather than doing one thing really well, their special asset, designers often claim, is the capacity to combine across realms. They describe themselves as "problem solvers," "facilitators," and "generalists." Using creativity guru Edward Debono's word, they often proclaim their "lateral" knowledge, derived from cross-discipline sensibilities in art and engineering.[14] They can "see" across a range of concerns: human factors—like ergonomics, readability, "interface design"—and marketability and ease of manufacture. Ambitious offices claim to provide a "comprehensive strategy" for a consistent "visual vocabulary," tactile feel, and instrumentation (e.g., controls appear and operate the same way) across a client's line of products. They may claim the role of organizational experts, helping integrate various activities within the client firm and smooth its relations with suppliers, other designers, and retail outlets. If they lack a relevant specialty, say optical scanning, they can bring in the right consultant. Rather than being limited to a specific product category, a good office can design anything, they say.

Put more informally—which is the way they talk among themselves—they can make individual products and whole ranges of goods cool. What is "cool"? For designers, "you know it when you see it," in the same way that "anyone" can see that Heimstra's heart surgery appliance is cool compared to the prior version. Cool are products that solve as many challenges as possible and *look* like they do. That is hitting the design sweet spot. To get to cool, designers use intuition (a trait they feel blessed to possess) honed not only in art backgrounds and design training. Their intuition comes from involvement, at least in the past, in more marginal arenas like theater, music, or free-thought movements that have expanded their thinking repertoires. Cultural currents that bypass others in the business world more often touch designers. As has been said of successful fashion designers, they have "an instinct for visualizing sharply what is perhaps nebulously and unconsciously desired."[15]

In terms of the object itself, good design involves working up good form and good function together as part of a single mind-set and practical accomplishment—"cool." I saw people designing the guts of electronic exercise gear and some basic medical equipment at one design office, part of the "total design and total engineering" the consultancy proclaims for itself. This means more than, for example, massaging a particular external form to accommodate a certain kind of apparatus inside and more than tailoring an internal mechanism to accommodate a preferred external form. When the process goes right, form and function—along with marketing and all the rest of it—are held in the mind together. This is what designers sometimes call "concurrent design" and engineers call "concurrent engineering." Even if a single person cannot keep it all in play at once, a product team can. At least at the high end of professional design, offices claim to give birth to products out of just such an interactive synthesis.

Clients may think they can second-guess designers because they commonly do have some experience with a particular task—they know a bit about toasting a piece of bread. They may not know much about art, but they know what they, and maybe even others, like. Designers express annoyance that deference goes to engineers, accountants, and "real" executives while those same experts often feel free to substitute their own judgment for that of the designer. So in addition to winning a client, designers often have to demonstrate why their views should count.

Designers typically work on a competitive basis; manufacturers may invite a number to make presentations. A standard pitch includes elaborate slide, power point, or video presentations of the office's general approach, its way of working with clients, its repertoire of services, and examples of past work. The office tries to convince that it is good at anticipating consumer demand and that it designs things that are easily and inexpensively manufactured. The pitch is about market share and longevity, dollar volume and production efficiency, as well as past products' cool features. A product that sells in big numbers and keeps selling a long time saves clients the costs of retooling and reorganizing their marketing and bolsters the designers' reputations as effective professionals. It becomes everyone's interests to come up with, say, a Ford Taurus—dominant in the U.S. car market for a decade—or Scotch Tape or the Toastmaster IB-14 pop-up model, the country's largest seller from 1947 to 1961. A subsidiary pitch is product reliability—appealing to companies eager to avoid the costs and headaches of returns, store complaints, and burdens on technical assistance lines.

Designers use their own offices to display their craft to clients. Design premises are modern and spare—no florals, antiques, or other pretty things. Designers' dress is similarly "architectural," in solid colors and simple lines, including (among men) the collarless, priestly appearing shirts favored by affluent culture workers in the mid-1990s. Such sartorial and object details reinforce design as practical and "hard," even though the settings are otherwise diverse, ranging from a historic London mews, a redone New York loft, or a sparkling Orange County office park. A number of them radiate superhigh technology. At

California's Designworks (partly owned by BMW), a full-size car pavilion revolves at the head of the conference room table. The consultancy has almost nothing in its interior, including the furniture, that it did not itself design. Some offices have turned items developed for their own use into marketable products.

Designers take some care to not overplay their aesthetic interests and backgrounds. In announcing one of its awards competitions, the IDSA called for each prospect to submit a product that "tells the world that good design is not just about aesthetics—it's about the bottom line!" (IDSA e-mail to members, March 8, 2002). Working under art-suspicious clients, designers may have to "sneak aesthetics in," according to a designer who has resorted to the practice: "If a client knows you're doing it to make it look good, they'll resist it. Sell it on function or cost savings." Veterans sometimes warn the young and "idealistic"—or other "beret types"— to face up to practical considerations and keep their artsy leanings under control. Indeed, some designers criticize products with aesthetic goals so high that production costs price them off the market. Some designers, those who do not win prizes, use *that* fact to sell themselves, trying to leverage corporate prejudice to their benefit. A full page *I.D. Magazine* advertisement from the old-line Teague Design office ridicules the competition with the headline quote: "LISTEN, I'M AN AWARD WINNER." The text then mocks the imagined competitor: "ENTER THE PRIMA DONNA: 'IT'S BRILLIANT, IT'S THE PINNACLE . . . IT'S FABULOUS . . . ' The ad ends with the tag line "AT TEAGUE WE DON'T WEAR TIARAS."[16]

Such bend-over-backwards positioning aside, virtually all designers are—to a degree—closet aesthetes, although they do not use words like "pinnacle" or "fabulous." Though all designers must be practical and some offices tend toward mechanics, the art part is what they, often uniquely, bring to the table. Some designers went to art school before design school; others were painters or sculptors. But as one told me, "I sensed my limitations as an artist." Some working professionals remain "Sunday painters." A prominent designer proclaimed in the IDSA house magazine, "we must have the courage to defend the beauty of a design, its emotional charge, its poetry."[17] In receiving a special personal recognition award from the IDSA in 1997, 90-year-old

Eva Zeisel urged her colleagues to "bring back the beauty and glory of the tabernacle . . . warmth and beauty . . . like in the olden times."[18]

Most designers do believe their aesthetic judgment makes for better products and, in part for this reason, helps stuff sell. Designers believe that beauty alone, even if it means just changing an encasement —what they call the "shroud"—can pay off handsomely. Ravi Sawhney of RKS Design showed me a hand-held gaming device that, after a fresh rehousing, moved into the number one sales slot from its prior seventh position. "People do read a book by its cover," says Sawhney. "They make a first judgment based on appearance of something and then they work to back up that first judgment. They may turn away from the product when other types of evidence do not confirm their first impression, but appearance comes first."

A product design can—and many do—fail utterly. The client can pay for a design that is too complicated to produce at the right price, inappropriate for its intended market niche, or with safety flaws that lead to expensive litigation and damaging publicity. If production goes forward on a bad product, it can destroy a company. Some products still involve vast development investment. The Gillette Mach 3 razor, introduced in 1998, took $700 million up front to make happen. A new automobile model can cost $1 billion to launch.

Clients do not gain much help from the design world in terms of figuring out just who is good or bad. There are no "Zagat" guides listing and evaluating product designers. And although they like to guffaw at the clumsy work of engineers or amateurs, designers do not often speak about their own mistakes or those of their professional colleagues. Unlike in the academic world, designers' conventions and periodicals contain no out-loud challenges of one another's work. Because designers are reluctant to acknowledge there is something a competitor can do better than they can, they seldom refer clients to other designers. Nor are there, as in show business or publishing, agents who make the match. Price competition also does not operate very well, given the uncertainties of just what one is buying or selling for a given amount.

do job well, so few are needed

CLIENTS

Gaining a client is both the opportunity to do a design and a source of constraint about how it can be done. Some designers gained their first clients through prior employment in design departments of manufacturers. Hauser Design, a leading design office in Southern California, arose when the principal's employer closed down. Many of the displaced manufacturing executives and engineers started their own companies, and almost all hired him, in part, says Steve Hauser, because he was the only designer any of them knew. His flow chart, made in about 1989, shows that about half his significant clients originated from the initial group of co-workers at the engineering company. The other clients were mostly in separate clusters of three to five firms or, on occasion, single firms that called him up based on magazine publicity or, in one case, his listing in the Yellow Pages.

The modes of referral—and such referrals are overwhelmingly important—affect the substance of products. In the Hauser case, the engineering orientation of his employer gave rise to a series of clients oriented in the same way, evolving into continuous specialization in medical instrumentation and related technical devices. In effect, the referral system creates a category of design office, one that goes on—and here I speculate—to provide a kind of stamp to a large range of products that have all been designed by the same office. The client base has a certain homogeneity, which gives rise to a similarity in the types of goods an office produces.

The system is by no means rigid; there are also processes that shift consultancies toward different kinds of clients over time (Hauser slowly evolved into a wider product range). One of my informants began in furniture design. After having successfully designed chairs for a client, the same manufacturer asked him to do a wheelchair. The result was more like a piece of furniture than prior wheelchairs. While changing, to a degree, the very nature of wheelchairs, the designer was now in the growing field of medical equipment. Manufacturers in this realm, noticing the success of his wheelchairs, hired him for "other" medical equipment, and that field is now one of his firm's primary activities. So style and features of a certain sort move from furniture to medical equipment, changing the nature of the medical stuff.

Aside from referrals from existing clients, new business can come through a range of serendipitous circumstances, some quite casual. A major California office got a first boost when the designer's jogging partner connected him to the electronics company for which he did the advertising. The "weak ties"[19] that people typically have with a large but non-intimate social network provide some of the client base. In another vein, Waterpik, based in Colorado, found that its designs were creating production problems for the LA-area aluminum fabricator it had engaged to execute the product. The aluminum company recommended Spencer Mackay, a local design firm, to make adjustments that would simplify production. When Waterpik had a new product to make, it turned to Spencer Mackay because the consultancy had solved the prior difficulty. Here the LA design office, and any specific sensibility it might have, gets into Waterpik through LA's role as a fabrication locale.

Face-to-face interaction between client and design office shapes the products, which is why some designers consider their products collaborations. A California-based designer spent 90 non-stop days with Compaq computer at its Texas location to work through a project. In another case, involving an international team, the U.S. client traveled to the U.K. designer every six weeks, and the designers went to the client approximately four times over the nine-month development period (this was in the early '90s). At various points, the designer presents recommended solutions in drawings or models or both. Visits to the designer allow clients to see and touch prototypes while simultaneously brainstorming, pointing, and manipulating. Videoconferencing, in contrast, does not allow physical contact with prototypes, or the ability to scan fleeting facial expressions and body language.

Although most designers speak of how "lucky" they are to have such "good clients," tensions arise from different priorities and status levels of the two parties. In one frequently told case (an extreme one), Chrysler's CEO, Lee Iaccoca, would walk through his company's design studios and order changes to his taste. He insisted on the boxy look and vinyl roofs that made most of his company's cars—and this seems a strong consensus[20]—the design duds (and poor sellers) of the late '80s. A more general, and subtle, complaint is that clients tend to overspecify what they want and in this way unduly limit possibilities. Designers prefer to be told the overall goal in functional or market terms. They don't mind being asked, in crass commercial language, to capture a certain percent of market share, as long as they are not told how to do that. They would prefer being told to find a better way to keep teeth clean than to be instructed to create a brush with a rubber nib. From the client's perspective, of course, there are already vast uncertainties, and specifying some of the parameters of the envisioned product is a way of limiting them.

Designers also come with certain urges stemming from professional ideals that are at least somewhat separate from corporate notions of a good product. They have heroes they would like to emulate, visible in their books, posters, and biographical articles consecrating the great designers, like Raymond Loewy, Henry Dreyfuss, and Marcello Nizzoli. Designers like peer recognition, as they display their plaques and press notices on the walls of their offices and reception areas. They are also proud when *Business Week, I.D. Magazine,* or the IDSA's well-turned-out publication, *Innovation,* publish their work. Professional notions of accomplishment thus also shade into what designers take to be good products. Clients may believe consumers prefer the trade-off of lower initial costs with less efficient operation and poorer durability than designers would like. Disagreements can revolve around different interpretations of consumers' aesthetic preference. One designer confided that working with a certain maker of household products caused him to seriously confront the meaning of his life, so awful was the design history of the product line. He eventually managed to "educate" the client to products that were, in his judgment, more attractive and appropriate. Some clients align more than others with the cultural framework of designers; for example, Silicon Valley firms like Apple or Hewlett-Packard are largely in synch with the tech-oriented design firms that have grown up around them. Garage tinkerers (and their creations), being unknown quantities, have less chance of finding a good designer than does a firm with more impressive bona fides. Novice clients have to be educated about what design is and why the fees only seem high. A few offices will not deal with novice clients at all.

Product success, say the designers, requires everyone to be on board; the engineers, accountants, and executives all must want the design to succeed. Without sufficient enthusiasm, too many "good reasons" will arise not to "move the envelope." Designers distrust judgments made by people who, in their view, have insufficient motivation to "make it work." Sometimes the problem is one of engineers trying to refine an existing mechanism, rather than striving for a different way to reach the goal. A former design head at Amtrak recalled a lot of problems with engineers for whom the prior version would always "do."[21] Not having the will to play, to appreciate fantasy or elegance, the employee will not expand enough sweat to engineer, source the right materials, or develop the marketing strategy.

Pricing design work can be a source of tension. What is a fair price to pay for someone to create a thing that does not yet exist and indeed that may, depending as it does on so many contingencies, never come to exist at all? Complications of all sorts can arise. Designers can misinterpret the clients' goals, can miss deadlines or delay so long that factories go quiet or a competitor moves into the breach. Clients can demand more work than agreed on, insist on unreasonable schedules, or refuse to pay for additional work that could not be anticipated, as when an early design has to be scrapped because the market changes or the competition gets there first. The client's decision at one stage may imply a greater or lesser complexity of design work for the next. Remuneration arrangements, as with substantive design decisions, thus have to be dealt with ad hoc, as projects move along.

Different methods of design pricing exist to deal with variations in types of goods and different expectations of their sales potential. Offices can collect a flat fee or they can take a percentage of gross sales—a royalty interest. For the designers, royalties can mean big rewards if the product succeeds. On the other hand, fees mean getting paid whether it does or not. The two different payment systems help different kinds of artifacts come into being. For a product that might be risky, perhaps involving a real change but a client without much money, a royalty arrangement may lure in a designer who comes to share a belief in the product's potential. But the designer may be taking on the risk of working with clients with inadequate resources to bring the product successfully to market—if the clients were rich enough, they would just pay the fee and keep the future profits for themselves. Working with such a marginal client could end up meaning the designers worked for nothing. Sometimes the product and the firm emerge together as a joint project, with the designers retaining an ownership stake—something that New York's Smart Design did with the highly successful Oxo Good Grips kitchen tools it developed with manufacturer Sam Faber.

For some other kinds of stuff, however, having to work under royalties (or joint ownership) would hurt the designers. For example, a corporation may want a product that, although unlikely to sell well, will add prestige to the firm, perhaps indirectly boosting sales of other stuff they make—for example, the way auto companies issue "concept cars" that bring attention to their brand. In other cases, a company may be willing to produce a small number of units to test a new market that it will enter only if there is good public response to an initial model. For these types of goods, royalties would not pay.

For the more established offices, relations between client and designer may become so closely aligned that the designer no longer has to compete for projects at all—the office is simply hired—and fees (or royalties) are established with little discussion. Over time, through repeatedly close and high-trust relationships, client and office become what business organizational experts call "quasi-firms," operating almost as a single entity. Indeed, office and corporation can become so blended that the client takes ownership stakes, as happened with Steelcase office furniture buying into the IDEO design consultancy and BMW investing in Designworks. Such efforts to more systematically conjoin centers of creativity with production activity presage a more general trend in corporate life that has big implications for the nature of future stuff (trends to be taken up in chapter 7).

DESIGN TECH AS A FORCE

Besides speeding up their development, new technologies for *doing* design affect products in more subtle ways. By the late '90s almost all offices in the United States used computer-aided design (CAD). CAD allows designers to alter their schemes rapidly; inputting change of a single dimension, for example, creates instant readjustments of all other dimensions. Electronic data interchange (EDI) permits direct linkage between designers' computers and those of clients. This means people with different roles can act on the same design scheme in tandem even at a distance, with clients responding on the work itself from afar. The great CAD dream, now only partially realized, is for electronic versions of a design to enter directly into an automated manufacturing process. The designer would ship the CAD program to the factory electronically and the finished goods would come out the other end.

Some designers, starting in about the mid-90s, turned their CAD-produced diskettes over to more specialized firms to create product prototypes. The process, called "stereolithography," results in a three-dimensional plastic model. At a more modest cost, a desk-top forming machine using ordinary potato starch can create prototypes by functioning, in effect, as a 3-D printer linked to CAD programs (year 2000 cost was about $10,000). Combining the new processes, a product like a new computer model can go from first discussions to manufactured item in six months or less.

Software may influence substance. The word processing program I use to write this book comes with a grammar check that motivates me to make some dubious "corrections" that, should others be acting similarly, will cumulatively shape writing in the English language. For the designer, the computer interface mediates in subtle ways. CAD is not a "prostheses of the mind" like the drawing hand.[22] A microsecond delay from the technology can kill a gesture. Particular CAD programs make some types of products easier to design than they otherwise would be, especially those with complexly irregular shapes (Frank Gehry's fantastical buildings like the Bilbao Guggenheim owe much to their designer's technology). Design awards now sometimes list not only the name of the client and the designer (unless prohibited by the manufacturer), but also the design software used to create the product— evidence that CAD is not just a tool but intrinsic to the outcome.[23] In actual practice, electronic media, drawing, and talk seem to reinforce one another. The "drawing is indecipherable until verbalized, and the words obscure until visualized."[24]

Three-dimensional prototypes similarly work with talk and various combinations of handwork and technology. Models and prototypes facilitate thinking through ergonomic problems and can be tried out in different situations, including wearing clothes or undressed, by those with more or less dexterity, and with different hand sizes and motor strength. Models are especially appealing to clients. "If I show you a picture of a spoon on a screen," says Jeff Smith of Palo Alto's Lunar Design, "and have one on the conference table, you'll grab the one in front of you and stop looking at the wall." Here too, the old-fashioned methods persist. Hand-built models, unlike those from stereolithography, can be made of materials tailored to the product (clay, wood, or foam) and then painted or covered in veneers to simulate almost any sort of finished surface. A designer can make adjustments to a hand-made prototype with barely a moment's hesitation, changing its weight or perhaps tactile feel. Handmades also can more easily simulate details like flaps and moving parts—something that may affect a client's willingness (pro or con) to accept such elements in a finished product.

INSPIRATIONS, PERSPIRATIONS, AND SUCH

When I asked designers about the source of their ideas, which I often did, they were nice enough to provide some answers, a number of which I will repeat. But I think it was a bit forced. Products come from too many places to lend themselves to an interview sound bite. Ideas—and bits of ideas—creep in at random times and places. Many designers keep notepads at the ready—in the car for drive-by sketching, by their beds to use in the middle of the night. Designers are apt to say their solutions "just hit." But there are some patterns in their responses.

Some say they "look a lot" as they move through life. Sometimes, they look more specifically, for example at air photos for shapes and textures formed by roadways, crops, and natural demarcations. They may engage in voracious magazine and web surfing, what Tom Kelley, general design manager at IDEO, calls "idea wading."[25] The Swedish designer Charlene Schlyter says she got a successful chair design from a calligraphy course in which she became fascinated with the letter "h." No matter what kind of products they work on, designers notice the constantly changing array of shapes, colors, and textures that people wear, especially young people. They are prone to visit hip spots like LA's Melrose Avenue or New York's Soho district. An earring might inspire a car accessory or fender shape. Architectural elements, including store and window fixtures, may suggest the kind of look consumers have begun to assimilate.

Not surprisingly, many designers keep up with art, going to galleries and museums. The high art commonly in their backgrounds enters into their stuff, sometimes in direct ways as when they are consciously working an Arp-like form into a lamp base or car fender. But they do not go too far, stopping well short of involving consumers in an esoteric art history lesson. To deliver the goods, the trick usually is to downplay, if anything, the high-end cultural knowledge that may be incorporated in the object. A designer may put Monet water lilies on a sofa, but unless aiming for a very select market, shoppers should not have to know about French impressionism to get it.

However vague their sources, designers believe they need to keep the ideas coming, and this, according to both the bosses and the line staff, requires "fun." Designers talk of how little money counts to their satisfaction, and indeed several consultancy owners say that salaries are their weakest motivator. Designers come in nights and weekends to catch up, advance new products, or develop "cool stuff" for their boat, car, or house (workplace parking lots do not empty out at five). Designers are free to come and go, rearrange things in their work setting, and wear what they want. There seem to be lots of parties and silly prizes (made possible by having in-house capacity to fabricate just about anything). Floor layouts are non-hierarchical, although the two or three top principals sometimes have conventional closed-door offices (principals are always designers). Almost all design studios have separate workrooms for model building—segregated because of the noise, odor, and dust. But all designers move freely through every space, often, for example, making their own models or working directly with those who do. People in design speak of a need to maintain a kind of creative intimacy in the studios, which may explain why, even as the profession has expanded over the years, the scale of offices has not much changed. Design works best with minimal layers of bureaucratic control, and small size means fewer layers.

Some offices try consciously to stimulate free thinking with the kinds of objects they keep around. At the Palo Alto offices of IDEO, "Tech Boxes" situated in the various work studios are filled with "neat stuff"; one had about three hundred items contributed by staff people from their various meanderings. Clients are encouraged to sift through the stuff both as a source of amusement and to loosen them up to imaginative solutions. Things and pieces of things turn colors when touched, ring in funny ways, collapse oddly, expand with gusto or quickly shrivel when exposed to body heat. In a direct product effect, IDEO's Dennis Boyle, observing this shrink-return feature, created a non-mechanical means for users to eject PC cards from their Apple PowerBook. Heat supplied by the computer battery shrinks a wire of the magic material, called Nitinol, which releases a latch that frees up a spring, and the spring shoots out the PC card. The Natinol wire immediately returns to its former shape, again ready to hold a PC card in place.

Toys are scattered all around IDEO's spaces (and several other offices I visited). Boyle speaks of toys as "congealed ideas." Toys need to delight, surprise, and be cheap. They can be remarkably simple, with few parts, or amazingly complex but fabricated in an inexpensive way (Radio Shack's $30 Armitron toy has about three hundred interconnected moving parts). Toys are kept within reach on shelves and on the floor so "you can grab them," "make a kinetic contact," think through their process "even as your eyes were looking for something else."

Beyond their work environments, designers approach tasks by drawing on their personal experience, most particularly their own bodily needs. Many goods are, after all, an extension of the human body, improving on activities already well practiced. Eyeglasses, binoculars, and telescopes extend the eyes, telephones the ears, can openers the hands. Some products derive from physical ailments of their creators or their kin. His wife's difficulties in handling conventional kitchen tools motivated Sam Faber to create the Oxo Good Grips line with Smart Design. The original creator of the Jacuzzi tub was a man named Jacuzzi who created the whirlpool bath to alleviate a family member's arthritis. Because they are typically neither very rich nor in abject poverty, designers come up with ideas that derive from experiences common to many others as well—a true marketing advantage. Not everyone is this way.

George Bush (the First) had never seen a supermarket scanner before a presidential field trip; Queen Elizabeth did not know the inside of a fast-food operation until late in the last century. In the design office there is no use for royalty of any kind. Instead, the life practices of designers are put to work in the way assignments are given out (swimmers are assigned goggles) or in the way designers come up with projects of their own. Designer Alberto Mantilla designed a baby crib for his son, Mateo, without realizing it would one day be marketed (and under the name Mateo). Another designer credited his mother-in-law, frustrated by the tipsy restaurant table they were sharing, for the challenge that led to a successful product: "make a better one; you're a designer," she said. So he came up with a table with easy-access finger-twist levelers built atop the foot of each leg.

Goods that end up with industrial applications also can emerge from ordinary life experiences. The "Menda bottle" is familiar to many people who have received an inoculation at their doctor's office. The special quality of the Menda bottle is that when the nurse presses a cotton swab down on the top, the bottle spurts up alcohol. So the clinician can wet the swab with the use of just one hand, allowing the other hand free to inject. The bottle's inventor, an engineer named David Menkin, created it after watching his wife's difficulty in trying to get baby oil on a swab while struggling to put a fresh diaper on their infant. He saw a need for a bottle that would dispense fluid upward and allow one-handed operation. Menkin's efforts to market it as a nursery product failed. But the Menda bottle became a mainstay in other applications, first in medical offices and then in a still bigger way in factories, or wherever else soldering operations take place (workers swab surfaces with acetone using one hand while holding the metal parts, or the soldering tool, with the other).

Another influence on product detail comes from mundane physical objects already part of the designers' immediate surroundings. The person who specified the dimensions of standard floppy diskettes thought the coffee stirrer he had in his hand was about the right size. As with some other decisions where standardization is more important than the content of that standardization—like which side of the road to drive on—using the stirrer's length was as good a method as any. The designers of Hewlett-Packard's first hand-held calculator measured the pocket of the shirt William Hewlett was wearing at the time when, taken with miniaturization possibilities inherent in semiconductors, he asked his team to come up with a calculator small enough to wear. That particular shirt ordained the dimensions of a piece of electronics.[26]

It is not all happenstance. Designers also do what they term "research." For example, they may create "style boards" (or "lifestyle boards"), assembling pictures of products, scenes, clothing, and other items used by the target group. This reveals the prevailing "design language" in play and stimulates new ways to fit a product into the tastes and needs of a given consumer group. A phone for teenage girls, for example, might be accompanied by logos of clothing they wear, CD album designs, pictures of stars, stuffed animals, and dolls that are popular with that age group. Designers want to provide the right "visual placement"—making the product right for its "design position." They may also perform a "product audit" in which they compare goods of all the competitors, packaging included. If their own product is cheaper or of lower quality than competing models, they may try to reassure buyers by closely following convention. If they have designed a more costly item, the method is to differentiate. Another technique involves taking competitors' products apart to see how they were made ("reverse engineering") and then try to surpass them in some way—re-creating the mechanics to get a better look or altering form to enhance functional performance. Designers commonly scrutinize the way consumers change a product after buying it, like putting stickers on phones, customizing cars, disengaging smoke alarms. These aftermarket alteration "studies" provide notions of how to accommodate consumers' actual practices or solve the problems they try to solve on their own.

Especially in larger and more sophisticated offices, designers may use techniques more familiar to social scientists like ethnographic observation, time and motion studies, and focus groups. To "do teeth" (that is, create a toothbrush) a design office may bring in dentists and hygienists and toothpaste makers; they may video people brushing or flossing and break down their movements. Designers might examine the number of required reaches they can cut from a product's use, perhaps how configurations and materials will minimize fatigue or injury.

Designers think through how human physicality interacts with objects in any setting and at all stages of the life course and daily round—including intimate acts and the products, like toilets and condom dispensers, that aid them.[27] Many in-house "studies" are notably informal, as IDEO's Kelley corroborates: "We have no time for detailed scientific studies at IDEO, nor does most of the rest of the business world. . . . We usually track down several interesting people to observe and talk to. . . . We'll blast out a query to see if anyone knows friends who fit a certain profile or who might let us watch them using an existing product or service."[28] A person described as "part anthropologist and part seer" (with a college degree in psychology) oversees these operations at IDEO.

Contrary to suspicions that corporate research is designed to foist new things on people who do not need them, systematic market research has, in the view of some designers, a conservative bias. Jeff Smith, founder of Lunar Design (Palo Alto), sees quantitative-based research as part of the corporate system of "antibodies" deployed to make sure something that might be dangerous does not get into the system. Given that the research is anything but exact, it can mistakenly kill excellent products, not just bad ones. The researchers "clinic the thing to death," says another major figure, Charles Pelly who designs for BMW. Market research isolates a product from the context of its purchase or use and cannot predict how it might catch on with time and exposure. Designers think they are the ones who project forward in terms of market preferences, whereas market research documents preferences in the present. But many designers welcome the research as a genuine guide for product refinement, or at least as a way to back up their intuition with "the numbers."

Ideas within a given consultancy often come from prior jobs carried out by the office. An office's dominant product type may influence the other things its people create. Although there are no crisp boundaries, consultancies tend to specialize—computers and electronics, for example, or medical equipment, or furniture, or display fixtures. Another type of divide is between design for consumers versus institutional applications (e.g., hospitals, laboratories, and factories) or retail goods as opposed to capital equipment. A consultancy that primarily designs computers might tend to turn out toys or vending machines that are computerlike, even if not otherwise technically distinctive. Clients may come to a given office because its designs have a look they are after (say, for a steam iron they want to look like a laptop) thus helping create, through the way consultancies are organized, a particular product model that might not otherwise exist.

Beyond patterns that make some sense, new stuff happens from what designers can acknowledge as "simple" dumb luck, even mistakes. Happenstance happens. The little Post-it at 3-M Corporation came out of experiments that produced an adhesive so weak it appeared useless. But a 3-M engineer and choir member named Art Fry used a piece of paper coated with the stuff as a bookmark in his hymnal.[29] After he loaned his choir book to another singer, it came back with a note written on the "bookmark," which had been placed on its cover. In this way, a new product was born. ScotTowels arrived in 1907 when the toilet paper machinery at Scott Paper company went haywire, producing the wrong consistency and shape. The result yielded a new product and set the still dominant size standard for paper towels and their holders. Of course, for mistakes to translate into products, the organizational and personal proclivities have to be right. 3-M does not just manufacture chemicals; it makes consumer goods as well. Scott Paper had a vast marketing apparatus ready to put a new variation to the test. Luck is never totally dumb.

WHO DONE IT?

One way of answering the question of where stuff comes from is to name an office or even the human being who came up with a product, akin to the way we might say that Edison invented the lightbulb or Michaelangelo painted the Sistine Chapel ceiling. The answer to the "who done it" question is seldom clear. Who invented the Post-it? The scientists who failed to create a strong adhesive? The 3-M choir singer who stuck the thing on a page? His choirmate, who was the first to write on it? Or the 3-M boss who saw the opportunity and gave the go-ahead for mass production? Among designers, there is little ambiguity as to who should get the credit for a modern product. They should.

They gave it form, and they (not marketing, engineering, or finance) typically came up with the conceptual solution that made it happen as a product. To come up with the very successful "Dustbuster" light-weight vacuum cleaner, the designer made changes in the size, controls, and appearance of an industrial shop machine. The Sony Walkman also combined elements already in existence—a tape player and head-phones. The company wanted a very small, portable tape player. But because speakers were then too large to fit the specified dimensions of the product, the designers worked it up with headphones.[30] Rather than creating a compromised cassette player, they produced a new way to lis-ten —privately and without ambient noise. If use and application are an intrinsic part of what something actually is, as most designers believe, the Walkman and Dustbuster were new inventions for which they can take the credit. Creation, in this sense, means seeing how the parts can be made to fit together; a "thing" exists only through the successful linkage across realms.

It bothers designers that when their products succeed, recognition goes to the manufacturers—who seldom even release designers' names (design consultancies, in contrast, tend to include notice of those who worked on the project). A designer working for a major corporation who had just won an IDSA "gold" told me it was "the first time in 27 years I have received any recognition for my work." Giving public credit to individual designers would risk talent raiding; such raiding might also, one can surmise, stimulate a rise in the status and income of design professionals. Not knowing who designed their goods, people refer to products by the name of the manufacturer (a "Black and Decker drill") or the store where they bought it ("an Ikea sofa"). It is unjust, designers might say, to publicly ignore Brooks Stevens as the person who created the steam iron and its holes (no more hand sprin-kling), along with stove knobs that do not burn hands. Why shouldn't Jonathan Ive, the California–Londoner who directed design of the I-Mac, have his name on the product itself just as Armani has his on clothing or Picasso has his on paintings?

Especially when the creators are dead and gone, they can some-times be recognized. So more people now buy "an Eames chair" rather than "an easy chair" or a "Herman Miller" (its manufacturer's name). In

France and Italy, where designers do receive greater recognition, the products are made distinctive by that fact, something that implies there would be product effects if the same pattern were to spread to the United States and other countries.

WHO DESIGNS AND WHY IT MATTERS

The nature of the humans doing design, including their ethnicity, race, and gender, influence what stuff can be. By IDSA figures, women make up only 11.5 percent of members; there are no data on ethnicity and race, but based on my own observations, the proportion of African-Americans, in particular, comes nowhere near reflecting their share of the U.S. population overall.[31] However apparently homogenous their own group, designers are well aware of diversity in how different types of people are built and function. They may speak, for example, of a product having size advantage when it will work for all between "the fifth percentile Asian female and the 95th percentile African-American male." Ford designers test products dressed in what they call a "third age" suit, with glasses and gloves, to simulate having the body and eyesight of a 70-year-old. Designers would all bet money (in effect, many do) that women and men have different physical capacities and logistical preferences. When Australian designers saw that more women were changing their own car oil, they developed an oil can handle needing less strength to puncture the can and with less likelihood of producing a mess.

In terms of gender, some designers say that women not only tend to design different things—by desire or office prejudice they concentrate in textiles, graphics, and housewares—but also design the same things differently. Not all designers think this way, and some outspoken women designers say gender makes no difference. Among those who think it does, one version is that men are more "performance oriented"—that is, they want the product to run faster or more powerfully or have more features. Women, in some degree of contrast, concentrate on the interface: how the product can be approached and satisfactorily used—its "affordances," as they say in the trade.[31] An in-house appliance designer told me her bosses (all men) "explained away" women focus groups' preference for her simplified washing machine control panel. Her comments were pungent, "If women did more designing, products would be simpler . . . I'd like to add up all the money that's been lost by white male arrogance." To heighten her male colleagues' appreciation of the importance of the human-product interface, a different woman designer says she persuaded her Japanese male clients to scrub their home bathrooms (presumably it was their first time) to show them the importance of cleaning ease for a toilet seat. All this runs counter to the critique that men design products to "ensnare" women;[32] if anything, women designers seem to think the "ensnaring" is the part men do least well.

Power tools were once designed exclusively by men and solely for men to use at work. But during World War II, women in U.S. factories started "borrowing" their tools for home projects (during the war more women had to do home carpentry and plumbing tasks as well the other domestic tasks). Power tool companies like Black and Decker, now the largest U.S. maker, noticed the trend toward home use and began producing home power tools after the war. At first the marketing aimed only at male consumers, then gradually shifted to include women. Such products now represent the bulk of Black and Decker's business with most power tools bought as gift items.[33] Changes in the domestic sphere altered the products. If there had been women at Black and Decker in the first place, perhaps the transition would have taken place sooner.

There are other plausible outcomes of designers' gender. A woman designer created a mammography device more sensitive to women's physical comfort that also, to aid the patient's calm, placed the woman physically closer to the technician. In dealing with other medical problems, like incontinence, both the physical and social predicaments of the patient are different by gender, and it may indeed save a lot of research effort if the person designing for the woman is also a woman. In design of ordinary outdoor metal furniture, a woman designer was thought to have given the product "a more delicate aesthetic" than would a man, or so I was told by a woman designer. Women may also design for smaller bodies. The La-Z-Boy recliner chair came out with women-scale models only after years of having the man-size version on the market.[34]

Still more subtly, women might take consultancies in a more "caring" direction. I notice a disproportionate number of women active in IDSA realms having to do with children's goods (hardly a surprise), but also in special sections and events having to do with ecological responsibility. They are also salient in public service projects. Australian designer Ruth McDermott won a public service award for designing a needle packet for an AIDS prevention program. Her design made it extremely difficult for a child or innocent person to access the contents, and impossible for the user to retrieve a used needle once it was returned to the case.

Given its relative invisibility, design careers may be especially vulnerable to subtle forces that guide one kind of person into the profession (or its subspecialties) and discourage others. The absence of design as subject matter in schools, the low numbers of designers walking the earth to "bump into" and the weak visibility of the field make it harder for a broad base of young people to have product design as a goal and then take the steps necessary to achieve it. Automobiles, being so central in the lives of boys, act as a draw, but even here there is no clear way to turn that boy-toy into a career line. For several male designers, their childhood dream was to design cars, "whatever that meant," as one told me. In still a different case a self-described "drawing-and-painting type of child" took a battery of school tests and was told he was well suited for work as an "industrial designer." But because he was not told what that phrase meant, he became an anthropology major, only years later finding the route to design. A knowledgeable U.S. Army officer first encouraged one designer now working in LA after spotting him, as a child, creatively assembling stuff out of rubble in a post-war Displaced Persons camp in Germany. A number of designers are from design families, having kin in product design.

Feminist commentators note that job environments can send signals that create enough discomfort to encourage women to go elsewhere. It is not a stretch to see the physical environments of the design offices as bespeaking not feminine welcome but "manly beauty, naked and unadorned," the trait admired by Vitruvius in his praise of the Doric column.[35] "Less is more masculine," as a contemporary commen-

tator translates the same sentiment.[36] The major American auto companies (at least GM and Ford), were self-consciously masculine during
their heydays. According to Mike Nuttal, head of the IDEO design
office, General Motors engineers called designers "clay fairies"—not
exactly making for an environment conducive to inclusion of women or
for relaxing gender anxieties among the designing men. Women were
not permitted to design car bodies for fear their presence would yield
"emasculated design" or inhibit the men around them from using sexual gusto to mold their phantasmagoric body parts.[37] The exaggerat-
edly pointed bumpers of the late '50s (which crushed on slight impact)
were called "Dagmars" at GM, a reference to a full-breasted entertainment celebrity of the day.

In the end, I do not know the full reasons for underrepresentation
of minorities or segregation of women, but note that employers advertising jobs in the IDSA's *Design Perspectives* want ads make no mention
of diversity goals nor encourage applications from underrepresented
groups. In contrast to past practices, some male designers now say the
inclusion of women is a necessity, whether for reasons of fairness or
because of the belief that women bring a distinct and valuable orientation to the design process. There is also the thought that in "the new
paradigm" (as designer Tucker Viemeister called it) both male clients
and women clients (who also show up more frequently on designer
radar) appreciate women's presence. That women are gaining a more
prominent role in design is plausible enough, given design's general
relation to the "outside" world—one of continuous interaction and parallel development.

Designers at any given historic moment carry forth the history, as
a designer-informant put it, of "the whole stream of what has come
before." Though other corporate actors are no less creatures of history,
the designers have the special role, in ways their practices indicate, to
connect "soft" sensibilities of art and culture with the "hard" production facts. Somebody has to do this amalgamation because otherwise
there would be no goods at all.

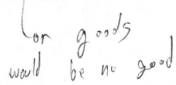

or goods
would be no good

Chapter 3

Form and Function

The great form versus function debate within design reflects analogous controversy in society. It raises the large issue of life's priorities: pleasure or business, expressivity or fulfilling practical need. In more concrete terms of goods production, the question is whether products ought to be made useful or beautiful. If not one or the other, then where should the "compromise," the "balance," the "line," be located? Asking which matters most or even what the balance should be, I will try to show, is fruitless. More radically, I believe that what appears to be form can alternatively be viewed as function and what is thought functional can be seen as aesthetic. But the fact that the argument takes place, and that people take positions within it, affects the goods. I want to show the way both form and function, as each is conventionally understood, enter into products. But in addition, I want to show how the debate itself, variously naïve or sophisticated, also lodges in the stuff.

For their part, designers think that both form and function matter for the creation of a good product. In their common refrain, "it's both." But they do not have a clear way to articulate just how and why both matter, something I try to remedy. To do so, I must document the less appreciated element, the "art part," as omnipresent in human projects and in ways often not realized. But I always understand art as connecting with all other aspects, technology and business included. I also declare that my "art" includes all the variants of "play, fun, display, and pleasure"[86] whether they end up as things hanging on walls, around necks, as songs to sing, or just new ways to be silly. I will try to show its presence in projects usually thought of as having little to do with such realms. As I gather up rhetorical steam, I can then turn to the debates themselves as a force in making up the goods.

Given the stance of so many commentators who champion one or the other—form or function, art or economy—studying the two under the same lens of appreciation runs against some substantial intellectual precedents. For some who champion the *practicalities* of life, art may be a good thing, but hardly intrinsic to the production process. Some schools of anthropology (but not all) hold that art happens historically only when a people generates enough material surplus to free up time and consciousness for the non-essentials. "Men eat before they reason," Marx said—and that means well before they decorate. In a contemporary vein, Petroski argues with characteristic succinctness that the "evolution" of modern products comes from their "usefulness," by which he means utility quite apart from any aesthetic considerations. Issues of aesthetics, he says in *The Evolution of Useful Things*,

> may certainly influence, in some cases even dominate, the process whereby a designed object comes finally to look the way it does, but they are seldom the first causes of shape and form, with jewelry and objets d'art being notable exceptions. Utilitarian objects can be streamlined and in other ways made more pleasing to the eye, but such changes are more often than not cosmetic to a mature or aging artifact.

"Design games," he says with seeming pride, "are of little concern to this book."[2] Some commentators more closely connected with the design world echo the sentiment. The *New York Times* design critic Philip Nobel has urged that "utility, not vanity, should drive change in design . . . that's one of the things that distinguishes it from art," he says. Rather than succumb to "style traps" and "glamour" (as he thinks they were doing in the year 2000), designers should engage in "can-do make-do problem solving."[3] From deeper within the business world, creating and appreciating art has always been suspect—viewed as something done by those who take up the unessential tasks, women and effete or neurotic men. Ornamentation and emotion are regions "that Western and particularly Anglo-Saxon society has defined as feminine preoccupations."[4] The business-minded, traditionally at least, give credit for corporate success to the virtues of competitive drive, including the capacity to exploit natural resources and labor.

Connoisseurs on the art side of the divide are equally wary. They may grant that practical resources can be necessary to physically sustain artists, but money and commercial considerations are otherwise a threat to aesthetic fulfillment. Indeed, instances of art serving business is enough to rule it out as art altogether. As Max Eastman said of artists who have "gone over" to commerce—reminiscent of Semper's nineteenth-century lament—the use of their work in advertisements is "an obituary notice of these men as artists."[5] Commercial art is thus an oxymoron. Art needs to be an autonomous antidote to the commercial, not corrupted in its service. Some go one step further to argue that art's value comes from its potential to *oppose* the economy, at least the economy under capitalism. When it is not obviously doing just this, one should be suspicious. Otherwise, preoccupation with the aesthetic, some left thinkers have argued, may deflect workers' attention from the conditions of their exploitation. That is why, it has been said, capitalism turns up the volume on high art "in periods of confusion and uncertainty"[6] so as to keep the masses humbled and distracted.

Out of this mishmash of art for art's sake, utility is all that's really needed, and the kinds of suspicions that can arise from mixing the two, how does one look for art in the goods and the process that leads to them? Some theories of art do leave a space for merchandise because they define art not in terms of how well the creation itself meets some canon, but in the way it connects to its context, however mundane. This means that ordinary things and miscellaneous experiences can be artful. Baudelaire was one who searched for an alternative "to the academic theory of a unique and absolute beauty." There may be something like intrinsic beauty for Baudelaire, but it needs an appropriate social and cultural context to come out—"the age, its fashions, its morals, its emotions." Unless the object can catch this second element of art's "double composition"—"the amusing, enticing, appetizing icing on the divine cake"—the first elements remain beyond "our powers of digestion or appreciation."[7] In other words, ordinary social currents are intrinsic to the art experience; they unlock the thrills.

I go one step further than Baudelaire and see even his "divine" base as coming out of social experience. For me, there is no limit to the excitement that even ordinary experience can generate when artfully invoked. What he and others take as divine are the large and small dramas of life juxtaposed in spectacularly particular ways: maybe its stormy nights, sexual thrill, a flowerpot, eating Rice Crispies, coming home from school, and all art one has ever seen before. Something becomes art through achieving in the viewer an intense lash-up of connotations, a congealing that gives emotional force even to details like a certain physical curve, minor indentation, or nipplelike bump. So complicated a melding clouds over the mechanism of the artist's accomplishment. Art happens when observers sense they cannot know how their response came to be. Whether it is a finial that so perfectly tops off a picture window lamp, a religious icon whose decoration and form evoke higher beings, a "magnificent" painting in some great collection, an awesome rendition of "Melancholy Baby," or a good magic trick, art represents uncanny accomplishment. One cannot easily think, "oh, I could do that" by this or that procedure. There is, as Alfred Gell put it, "the spectator's inability mentally to rehearse" how to make it happen— a "blockage" in cognition that creates "fascination" or "captivation."[8] Mystery refracts back upon the senses, in ongoing, instant-by-instant loops, intensifying the experience. To at least a degree, this is also how a good toaster works.

With home appliances, as with other media, judgments change; people come to understand the object only too well, causing the mystery to erode, the trick to become old hat, the "manipulation" to become transparent. People may come to understand there are institutional mechanisms that support, celebrate, or reinforce one object as opposed to another. An artistic thing can then be demystified for what it was all along—just a style, perhaps a result of advertisers' enticements and thus no longer experienced as authentic. As mysteries yield to clarifications, creators produce new mysteries to be again demystified. As with choosing first names, certain people lead, being first to see through the stuff of the prior generation or that came earlier in their own lives. The old—at least the proximate old—no longer intrigues. This adds in, from the world of art, a further elaboration of the underlying mechanisms of fashion.

From their loftier and more refined positions ahead of the pack, elite critics can regard ordinary people's fascinations as wasteful kitsch, armed as they are with enough cultural capital to see the contrivance. But elites lack a sufficient awareness to demystify their own prized goods—although when they do, they chuck that stuff too. It would be a step forward to see all goods as mysterious works of art to their admirers. Then we could more fully understand how the seduction process works—just how products become powerful through the particular way they combine art and utility.

HIGH CORRELATION

That designers themselves think "it's both" is evidence in itself for art's significance. They may be somewhat self-serving in making the claim, trying to exploit their artistic capital, but they do have a lot of evidence based on business experience. They perceive a high correlation between stuff they judge as having good form and stuff they judge as highly functional—a correlation that yields market success. In the car industry, it is clear to them that the Japanese and German designers used no form-function trade-off to produce the cars that so drastically eroded the domestic Big Three. Aesthetics do not dictate car reliability or a quieter ride, but aesthetic speculation, carried out with focused enthusiasm, may offer frameworks for technologies that otherwise would not exist. Loving a look, design practice indicates, can stimulate dissatisfaction, experimentation, and reconfiguration in ways that increase technical skills and capacities.

Just as valued form and function may "naturally" align in products, people who specialize in one or the other—artists compared with, say, engineers, are less different than stereotypes imply. Every artist must, as Howard Becker has carefully observed, face the mundane.[9] There are material matters of pigments, solvents, durability, weights, scale, and interrelations among parts. There are organizational issues having to do with agents, dealers, galleries, preparators, critics, and patrons without whom the work could not successfully exist. The artistic output at the end stands as an encapsulation of the practical vicissitudes through which it has come to be—as well, of course, as the "magic" the artist brings to bear in making the combination happen. If the art is a solution, it cannot occur without the problems it has come to solve and those problems are, in considerable degree, practical ones. Indeed one's signature becomes what one makes of such limits.[10]

Leonardo did top-grade weapons as well as murals, and the same talents that make his works recognizably excellent for art connoisseurs plausibly helped his products be more effective in war. His notebooks make clear the Renaissance Man never stopped, and that includes his assiduous efforts in promoting his projects to patrons—whether pitched as art, entertainment, science, or some concurrent combo. Renaissance man lives on. In Zen terms, what might be going on then as now, is "mindfulness"—the propensity to focus and, in effect, let all parts of the individual brain as well as group intelligence work through toward an effective solution.

REPRESENTATION

That stuff typically has to be represented before it can exist is so obvious it is seldom remarked upon. Da Vinci advanced the skills of drawing to advance the prospects of his production goods. The development of linear perspective, critical to any realistic representation of objects, came from the drawings of Florentine sculptor and architect Filippo Brunelleschi, who applied the technique in 1425. In the way that people can experience a coastline through a map rather than being there, they can have some image of an object or production process without direct experience of it.[11] In mass production, specificity becomes especially important because extensive investment has to be made up front before a single item comes into being. Patents require precise representations of parts, how they combine, and how they will operate. Having a representation of a prospective thing amplifies the potential for

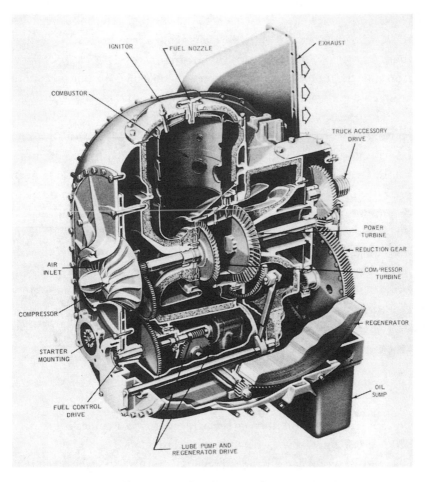

*Cutaway view of an engine. Photo courtesy of Alexander Levens Estate
(From Graphics: Analysis and Conceptual Design by A.S. Levens.*

enrollments among clients who give the go-ahead, investors who are needed for the money, distributors who commit to an inventory. If the product is to go before focus groups, the model, sketch, or prototype must be right or the research will be invalid.

Drawings and models integrate across time because they provide a way for different actors to come into the process at different moments. Many of us have had a chance to see the process when watching workers combine in constructing or remodeling a house. As subcontractors comes along, each checks the plans to get oriented and coordinate with those who came before and will come later in the process. Drawings (hard copy or computer-based) also integrate across space as they travel from one location to another within a factory or from one factory to another.

The precise mode of representation, the skills at hand, and the art conventions in use, affect the product outcome. Technical drawing underwent the same sequence of styles in the fifteenth through nineteenth centuries as did the other graphic arts.[12] Sophistication grew in use of multiple perspectives, shadings, and the other artistic tricks to communicate proportion and kinetic relations. It was not until well into the twentieth century that cross-sectional or "cutaway" drawing came about, a form of non-representational art coterminous with early modernist painting and budding surrealism. Max Miller's cutaway aircraft drawings for plane manufacturers in the United Kingdom during the interwar years receive part of the credit for making the aircraft's production feasible,[13] as with engines and artifacts of all kinds. Ways of representing imagined things helps make them things in fact.

ART AS PIONEER

Besides representation, there are other ways that art comes before useful object. Things now seen as functional developed out of things not evidently functional at all, indeed precisely because, in some cases, they appeared "merely" arty. That meant they were let alone, perhaps to be later tinkered into something considered useful. No one has argued the point more boldly than the MIT metallurgist Cyril Stanley Smith, who turned from what today we call materials science (and a career that included the Manhattan Project) to larger analytic frameworks later in his life. Smith says that aesthetics, desire, and "play domains" were the engine of materials innovation. He speculates that those who first molded baked clay, circa 20,000 B.C., were making fertility figures,[14] not utilitarian objects. Artifacts from the Neander Valley in Austria, circa 35,000 years ago, show detailed chipping and coloring.[15] Flutes carved from bone go back that far. Evidently the early technologies only later became the basis for pots, cups, and vessels. Humans used copper metallurgy to make ornaments prior to creating knives and weapons.[16] This runs against the claim that, as Petroski puts it, tools are "the first artifacts of civilization."[17]

Cyril Stanley Smith sums it up: "Paradoxically man's capacity for aesthetic enjoyment may have been his most practical characteristic for it is at the root of his discovery of the world about him, and it makes him want to live."[18] Cultivating and transplanting flowers, says Smith, preceded crop agriculture, and "playing with pets probably gave the knowledge that was needed for purposeful animal husbandry." He speculates that "pleasurable interactive communal activities like singing and dancing" gave birth to language itself. This leads him to the idea that "aesthetic curiosity has been central to both genetic and cultural evolution."[19]

From other sources, there is a suggestion that weaving fabric for decorative costuming and ceremonial events presaged the use of nets to trap animals and vessels to carry goods. "When people started to fool around with plants and plant byproducts, that opened vast new avenues of human progress," says archaeologist James Adovasio.[20] Dutch historian Johan Huizinga wrote in 1938 that "the whole mental attitude of the Renaissance was one of play."[21] These claims may be hard to prove—especially notions like singing before language or pets before animal husbandry. But the bias in our thinking is evident in the way we put the burden of proof on the idea that the art could not have come first—or even simultaneously. We naïvely take as given the primacy of utility.

Evidence from within the industrial era is more clear-cut. Smith describes a host of metallurgical discoveries in which the aesthetic presaged the mechanical. Blast lamps to make decorative beads led to the modern welding torch, forming the basis for modern steel production. Depositing metallic coatings by means of electrolytic currents owes its origins to layering gold, silver, or copper on baser substances to produce jewelry and decorative medals.[22] All copper and aluminum came to be produced through electrolytic reduction. The same process led to inexpensive production of conductors and integrated electronic microcircuits, including those used in computers and microwave equipment.[23] Across the industrial board—mining, missiles, textiles, chemicals, and plastics—the art application, at least as often as not, came first.[24] Materials and techniques that have spiritual, playful, or aesthetic value help hold a place, providing the space for improvements to develop, for the complementary elements to arrive and maybe for what is later regarded as the efficient solution to come into being.

BUILDING MARKETS

The artistic—including the subtleties of detail—creates markets. In the pleasure of feeling the texture of a doorknob, hearing the sound of a computer click, or taking in the look of a dental drill, the sensual makes people want things. Of all the realms of productive seduction, automobiles are perhaps the most noticed and, other than armaments, the most consequential of objects. Creation of cars depended on the invention of the wheel. Exactly how that came about can only be a guess, but the one by Jane Jacobs is that people made small solid circles, perhaps out of ginger root or squash; maybe mothers entertained children by twirling the vegetable slices on sticks. Then may have come toys of more durable materials. In terms of dating the event, archaeological evidence suggests the wheel came around about five thousand years ago, with the first ones used for ritualistic and ceremonial purposes— carrying effigies of deities or important persons.[25] Apparently closely linked in time and function, wheeled vehicles came into military use as chariots and battle wagons.[26]

But the next great advance, and it came several thousand years later, was the bicycle, invented in France as an amusement for rich and agile gentlemen. Subsequent technical refinements in the United States led to the "bicycle craze" as production boomed over the 1892–1897 period, with women joining in the sport. The bicycle's subsequent "serious" use as a basic mode of transportation (in some places) came only after mass automobile production was under way in the United States. But in the meantime, the bicycle brought on important technical innovations like the pneumatic tire, breakthroughs in ball bearings, seamless steel tubes (for the bicycle's frame) and the first use of stamped sheet metal (in 1890), thus replacing the more expensive foundry method for forming parts.[27] The socially significant bicycle riding public created societies that lobbied governments to build better roads.

The car industry similarly was born for fun, as a plaything for the rich—not as a rational device to move people and goods. The first car, created by Benz in 1886, was ridiculed by the head of the German patent office, who declared that the internal combustion engine, which then was thought appropriate only for stationary applications, "has as little future as steam for motivating road vehicles."[28] Others referred to it as the result of Benz's "mad obsession," consumed as he was by speed at any practical cost. Chevrolet, who started one of the early companies that was to become merged into General Motors, was a racing enthusiast, as were other U.S. car builders. The races, well publicized and greeted with sensation wherever they were held, helped spark general interest in automobiles.

The look of the car became no less aestheticized. Roland Barthes not altogether approvingly recorded the "intense amorous studiousness" with which people at a 1950s Paris exhibition admired a new-model Citroen car: "the bodywork, the lines of union are touched, the upholstery palpated, the seats tried, the doors caressed, the cushions fondled." Cars, said Barthes, "are almost exactly the equivalent of the great Gothic cathedrals . . . conceived with passion by unknown artists, and consumed in image if not in usage by a whole population which appropriates in them a wholly magical object."[29]

The history of car production displays what goes wrong when makers think the car is merely a device for transit. Understanding the automobile as magical object was not in Henry Ford's repertoire. As Michael Schwarts and Frank Romo note, his production equipment gave no consideration to the possibility of periodic design changes. Hence "the boxy body of the Model T . . . was maintained long after the technology was available for a more streamlined design because the metal stamping machines that were installed in the Ford plants could not create curved panels."[30] Ford's production tools could do only one thing, albeit one thing well; half of them had to be scrapped when he finally did make the move toward "styling." Because his machines were also so close together on the shop floor, as a matter of efficiency, there was too little physical space to reconfigure them. Before retooling in the latter

1920s for its first style-oriented car, the Model A, Ford laid off massive numbers of workers and lost $18 million, providing "the most expensive art lesson in history."[31] Henry Ford's philosophy of "any color you want as long as it's black," lowered his company's market share from 55 per cent in the early '20s to less than 15 percent in 1927.[32] General Motors' cars outsold Ford's, and at higher prices. So in addition to whatever organizational smarts GM had over the competition,[33] the aesthetic was a distinct GM edge. The company brought in Harley Earl, who had earlier gained some fame customizing cars for LA movie stars. Beginning with the inaugural project for which he had full responsibility, the 1927 La Salle car, GM began its solid run of profitability. The world's first automobile styling department was GM's, and it was set up under Earl's direction.

After first innovating with color, including two-tone styling, Earl moved GM into deeper changes in body shapes. To gain a more rakish line, Earl smoothed steel over a built-in luggage compartment (today's "trunk" or "boot") to replace what had begun as, in fact, a bolted-on trunk.[34] This also became the place to put the spare tire, which could then come off the car's exterior. To mold steel into the shapes he needed, engineers created dye casts to follow the desired forms, including the "sporty" GM hardtop arrangement. GM developed simultaneously a special steel that was "flexible enough and strong enough to endure the tremendous strain" of the molding processes.[35] The streamline look, with a rolled steel body, enhanced the car's aerodynamic efficiency, decreased the number of its parts, lowered labor costs, increased security against theft, and quieted the ride. Analogous taste and engineering changes moved through appliances and other transportation equipment. One of the more famous was Raymond Loewy's first streamlined locomotives for Pennsylvania Railroad, eliminating rivets he thought made the train look "unfinished and clumsy."[36] The new design saved millions in fabricating costs.

By the '50s, the U.S. car companies moved into what Edson Armi (one of the few art historians to take cars seriously) calls "more irregularly sculpted cars (that) have more in common with the automatism of postwar expressionist painters and their biomorphic fantasies. . . ."[37] with, in the case of the flagship 1957 Cadillac, "Duchamp, Gropius and

Marinetti all commingled in the tail fin."[38] Despite the great appeal these products first had, things again changed—in terms of popular taste as well as the engineering and sales performance of the U.S. vehicles. The Big Three lost out to foreign producers who eschewed Detroit's chrome bucket reruns. Designers often disagree on aesthetic issues, but nowhere have I found a designer praise U.S. autos of the late 1970s and 1980s. *Fortune* magazine, in a 1988 review of "five products U.S. companies design badly," listed cars, making an exception for the Ford Taurus.[39] Cars from Germany, Italy, and most triumphantly Japan have been more highly regarded for their styling, fuel efficiency, and—with the exception of Italy—reliability. The combination of failings in the U.S. product devastated Midwest economies and eroded billions in corporate worth. All this, I would argue because, at least in significant degree, U.S. makers were unable to find the right art when they needed it.

FULFILLING BASIC NEEDS

At every instant in the history of social life, as Braudel summarizes, "man feeds himself, lives and dresses . . . but he could feed, live and dress differently."[40] Even as people fulfill what might seem fundamental material needs, the psychological and cultural realities they attach to their goods become as firm and incorrigible as any physical compulsion. The proof of this pudding is that, at the extreme, people will indeed die rather than eat the aesthetically wrong thing or, as in the case of anorexia, go without food altogether rather than risk appearing unattractive. With death somewhat less certain, they will drive recklessly, drink excessively, or smoke tobacco. Cigarettes may be a health menace ("coffin nails") but they also imply the romance of Bogey and Bacall, mysterious travels, or living on the defiant edge. These are involuntary associations; like lost loves, we can't get them out of our minds. In Richard Klein's strong statement, "cigarettes are sublime."[41] Pleasure comes not just through biologic addiction, but through social and symbolic appeal, including the flirtation with death itself. "To be on the wire is life; the rest is waiting," the acrobat Karl Wallenda explained in returning to his act after a member of his troupe met death in a Detroit fall.[42]

Such inclinations influence products, the economy more generally, and all the institutions in which the economy is embedded. Culinary preferences among some fifteenth-century Europeans (along with people's desire for glitter) stimulated the great treks and voyages over the earth, forever changing all that came after. Starting at least as far back as Roman trade in the time of Alexander and Chinese traders at the time of Marco Polo's journeys, sponsors were involved in a pleasure business—a kind of entertainment economy—rather than a utilitarian search to increase caloric intake.[43] European elite taste for sugar led to slave plantations of the New World, among other social and economic consequences.[44] Taste for coffee and tea, also filling no nutritional needs, brought analogous transformations in domestic production systems and population displacements, including the transformation of Latin American peoples into virtual coffee slaves.[45] Every such food preference carries with it a distinctive goods regimen. Asian diets of small cut-up pieces work with chopsticks; U.S. steak eaters need sharp knives; dope smokers need bongs. A world of culinary products (pots, pans, blenders, serving plates) rises and falls depending on what is being imbibed and how it is prepared and served.

Like food, bodies need a place to rest—but given the changes across time and place in how this is done, the rest is sensual history. The bed is anthropologically odd; most people slept on the floor, shared large platforms, or used hammocks. Chairs are also unusual among world peoples, most of whom squat, or sit cross-legged or flat on the ground. Islamic peoples traditionally do without furniture, making both home and public life on elaborate rugs. From the archaeological evidence, chairs existed as early as the Neolithic Age, but as an expression of authority rather than for relief from standing.[46] Pervasive among the Greek and Roman citizens, slaves did not use them nor did those in the conquered territories. In depicting the diners as sitting, Da Vinci upgrades Jesus and his group, who were too lowly for chairs; they would have been on the floor that night just as on other nights. The chair disappeared even in the West during the medieval period for purposes other than to signal status. It is a misunderstanding to think of today's furniture reproductions of "period" pieces as simulating prior ways of life without realizing they were used by only a small segment of the population at the time—and for different purposes than they are now put.

With the eventual triumph of chairs, at least in Europe and North America, came what we might think of as the "chair style of life" involving related sentiments and artifacts, including the commode and tables of an appropriate height. Higher seating altered the placement of windows and increased the liabilities of low ceilings. Chairs have become part of the methodology of respect and rectitude.[47] Victorians, perhaps emulating medieval clerics, identified sitting up straight with moral virtue. For this reason, it was more important to sit up straight at home compared to the less morally charged environment of the office, where slouching was more acceptable—something of a reversal of the contemporary norm.[48]

The chair's danger to posture, bone development, and healthy defecation is evidence that something other than inherent functionality lies behind it. Use of chairs is actively *enforced*, starting with the hard work of training children to sit. As architecture professor Galen Cranz testifies from woeful personal experience, the naturalization of the chair becomes evident to those who might otherwise ease their back pain by lying on the floor to conduct business or enjoy themselves at dinner parties.[49] To do so would breach normal social life. The chair's symbolic value and the physical necessity now reinforce one another. Europeans and North Americans have lost the technique and muscle power to squat. The chair's durability is locked in because it has lashed up with so much else, indeed invading and snatching our bodies.

Clothing is another necessity we could often do without. People exaggerate its health benefits and other practical gains. So a furry lining supposedly helps ward off a cold even though bacteria and viruses —not a failure to stay warm—cause disease. But clothing does incubate and help spread vermin and dangerous microbes, especially when adequate laundering is not feasible. Ankle support was thought to be a health necessity at the turn of the century, thus creating high-top shoes for women, whose ankles in fact were made weak. As with chairs, shoes do little for the body; even purportedly comfortable ones would probably be best left off under many circumstances.

Use of clothing at all is sometimes a fashion "extra." This is obvious enough in the tropics where most people today wear full-on dress despite its functional superfluousness. But even peoples whom we might think required garments because of harsh climates could exist through their own skin. Indigenous peoples of Australia and Tierra del Fuego apparently kept warm through diet and exercise.[50] Alternatively, no sensible person should ever wear clothes in a New York summer, but millions swelter in them on the city's sidewalks and require air-conditioned interiors to offset the burden. Of course what is involved is an aversion to social stigma, something that even minor errors can attract. Wearing the wrong blouse when visiting relatives can mark a betrayal of "sartorial conscience," even risking effrontery.[51] More radically, a person who walks downtown wearing only underwear (or forgetting a sock) undercuts a whole life of competent living. As the U.S. cross-dresser Ru-Paul says, we are each born naked and all the rest is drag. Analogous to the ways "precision consumption"[52] works in other goods areas, working the drag—among those who produce and those who buy—makes up the stuff. This art of dressing is as important, personally and economically, as utility.

Leaps and Visions

Getting to a new thing, even if only by small and incremental steps, requires leaps. Art helps leaps, something that engineers and scientists often acknowledge—at least in their memoirs. Necessity is not, Cyril Stanley Smith emphasizes, the mother of invention: "A man desperately in search of a weapon or food is in no mood for discovery; he can only exploit what is already known to exist. Discovery requires aesthetically motivated curiosity, not logic, for new things can acquire validity only by interaction in an environment that has yet to be."[53]

Children, Baudelaire explains, are always "drunk" with inspiration, always "in a state of newness," and ready to take on the world unburdened by practicalities or conventions. This is the element that even in adulthood makes the creative difference; "genius," says Baudelaire, "is nothing more nor less than childhood recovered at will."[54] Or as I heard a designer quote somebody wise, "get out of the day and into the play."

How does this inspiration work? Images "just hit," as the designers say. These are not the full-on solutions, but rather insights that then stimulate more precise working out just how an imagined solution will take shape. Such "preanalytic visions"[55] offer a glimpse of the ultimate solution, the form it might take, and for the creator, the thrill that goads the tedium that may lay ahead. The imagined and idealized outcome becomes a template, a basis for judging alternatives, that leads one solution to replace another. "There is no doubt," says one reviewer of the history of inventiveness, "that nonscientific, even nonverbal, thought plays a crucial role in all invention, including that of engineers."[149] The art testimonials pour in from the famed. "It is more important to have beauty in one's equations than to have them fit experiment," writes physicist P. A. M. Dirac.[57] Andrew Strominger, the contemporary string-theory physicist, is guided by "a sense of aesthetics, of what would be the most satisfying possible answer to the problem. I would say: Gosh, wouldn't it be nice? And then try to prove it."[58] Einstein, the genius himself, followed the same version of scientific method.[59]

We all think in pictures, and those pictures have objects, and those objects have affective connotations. Experiments show it is harder to learn logical propositions when expressed formally ("If a, then b") compared to expressions that incorporate "real" objects ("If Socrates is a man . . .").[60] Similarly, it is easier to solve analytic problems based on assumptions of speed, time, and distance by attaching a scenario of trains leaving stations than trying to hold it all as mathematical symbols. By utilizing known cultural objects, including spatial and geographic phenomena, people can more easily manipulate dynamic scenarios. That is a principle of the desktop metaphor in Macintosh and Windows. "In order to remember a long sequence of ideas," a cognitive scientist explains, "one associates the ideas, in order, with a set of landmarks in the physical environment."[61] Coming from the other direction, geographer Yi-Fu Tuan says "transient feelings and thoughts gain permanence and objectivity through things," which then become repositories of meaning.[62] Objects and landmarks do their "thought jobs" because they are affectively redolent. This dual nature of objects as both material and emotion is consistent with emerging notions about how people manage to think at all. Affect makes objects into utilities of mind.

It is doubtful, as held in the common stereotype, that art and practicality reside as separate realms lodged in different parts of the brain, left versus right. More advanced cognitive science presents a different picture. At a very basic level of brain functioning, art and utility not only operate in conjunction, but presuppose one another. People who have had accidents that leave them with lesions in a certain part of their brains (the ventromedial frontal segment) show both severe loss of affect along with diminished capacity to reason their way through ordinary life problems. Experiments with such individuals show, writes cognitive scientist Antonio Damasio, that "the powers of reason and the experience of emotions decline together," even when some other skills like memory for facts and language remain strong. Feelings, based on emotional sensations, act as "somatic markers" that help establish priorities of what to think about and in what order. They are, as Damasio puts it, "boosters to maintain and optimize working memory and . . . scenarios of the future. In short, you cannot formulate and use adequate 'theories' for your mind and for the mind of others if something like the somatic marker fails you."[63]

Emotional traces give objects and the thoughts they carry differential salience. This makes them hierarchically available for complex combinations over time.

This supports the idea that whether as designer or consumer of an object, people do not recognize form and function as separate elements to be weighed as more or less valuable compared to one another. The solutions come as a single gestalt or "blend"[64] rather than as separable "additives." This clarifies why people often have trouble explaining just why they like something and why designers have trouble specifying how they gain ideas. It misleads to think of people, groups, or brain parts as hyper-specialized to one kind of capacity or orientation as opposed to another. Seeing a chair, one may take in the fact of a certain durability or rest for a weary body, all merged with the thrill of red velvet upholstery like that upon which Marilyn Monroe once reclined or John Wayne shot up. The practical and the sensual merge as one: seeing durability may bring pride in having acted soundly in acquiring (or designing) such a chair; anticipating a resting place invokes past rests, a good book, or nice dreams. When apprehending an object, aesthetics and practicality combine as the very nature of the thing.

I do suspect there is one way that the aesthetic must be the more basic, and that is in motivating people to do all this combining. Life is a job, including the moment-to-moment cognitive work involved in doing all this unceasing blending. If there is a master force out there, it can be identified—and here I overlap with the spiritualists of the world, particularly those who write song lyrics—"it's still the same old story, a fight for love and glory." That is why, once again, we see so much "irrational behavior" whether in the world of goods or any other realm of human activity. Products are not merely a matter of function or thrill, but both in a single case and across all the stuff that comes our way.

FINE ART

Among the objects that act as landmarks for thinking, especially for certain kinds of people, are works of fine art. The links of fine art with the production and appreciation of ordinary goods were more evident before art institutions so strongly took on their "beyond-the-goods" elitist stance. In the early part of the last century, New York's Metropolitan Museum of Art had "laboratories" and workrooms in which designers mimicked items in the collections to create lighting fixtures, inexpensive jewelry, soap wrappers, toothpaste containers, and lampshades.[65] The Brooklyn Museum had similar operations; the Museum of Natural History offered lectures for retailers on the art of the Mayans, American Indians, and other groups.[66] In Britain, the Victoria and Albert was consciously created for its commercial applications.

Some of the evidence left behind is obvious, especially in the realms of clothing and textiles. Recognized avant-garde artists like Sonia Delaunay and Natalia Goncharova ended up in Parisian couture in the 1920s. Artists like Leger, Dufy, Dali, Schlemmer, and those associated with movements like the Wiener Werkstatte, Bauhuas, futurism, and constructivism designed clothing. Because people change their wardrobes so fast, compared for example to their bathtubs, each moment in art history has a chance to quickly register. Chanel, responding to modernism, created dresses and suits with rectilinear lines, celebrated for "the working beauty of the garment in wear."[67] In the mid-1960s Yves Saint-Laurent turned Mondrian directly into a

Piet Mondrian. Composition, *1929. Photograph by David Heald*
©The Solomon R. Guggenheim Foundation, New York.

cocktail dress—a concept later knocked off in dresses and, among many other products, in cigarette lighters.

The theater—and then later the movies—is a halfway point for images on their way from art to goods. Besides their work as set designers, modern artists created stage curtains and character costumes—people like Matisse, Leger, Chagall, Picasso, Miro, Depero, and, in the present day, David Hockney. The neo-Greek costumes worn by dancer Isadora Duncan helped launch the Hellenistic dress styles that we associate with the post–World War I years.[68] This style later became the "flapper look" as it drifted further from the Greek prototype.

Art visions can also translate into new means for war. Besides innovations in painting, literature, song, poems, and theatricals to encourage fighting and sacrifice, the First World War marked the coming of a

Yves Saint-Laurent Cocktail Dress, Autumn-Winter, 1965.
Victoria & Albert Museum; ©V&A Picture Library.

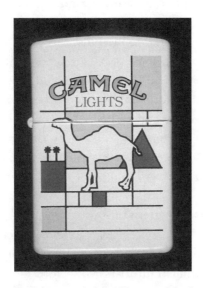

Mondrian to a cigarette lighter. Photograph by Jon Ritter.

different mode of battle dress and choreography. Overhead bombing, new at the time (from long-range artillery and then planes) turned visibility from an advantage into a liability. Intimidation through displays of fierce regalia or redcoat power dressing was over. It was a time for camouflage, which came to the French Army via cubism, a form of painting that eschews literal representation but relies on precise placement of line and color. The developer of the technique, Guirand de Scevola, was explicit: "In order to totally deform objects, I employed the means Cubists used to represent them—later this permitted me, without giving reasons, to hire in my (army) section some painters, who, because of their very special vision, had an aptitude for denaturing any kind of form whatsoever."[69] By the end of the war, three thousand artists were working as camoufleurs. Avant-garde colleagues in architecture were more or less simultaneously responsible for some of the fortifications along the Maginot line, developed out of fanciful pre-war experiments in sculpture and bent-steel concrete forming along with interrelated engineering discoveries.[70] The twin technologies of camouflage and Maginot line probably prolonged the war to end all wars by enhancing defense; otherwise artillery and tanks would have wiped out bright armies less secure than those surrounded by molded concrete. We had a durable system of death and misery with art and mechanics combined in destructive standoff. Bad stuff.

Along with the military museums, fine arts institutions like the Met feature armor and hold special shows on historic military gear. According to the Smith and Wesson handgun product manager Herb Belin, "A firearm is no different from any other product. . . . Its design is based on engineering and aesthetic needs."[71] Perhaps it is easier to use a handsomely designed U.S. M16 or German G3 rifle than a clumsy Soviet-styled submachine gun such as the Kalashnikov AK47.[72] Military parades, gun shows, and battle reenactments testify to public fascination.

As with the usual pattern of interactions, war goods go back into the art they came from, affecting the goods of peacetime. The futuristic bombs and bomber planes used in World War I inspired, in one famous genre, the Italian futurists, whose forms—in still another iteration—turn up a generation later in U.S. car styles as tail lights, bumpers, and "rocket" insignia (the Oldsmobile icon, even before Sputnik) and rifle sights (Chrysler Imperial tail lights, circa late 1958).

Given the art-merchandise linkage, idealistic movements have consciously tried to mobilize art to inspire goods that would be socially beneficial. In the late nineteenth-century British Arts and Crafts school, William Morris and his associates created home products with natural motifs (flowers, trees, leaves, acorns) modeled after paintings of the day, including the romantic idyllic landscapes of Gwynn-Jones and Lord Leighton. Such furniture, wallpaper, dishware, fabrics, and bedding, based on nature, would ennoble their users. There were variants across Europe and North America of explicit match-ups between art currents, merchandise, and a social vision—De Stijl in the Netherlands, Mackintosh in Scotland, secessionism in Vienna, art nouveau in France, Craftsman in the United States.

It was the creators at Bauhaus who most explicitly and consequentially advocated linkage of art, merchandise, and social vision. Almost in reverse of the Arts and Crafts groups, Bauhaus celebrated the potential of machine-made goods to provide a more honorable aesthetic and egalitarian social order. Funded by the German government and active between the world wars until closed down by the Nazis, the school housed painters and sculptors, architects, and the type of people later to be called industrial designers. To see the fine art in a Bauhaus chair, compare the painting of Piet Mondrian with Marcel Breuer's "Wassily" chair (on the next page)—which takes its name from Breuer's painter friend and the chair's inspiration, Wassily Kandinsky. Entire institutions and vast public facilities (corporate headquarters, airports, restaurants, dormitories) continue to be outfitted with Bauhaus models. Although many of the Bauhaus "classics" had sales success, the still greater economic consequence comes from the imitations and their stylistic influence on other wares. First through Braun home appliances and then to the other German makers, the Bauhaus idiom influenced virtually all producers.[73]

Of course, fine art offers vision from afar as well as through proximate contact. Operating more or less independently in the United States, Harry Bertoia, himself a lifelong artist, attributed his classic steel-rod or "diamond" chairs to Marcel Duchamp. "I wanted my chair

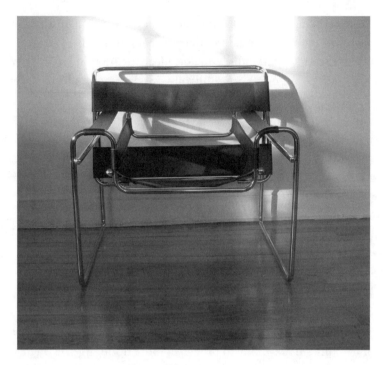

"Wassily" chair by Marcel Breuer, 1925. Photograph by Jon Ritter.

to rotate, change with movement, like the body in Duchamp's 'Nude Descending a Staircase'" Bertoia said.[74] This chair has been vastly imitated, with the wire back appearing in kitchen dinette sets, folding card table sets, and a large run of garden furniture.[75] (The next two pages exhibit the line of descent.)

Matisse and Kandinsky can end up in a tub. To stand out from the competition, the bathroom fixture maker American Standard hired the British designer Robin Levien to create a bathtub that would anchor its other products in the affluent segment of the market. Plumbing products are often sold as ensembles, so if you lose the tub sale, you may lose the sink and toilet as well. Especially if a firm like Jacuzzi—the "hot" maker of expensive tubs—were to buy up a sink/toilet producer they would then have a complete range to threaten the more traditional brands like American Standard. In a 37-page booklet the designer documented his borrowing from Matisse and Kandinsky to create the

*Marcel Duchamp. "Nude Descending a Staircase No. 2," 1912.
©The Philadelphia Museum of Art: The Louise and Walter Arensberg
Collection; ©Artists Rights Society (ARS), New York/ADAGP,
Paris/Estate of Marcel Duchamp.*

Harry Bertoia, Diamond chair, 1952. Photograph courtesy of Knoll.

Wire garden furniture knockoff, circa 1980. Photograph by author.

"single geometric alphabet" of circular arc, large wave, small wave, and straight line that went into the tub's "playful balance." The "Wave" series, produced in a variety of models, was never intended for mass sales but consciously used high art to establish the clients' presence in a particular niche. Sales were sufficient to meet the product's goals, augmented by an unanticipated boost from markets in the Middle East.

The Wave bathtub broke with prior tubs. Ordinary tubs are symmetrical with hot and cold controls on either side of the tap at the tub's foot. In the Wave case, the tap is on the side about where an outstretched hand could reach the flow, and the temperature controls are also on the side, but in easy reach of the hand. This tub can trade on asymmetric images put in circulation by certain modern artists and the emerging deconstruction architects. It is a break with classicism and Victorian aesthetic conventions. The tub is also safer and more comfortable than conventional tubs, but much pricier—as much as ten-fold the cost of base models. The same art "groundwork," I would argue, helped the success of the more basic Ford Taurus by allowing dashboard controls to be clustered around the driver. This was a reversal from prior dashboards using an aesthetic of rectilinear symmetry. The new design helped make cars safer by lessening the stretch of short-armed drivers trying to reach for radio dials.

Even seldom seen infrastructure is affected by art. Pipelines, in homes and factories can tend toward formal rectilinear symmetry, as for example when a fuel supply must make connection to two different valves. Compare this kind of installation with one that allows an asymmetrical linkage through a shallow-angled branching as shown in the drawings on page 81. The symmetrical version may look neater, but the right angles raise energy pumping costs. The alternative version works better, makes less noise, and is more eco-friendly.[76] It has been resisted because so many involved in the process, including professional engineers, defer to classical neatness. As with other art-to-product routes, the path is not so self-conscious as the Wave designers' record of Matisse-to-tub. Art just merges with life and work experiences, available as part of the blend that makes things thinkable.

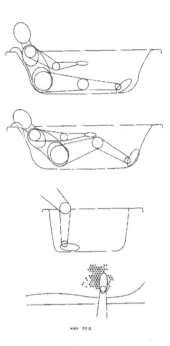

Tub study, inspired by Matisse.
©Studio Levien.

Tub study—ergonomic exercise.
©Studio Levien.

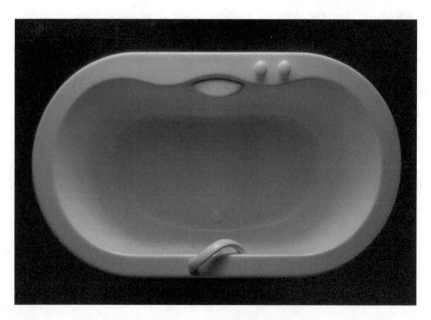

"Wave" bathtub as marketed. ©Studio Levien.

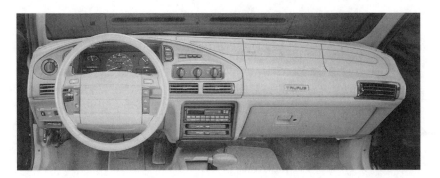

Ford Taurus dashboard. ©Ford Motor Company.

Geometric symmetry, Pontiac car dashboard. Photograph by author.

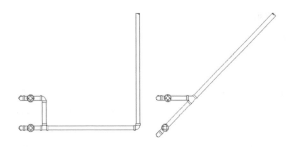

Symmetrical and right-angle pipes vs. asymmetrical. Drawings by David Paul Collett.

THE SEMIOTIC HANDLE

Whatever its original inspiration, the management of aesthetic detail helps determine the specific ways a product will be useful and durable. The polka dots or a favorite Disney motif on a child's bedding is more likely to secure a comfortable night's sleep (for both child and parent) than putatively more "functional" hospital whites.[77] When decoration is a "technology of enchantment,"[78] it is as efficacious as any other form of technology. The enchantment details have to be just right, appropriate to the users gender, age, and so forth. Individuals can be attracted to an object but "wrongly" attracted, for example. Form may excite a pull on the wrong lever, or in the wrong order, with an unsuitable grip, or for an inappropriate application. If the push-down lever of a pop-up toaster beckoned not just a single finger, but the whole hand, the force could damage the mechanism. Scholars now understand that all objects tell a story, have a semiotics that people "read." Every material object thus works through its *semiotic handle* and that kind of handle, as much as any other type, affects what something can be by making it attractive in the first place and specifically useful in practice.

I am not making the more familiar argument that objects should be shaped to make them more useful in a conventional sense of utility. In his influential book *The Design of Everyday Things* Donald Norman condemns design that puts aesthetics ahead of functionality. Instead, he thinks, products should be shaped to provide affordances, their very form should instruct the proper use. He praises, for example, faucet handles on some airplane washbasins that invite a downward pressure by having concave indentations that cradle the finger. I like the faucets he likes and hate the VCRs, with their long booklets of instruction, that he condemns. And everyone should worry about nuclear power plant control panels set up as a uniform array to give them a "modern" look, if that means plant operators will be confused in approaching them.[79] But in opposing aesthetics, Norman does not seem to realize that aesthetics are the basis of his affordances. Faucet handles do not simply have indentations; there are indentations and there are indentations. The ones praised by Norman invoke surrealist forms of sculptor Jean Arp—an imagery that many jet-era customers can find, literally and pre-

cisely, attractive. Just exactly how a physical element will act as a "come-
on" depends upon the designers' ability to catch the cultural sensuali-
ties of the moment and the group, and mobilize them for the
push-down goal. The "before" version of the open-heart surgery device
(fig. 2.2), ugly to most contemporary eyes, would likely have been intu-
itively friendly for a mind shaped by ninteenth-century mechanics. But
given the art-historical and consumer goods moment of the late twentieth-century, the molded shapes of handles and forms of the "after"
invite the more healthy usage.

Getting the right semiotic handle affects utility in capital goods,
both in the sense of helping them sell as well as enabling production
through their use. In awarding a prize to Uvex Designers for Genesis
protective eyewear (worn in industrial applications), the jurors praised
the lenses as "successful because they make you want to put them
on. . . . And once you've got them on, they're so comfortable you're in no
hurry to take them off."[80] The aesthetics of forklift trucks also seem to
matter, whether because it helps workers do a better job or just because
factory owners like to buy stuff that looks good—or both. Crown
Equipment Corporation's decision to break the U.S. industry mold by
hiring a design consultant in the early 1960s resulted in crisp Bauhaus
lines on their forklift trucks. The product won the IDSA "gold" (shared
that year with the Ford Mustang), and launched the company toward
market dominance (with annual sales of $600 million by 1995). The
founder and CEO, Thomas Bidwell, says that although he is "from an
industry that bends heavy metal . . . we used design to build our company.
. . . Design was our edge."[81] He recalls that people think his customers "are
the tough guys who chew cigars." But "I never did buy that. . . . This guy
buys suits. He doesn't turn his senses off when he goes to work."

The right semiotics will be of one sort for an airplane sink, another
for a skateboard, and still different again for a chair that certain people
will find worth sitting in. In some cases—for example, products for
young "techies"—it may be important for the product to look hard to
use, or may be hard to use in fact. If not, people will avoid it, and it will
have no use at all.

After generations of being focused on exterior decoration of people's pots and baskets, archaeologists increasingly now recognize that

what they called "style" goes beyond what is on the surface. Even just in physical terms, style is not merely a surface add-on, but involves proportion and shape, the thickness of the rim or lip of a vessel, the flanging of a bronze ax.[82] Vessels must hold things that people can, given human physiology, manage to carry, but they otherwise can be vastly different— archaeologists call this potential for variations in the way the same thing can be accomplished "isochrestic" variation.[83] Style is not something opposed to function but contains it. So form and function, rather than bespeaking opposition, are the conjoining mechanism through which a particular people at a particular moment get something done. This settles a false dichotomy and provides a way to understand why in looking at contemporary product realms, "it's both" keeps coming up.

One way to see how the process works is to examine instances when things, either by accident or through deliberate calculation, go "off"— when the tension between apparent form and apparent function gets manipulated in a way that notice must be taken of form-function as a *problem*. Duchamp could generate outrage with his 1917 urinal because it juxtaposed what was then "simply" a functional item with a setting in which its function could *not* possibly be fulfilled. The subsequent practice of sticking other ordinary utilitarian objects into a setting in which they cannot function raised eyebrows until this latest twist in modern art—using "found objects" alone or in assemblage—itself became routine. The magic went out because people, just by seeing it repeated and maybe practicing it some on their own, learned just how the shock was generated. Just as I imagine the very first "real" urinals to have been a rush that dissipated over time, so it was that the first art gallery urinals lost their effectiveness.

Artists repeatedly try to intrigue with form-function confusions. It was used in a garden bench entitled "Reserved: Seating to be shared with flowers." As shown in the picture that follows, a human-scale garden bench has large holes across the seat with artificial flower heads poking through. There is just barely enough space to partially sit between them—is it "really" a bench? "Only" an artwork? By putting the piece at the edge of this presumed boundary, the artists thwart the normal habit of classification, thus stopping some traffic and producing some wonder.

Garden bench art piece. "Reserved: Seating to be Shared with Flowers." ©Michael Anastassiades, Anthony Dunne, and Fiona Raby.

Closer into the product realm, some useful artifacts carry an artful tingle of uselessness as part of their appeal. In her line of home furniture, Maya Lin (creator of the Vietnam Memorial) has side chairs that put the body slightly off-center—deliberately awkward for those whose sense of comfort means having symmetrical access left and right. Her chairs require a certain twist in the sitter. As she explains it, "It's almost a subconscious way of making people pay attention to their surroundings."[84] In this "making people pay attention," the chair operates as a piece of art, continuously intervening in the body's movements and the sitter's experience. As with any such effort, the issue is not whether the chair is fundamentally dysfunctional, although keeping the body moving is thought by many experts to be physiologically best. But it wouldn't matter if it were ergonomically awful. If people so much enjoy "a Maya Lin" that they buy it and use it, then it has the right affordance to make it a success all around. Her chair is radical because it pushes against

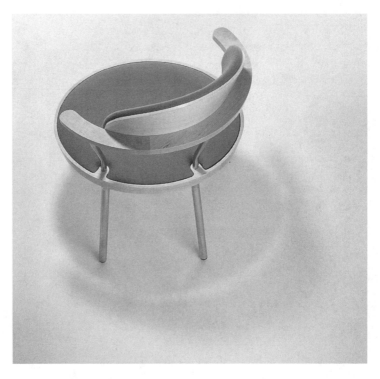

Chair by Maya Lin, The Earth is (not) Flat. Photograph courtesy of Knoll.

understandings and customs of what is the ideal form-function mix, the type-form convention, for a chair.

MAKING LOVE

Productive projects require coordination among diverse actors; there must be a way to "get it together"—to enlist enthusiasm as well as create a common understanding as to what a shared enthusiasm should serve. Art, not just in regard to representations in plans and prototypes but also narratives and song, coordinates diverse individuals and groups by tacitly providing shared understanding of "what this is all about." We know the details involved in even a single life project are always too numerous to explicitly state, that no list of rules can incorporate all that needs to be known and done.[85] Whether making a movie or a line of dishware, some alternative mechanism is required to seduce diverse agencies and actors into a coherent effort and to give them "the feel" for the desired outcome. It is "art"—sometimes a painting (like a Matisse bather), a metaphor (like "the tabernacle"), or a fantastic aspiration (Steve Jobs's drive for products "insanely great")—that radiates visions that span across actors and industrial segments. Art brings enrollment.

Before Edison could have his lightbulb, a lot of different actors had to sign on. Edison overtook his competitors (like Swan in England) not just by coming upon a good gizmo, but by organizing other aspects of the industry into being—investors, power sources, and government cooperation to stage street lighting exhibitions.[86] This coordination was no doubt part of the "perspiration" he said was crucial to his success. As reported in firsthand accounts, seeing streets lit by electricity filled hearts with rapture, helping overcome not only organizational impediments but also fears of so inexplicable and dangerous a technology (gas lighting also gained its early acceptance through uses "for effect and display as much as for utility").[87] Colored glass followed, evolving into Tiffany lampshades to add further glory to displace the dark. A bandwagon builds as people find it easier to love something others also love—something we see at performances when people joyfully join with one another in offering a "rousing" applause.[88] A crowd of affections becomes a virtuous mob as aesthetic contagion spreads. Impresario of it all, Edison prevailed.

We can look, using the same ideas, at why a big contemporary project can fail. Over 24 years of planning and prototype efforts, the sponsors of an ambitious automated French railway project called Aramis spent large sums and extended great energies before finally giving up. In the end the project could no longer hold together; the diverse participants—politicians, bureaucrats, financiers, technologists, media, and public groups—no longer operated in common orientation toward it as something worthwhile. In his detailed account,[89] Bruno Latour chronicles how so many pieces needed to be kept together more or less at once and over an extended period—something that only "love" could do. When segments of the coalition fell out of love, the prospect of a lash-up for Aramis came to an end. Latour found "love" in his study of

French transit in the same way Cyril Stanley Smith found it in the toys—as well as art—that he perceived to be the core of technological change. "All big things grow from little things," Smith writes, "but new little things will be destroyed by their environment unless they are cherished for reasons more like love than purpose."[90] Or, from a different context and put another way by jazz maestro Duke Ellington, "it don't mean a thing if it ain't got that swing."

CHICKENS AND EGGS

I have tried to clarify why "it's both." For any product, form and function are always bound up. Partisans can choose to praise one over the other. Historians can notice that the "art" came before the utility or vice versa. Consumers can explain they love it because it works or because its so pretty. But within the mind, biography, and history, form and function interact as they mutually determine what something turns out to be. We are, with form and function, with art and economy, at home not just with chicken and egg, but chicken in egg and egg in chicken. There are no independent variables in this henhouse.

I think the root of confusion is the common assumption that instrumental rationality is the core of human activity, an idea reinforced not only by academic fields like formal logic and economics but by almost everyone's retrospective accounts of their own behavior. Whether in science articles, history books, or even therapy sessions, folks "clean up" their messes to provide an orderly story.[91] In part this is because it is nearly impossible to recapture the complex textures that make up human activity and in part because we are expected to have performed in a way sufficiently "rational" to make a tidy accounting possible. We are supposed to mesh our accounts "with the juridical, ethical or grammatical legalism" in which we each find ourselves.[92] Indeed, to try and make conscious the artful mechanisms through which practice occurs undermines the very capacity to succeed at that practice— like trying to ride a bike by thinking through how it can happen.

To speculate ever more widely, I surmise that people do sometimes recognize, as evidenced especially in their poetry, religion, and song, that life's ends are artistic. But even if they reach these "heights" of spirituality, folks understand the means for reaching such ends as—at least in the United States and Europe—practical strategies. At each moment individuals tend to exaggerate the role of the utilitarian. The artful pleasure always beckons on the horizon—pie in the sky, by and by—or when nostalgic moments recall the meaningful moments of a spent life. Whatever wisdom this implies for enriching our existence, the relevance here is that the underplay of art, both as an end and as a means to reach that end, inhibits understanding of how new things happen.

The right form-function combination makes for a successful product, but the durability of that success depends on the type of artifact, its market niche, and the cultural moment. We now examine why some things—like stripes on underpants—change a lot, while things like diamond rings seem to go on forever.

CHAPTER 4

Changing Goods

As with first names, internal mechanisms and external forces make both change and stability part of the goods story. Parallel to the strain any of us can feel about whether to change job, car, or diet, forces in the artifact system simultaneously augur for stability as well as for doing something new. Tension is everywhere and probably always has been.

Even the bugaboo of "fashion"—a never-ending flux of socially mandated change—has been around quite a while. Just how long? Some point, usually accusatorily, to the rise of couture in the late nineteenth century—when "dictate" from Parisian ateliers created yearnings for the new.[1] But earlier dates are also cited, starting when mass manufacture made consumer goods plentiful enough for people to use commodities to follow trends and distinguish themselves from others; fashion textile prints were widespread in the late eighteenth century.[2] And still earlier dates surface: fashion magazines showed up in Paris in 1677. Earlier still, French royal courts stimulated change in furnishings and dress, with each successive monarch setting off new styles.[3] About 1350 European men's jackets grew shorter—a fashion change, the historian Fernand Braudel calls it.[4]

To the east, a surviving Chinese document from 1301 A.D. contains advice as to what kind of writing brushes, ink, and hardwood furniture one should properly have, including recognition of what we would consider a vogue for emulating others.[5] Artisans of the late Chinese Ming dynasty (sixteenth century) created porcelain and silks, a world of "superfluous things" in a "relentlessly fluid game of emulation."[6] Evidently "the ferocious pursuit of getting and spending has a long history. The feverish pursuit of fashion is just as ancient," says Neil McKendrick after decades of study in the history of consumption.[7] All this makes a search for "the beginning" seems pointless; there may never have been a time of unchanging objects locked in the "still waters of ancient situations."[8]

One cause of change, forceful in any era, is contact among strangers and groups, whether coerced in conquest or more voluntarily in trade, intergroup mating, or happenstance. Some now "classic" Greek motifs arose from contact with Pharaonic Egypt, as did more basic changes in design and construction technology. Within Greece, the architectural motif of the acanthus plant (used atop the Corinthian column) evolved in this way from simpler to more complex forms to yield what we now take to be their classic shapes.[9] The Greeks' and Romans' foreign exploits brought them not just design motifs to imitate, but the convenience of slaves, which also affected their goods. Togas, which themselves were a fashion item—they varied by weave and material as well as by clasps that changed in elaborate ways—made the left hand largely useless. This feature could work only when others were available to do hard labor and to serve. Access to slaves and the toga, along with body stance and mode of gesture, made up a coherent configuration—lash-up of body, costume, and social organization. As access to "help" waxes and wanes among specific groups, their stuff changes.

Whether in contemporary design studios or ancient craft settings, the creators have their own pecking orders of emulation, based on personal and professional admiration and disdain. Anthropologists report that Luo potters (people in the Lake Victoria region of Africa) would add a motif used by an especially popular potter to their repertoires, just as a personal antagonism led them to deliberate differentiation.[10] Change also happens because of human limitations in ability to mimic one another and conform to those traditions they value. As with parents who choose wrongly in trying to provide their child with a common name—because its time may be up just at that moment—people are limited in their capacities to imitate other conventions of their time and place. Given the large number of items, motifs, and ideas that exist even in so-called simple societies, reproduction is a challenge, one bound to small errors or even large mishap. Imagining unchanging style presumes that people can unproblematically categorize just what fits or does not fit the canon of their moment. This is a doubtful proposition, given changes in weather, membership, personality, technologies, and contact. Every instance is a chance to get it wrong; as a single new detail gains acceptance, ramifications occur in other parts of the composition that also need adjusting.

Commentators easily exaggerate similarities within bygone groups—at the extreme putting human figures in natural history museum dioramas "as a changeless natural species ."[11] Also not helping matters is the tendency for the "indigenous" tourist industry to select certain artifacts as the essence of the traditional and to churn them out as souvenirs. Malinowski reported difficulty in appreciating the small differences in Kula people's goods that made them more or less valuable in trade—it "took a connoisseur's eye to spot the differences."[12] It makes a good thought experiment: What would future excavators from a culture that did not use chairs (or blouses or computers) make of them if unearthed in the absence of contemporary commentaries, advertisements, and other documentation? If the discovering people found them utterly strange and useless, it might take some special subtlety to see the kinds of evolving differences that mean so much in today's context. A "traditional" artifact (or event) is only "traditional" when, Gell puts it, "viewed from a latter-day perspective."[13]

Change itself can be part of a venerated tradition. Tamil women used colored and white powders (some still do) to create home threshold floor "paintings" every morning to honor the cobra deity of fertility and, in their mazelike complexity, ward off or ensnare demons.[14] Within this genre, thousands of variations arise in response to fashion as well as convention.[15] In "traditional" Bali, dance was and still is a basis of competition among village troupes, and innovations are made continually in moves and stances.[16] Indigenous American peoples such as the Yurok-Karon of northwestern California worked the twigs, roots, and grasses of their baskets into a never-ending variation of new styles, which they recognized as passing fads and which did not detract from more constant designs they also used at the same time.[17] Slaves in the U.S. South dyed their plain rough clothing with bark from local trees and found ways to create ornamentation on their bodies and headgear. As with other poor people in their era, they apparently responded to the local social currents, purchasing such goods as tea, buckles, and velvet with their meager resources.[18] From whatever combination of forces, slavery—according to one historian—"helped create a people keenly interested in fashion, intensely aware of personal style, and fervently committed to expressiveness in their everyday life."[19] Prisoners and soldiers struggle to adjust and modify their uniforms; Mennonite women manipulate collars, cuffs, and buttons to resist conformity.

For Veblen himself, "no class of society, not even the most abjectly poor, forgoes all conspicuous consumption" or deny themselves "all gratification of this higher or spiritual need."[20] Veblen's complaint was that anonymity under modern conditions increases the conspicuous waste of goods. But contemporary extravagance, distinct in volume and material waste, is not evidence—even for Veblen—of radical break. Newness, just for the sake of the new, "serves to detach the grip of the past in a moving world."[21] "To introduce difference," as Bourdieu says, "is to produce time."[22] That is a good basis for thinking fashion is not news. If goods did not change so quickly in the past as they now do, this probably less reflects any essential psychological or fundamental difference in the way of doing things than limits in technology and opportunity.

Just as there was more change among past peoples than often meets the eye, so there is more stability in the modern world than might be thought. Individual choices change gradually, as when "new" first names build on old first names—adding the "lyn" sound to the more common "Mary," for example. And some names, even in the United States, like "John," remain over generations. A given product does not easily pass away just because of changing whims or even if some other item performs the same task in a better way. The Gem paper clip has been around since the late nineteenth century and shows no sign of letting up, even in the face of innovations, including colored plastic versions (less likely to dent paper or rust), and the advent of the stapler. The Gem clip has become familiar enough to be workable to large numbers of people, to have encouraged cheap methods of fabrication, and to have prompted other uses—such as a place marker or wire tool for retrieving diskettes from computer drives. It has become a handy friend and virtually defines the product type. Nor did the computer do in the paper clip—or paper or file cabinets. The "paperless office" was a chimera; computer users need the security of hard copy, and they use the computer to produce even more of it. This is not to say, of course, that once something exists, it inevitably becomes permanent. But changing one thing means having to have other things change as well, including fears and enthusiasms. All the past mutual enrollments press to keep something if not as it always was, then at least not that different from before. The system has inertia.[23] If anything, the denser array of enrollments that come with a richly complex society may increase inertia rather than decrease it.

The inertia we see in the paper clip—or goods that last "only" a decade or generation, like the Toastmaster IB-14 pop-up—corresponds to the parallel phenomena at a deep cognitive level. People think in blends, and goods also come in blends. We can imagine these composites—consistent with archaeological ideas on the linkage of form and function (as in chapter 3)—as styles. Style means recognizable coherence among things that are at least somewhat distinct in what they do and how they appear.[24] For my purposes, style is both the actions of people who make things cohere and the visible achievements of that activity. Style provides stability in that individual items are not free to change willy-nilly on their own; they have to work within a larger context of how things are done and get recognized.[25] Clinician Oliver Sacks says that this aspect of style involved in recognizing coherence and adhering to it "is neurologically, the deepest part of one's being, and may be preserved, almost to the last, in a dementia" (he is speaking of actual Alzheimer's cases).[26] The philosopher John Dewey pointed out generations ago that "habits" free us to entertain innovation. It is reasonable that people should, at least on some occasions and in regard to some objects, expect the material fodder of personal and social habits to "keep still."

Plausibly enough, then, when things do change, there are forces at work that cause the change to be gradual and small, rather than sudden and large. The close study of changes in surface decoration and images on Polynesian artifacts indicates they underwent only minor variations over time. For example, creators may reverse a stick-figure leg design by pointing feet inward rather than outward. Motifs change in this modest way, evolving along "axes of coherence."[27] It happens like this across different types of objects as well as over time, for example when a decorative element travels from a ceramic pipe to a small bowl to a larger one and then an urn. Working under what Gell called the "principle of least difference," successive innovations involve "the least modification of neighboring motifs consistent with the establishment of a distinction between them."[28] So new styles emerge from prior styles. The results are not unlike the marginal differentiation once associated with U.S. car makers' annual design changes. In the words of a designer I spoke with, "we edit here."

Even within couture and high fashion, where radical change is often thought to be de rigueur, year-to-year style alterations are subtle adjustments of prior versions. This is what appears true from a systematic comparison of high-style women's clothing over the period from 1760 to 1960.[29] Thus even fashion change corresponds more to the principle of least difference than to radical shift. Any designer must, in product design pioneer Henry Dreyfuss's words, "be able to anticipate the public's desires, yet guard against being too far ahead."[30] Once again, this does not mean that some "fashion forward" producers, for example in a realm like couture, do not sometimes try (and succeed) in shocking.[31] But when they do so they are creating artistic spectacle, not clothes people will wear—and even the shocks are in line with aesthetic fashion of *that* world and what the first adopters will find almost practical. The avant-garde deploys just the right kind of outrage that will sell their more conventional goods on the racks.

Small variations, however limited in their scale, do mean a lot. What, after all, could Marilyn Monroe have done with a name like "Mary Monroe"? A furniture company rep in the LA Design Center waxed eloquent to me on the innovative use of a single oval covered button on the back of an upholstered chair as setting it apart from "what everyone else is doing."[32] Details in merchandise, as in conversation, diction, and body movements, are seen even when they are not noticed—"unspeakably significant,"[33] in Balzac's characterization of what he thought of as the moral universe of merchandise specifics. So it is that while contemporary commentators can so easily perceive change in the familiar world around them, they miss the small variations that happen among people who are distant.

TYPE FORM: SOME SPECIFICS OF STABILITY

Designers notice that most items—cars, houses, and bathtubs—achieve a widely accepted "type form," as some of them call it. Consistent with the least difference principle, people resist variations that depart too strongly from what they think "a thing like that" ought to be. Although designers may at times balk at what they take as overly rigid expectations, they know type form well as something to work with or at least work around.

Adherence to type form is a reason that new products often "unnecessarily" resemble a prior item that performed a similar function. Hence the first cars looked like carriages without horses; Benz called his first version the "oil spirit motor tricycle," and it had three wheels in tricycle format. Archaeologists call functionally unnecessary imitation "skeuomorphism." A familiar case is the architectural dentil adorning the cornice of Greek buildings and persisting in neoclassical architecture. Though they play no functional role in buildings of stone, they mimic the familiar protruding ends of wood joists and helped bring acceptance for the "new" material,[34] becoming an essential element of the classical style. Another architectural example is the layout of the House of Commons; it replicated the choir section of the Royal Chapel that Parliament had "borrowed" from the Royals for its first meetings. The building burned down several times, but in each instance the replacement repeated the original scheme—in this case, one not exactly functional for parliamentary use in the first place. What was originally, in today's language, an "adaptive reuse," came not just to define the British parliamentary environment, but sanctify it.

Type form particularly constrains products that consumers do not often replace—what are called "slow turn" goods. Even small variations may find resistance when people plan to buy only one model over a gen-

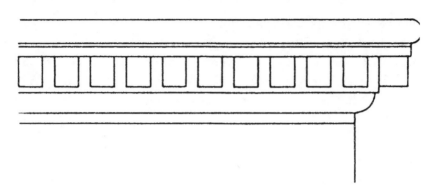

Architectural dentil. Courtesy of Glenn Wharton.

eration. When people purchase a bathtub, they know it may be for a lifetime, so they choose one with a prior satisfactory history. Slow turn generates conservative design. Various products fall on different points of the fast-slow continuum. Automobiles turn faster than, say, farm machinery. In clothing and music CDs, stuff is cheap enough to generate very fast turn. Entry is easy for new producers who are quick to respond to changing tastes and consumers are ready to take chances with a fresh approach. But even in realms of fast turn, subcategories can have highly developed type form. Despite efforts by the formalwear industry to encourage novelty, men who own tuxedos do not wear them often enough to justify the expense of variety. This means the one in the closet needs to be conservative. At the other end of the sartorial spectrum, Levi "501" jeans also became a standard retail item for decades—a virtual fetish. It led to countless "jeans-like" imitations, but always revolving around the Levi original. Other standards include khaki pants and skirts and the Izod cotton piqué knit shirt (the one with the alligator); the Land's End imitation alone sold more than 10 million copies, although with evolving color variations.

Cognitive Limits

A first constraint on change comes from human beings' cognitive limits; if objects are to serve as the mental landmarks that allow thinking to occur (see chapter 3), *everything* cannot be in continuous flux. In a more everyday way than we are sometimes consciously aware, there is limited time to learn new tricks. I suspect there is a better software program than the one I use to handle the citations in this book, but I am not going to take it on at this stage of my writing.

These limits translate into goods production. The oft-cited historic example is the QWERTY keyboard that, despite its ergonomic and speed inefficiency, just goes on like John.[35] Typewriter keyboards are built into people's fingers and minds through rote training—there are no mnemonic devices for figuring out how it works. Mastery is not to be given up lightly. Hence when the computer came along, it had to fit the old order—the skills and customs bequeathed by prior goods' configuration. In the contrasting case of touch-tone telephones, the adding machine was the keyboard precedent, one with a bottom-up array (lowest numbers at the keyboard base). But since few had mastered the adding machine and because it takes less effort to learn the relevant skills anyway, Bell Telephone could switch to a top-down layout when replacing the old dial mechanism with a keypad version.[36] In the early history of home radio, push-button controls dominated, rather than toggle switches or pull levers, despite what some have argued was their inferiority in dealing with signal drift.[37] People may similarly prefer analog to digital indicators on things like dashboard gauges because they are cognitively accustomed to the old-style movements. And that may be enough to keep them in use.

Cultural Meanings

Another kind of stickiness comes from cultural meanings, "cultural" in the sense of an identifiable social group's shared orientation of how things should be. Analogous to the traditions in various societies of naming children from a small repertoire drawn from deceased relatives, religious artifacts tend to resist change. Although books in general are fast turn, Bibles are not and resist alteration of type-form. Bible publishers avoid contemporary graphics, experiments in formatting (oversize or cutouts, or odd-shaped pages) or novelty treatments like scratch'n sniff. Ceremonial goods in general tend in the same direction—think of wedding dresses. People insist their wine come in glass bottles with a cork top, despite the fact that paperlike cartons can keep a vintage equally well—they were tried but failed in the marketplace.

Pillar taps. Photograph by Kirstin Dougall.

Plain metal screw tops (with plastic liners, of the type used on only cheap drink) are better to keep bottled wine from going bad, but people resist buying wine that way.[38] Adhering to the principle of least difference, some wine makers are replacing real cork with cork-colored plastic versions that can be removed only with corkscrews. It's less convenient than screw tops but keeps the ceremonial aspect alive.

Particular cultural contexts affect the nature of type form in different ways. British bathroom spigots or taps, as they call them, are a mystery for Americans and many others in the world. Still in the new millennium, separate, unconnected hot and cold "pillar taps" account for the majority of sales. Hot comes out of one side of the sink and cold out of the other. In using British sinks, I rush to get my business done under the "hot" during those few moments before the scalding sets in. I know the approved method is to stop up the sink or tub and fill with appropriate proportions of hot and cold to get the right mix. Presuming there is a stopper around, this takes time and if the solution turns out too hot, one loses more time making adjustments, including the pain of reaching into hot water to retrieve the stopper. From a resource point of view, this system loses hot water down the drain and cold water to rebalance the mixture. When I asked a friend in London why he preferred separate taps over what the British call the "mixer tap" he fell back on a cognitive, rather than cultural, explanation: "You know where you are." Others insisted UK plumbing was incompatible with mixer taps. I pursued such explanations at the British Bathroom Council, two British designers of bath fixtures, and several bath fixture shops. There is no technical constraint. The stores sell mixer taps or pillar taps based on people's sense of fashion and whim. Customers do not discuss their infrastructure circumstance, nor is it relevant for them to be asked. Unconnected pillar taps persist as a matter of style preference, maybe reflecting a vogue for "Edwardian looks" in the bath.

Besides national difference, type-form content often varies among groups in other ways, including by gender. So we end up with pink for girls and blue for boys, large and heavy for males (or larger number of controls and knobs), even when there is no clear functional reason. Bell Telephone made its "princess phone" diminutive not because women have smaller ears or fingers; they did not need to service gender, they needed to signal it. Motorbikes, like the Harley Davidson, are deliberately loud with exposed engine parts to help provide an "exaggerated look of fierce power"[39]—a "mechanical sexism," in Dick Hebdige's phrase.[40] In contrast, motor scooters are marketed to women as well as men and have their engines "dressed" (that is, enclosed). Italian maker Lambretta quickly discontinued its "undressed" 1951 model because of poor sales.[41] As a matter of type form, and linked to gender, motorbikes come undressed and motor scooters dressed. Women's bicycles, with the dropped frames originally designed to handle large skirts, are more easily mounted by anybody—and also offer more comfortable rides. But now, even with the heavy skirts gone, men do not go near the dropped frame. Females often use the male diamond form frame, as for competitive racing, but the "girl's bike"—like girls' names—stigmatize those of the opposite sex. They thus remain gendered, and hence when bikes are done up in pastels and with feminine baskets, they are of the dropped-frame variety.

Cultural context and historic time influence how color and texture play into type form. The popularization of the germ theory of disease led to a new anxiety of cleanliness, prompting appliance makers to sheath kitchen equipment and bathroom fixtures in white porcelain. When hard-scrubbed to a high gleam, such shiny whiteness could proclaim family protection.[42] Some of these goods have since gone through stylistic changes (pastels hit big in the '50s, followed by—in rough U.S. sequence—avocado, harvest gold, gleaming black, brushed steel). The bathtub is an especially hard case of germ consciousness. Its obdurate surface, of whatever color, provides cold, hard discomfort and is a frequent cause of injury and death. Softer, resilient plastic tubs have been unable to find a good market. Compromised plastic versions, still rather hard, are used in more down-market settings to save money—a case of the less well off having a safer experience than the affluent.

White can have other meanings; it signifies mourning in some parts of the world.[43] Black also varies, connoting death in Europe but rebirth in Egypt. Red is a favorite for sports cars in the United States, but doesn't work well in China, where red is the color for mourning—and is politically charged. Splashes of color can be used to imply "fun" in products; in the mid-1990s I was told that Spaniards prefer such goods (and also amusing shapes, like a steam iron with ears). Americans want black on black in their high-fidelity equipment, which once was the preference among Germans, who later moved on to a small use of color (like a spot of red) amid the black.[44]

Type form also has sound that varies across cultures and product. Compared, for example, to Japanese, Americans typically have high tolerance for loud products—their dishwashers, washing machines, and vacuum cleaners make more noise than those in other countries. While larger houses allow Americans to distance themselves from whirring motors, they may take loudness as evidence of serious capability (the Harley effect). On the other hand, Europeans, according to a GM official explaining their taste for stick shifts, "prefer the acoustic acceleration experience, whereas for Americans the big selling point is a quiet car."[45] But not for all car models; Chrysler made its 1963 turbine cars deliberately louder to imply jetlike speed.

Type form also has touch; besides the hard smoothness of tubs, each part of the car has a specifically favored feel (and sound). So it goes across the goods: pens can be, depending on time and place, hard or a bit soft but not sticky; refrigerator handles must not feel warm; keyboard keys ought to be springy. Sensations of slime or anything resembling the texture of human wastes seems wrong for any product among virtually all peoples.

Talkability and Taboo

Products differ in their "talkability"; some goods, or at least their key attributes, appear to be unspeakable in any culture. This greatly reinforces type form because marketers cannot tout features and users do not spread word informally. In the extreme case of the toilet, marketers cannot discuss what the product actually *does* (even the word "toilet" is not used). So they bring up aesthetics and water savings. The closest I've seen advertisers come to a straightforward toilet pitch is in an ad by the global maker "Toto," which carried the headline: "Its FORM speaks to those with an eye for beauty. Its FUNCTION speaks to those whose eyes are floating [*sic*]." Given this peculiar way of having to talk, there is little incentive for toilet designers to develop a functionally superior product.[46] Indeed if the resulting product would look off type form, there would be no way to explain why, and consumers would avoid it (toilet accessories, like plungers, carry a similar liability).

But clearly, there are reasonable alternatives to the toilet as we know it. The so-called Turkish toilet, which requires a squatting position, is ergonomically superior and more sanitary. "Thighs against abdomen provide the stomach muscles with the support they need for pushing action," according to a closely reasoned analysis.[47] Less skin touches what others have touched and with less chance of contact with fecal matter. But toilets of any sort have their own lash-up, including a forbidding discourse of distaste and ribaldry. To change toilets would require discussion of how the body works, the need for a different physical approach and sense of dignity. Clothing would also have to change so that lower-body garments could function without becoming soiled; plumbing infrastructure might also need to change. An effort, unsuccessful, was made to adapt to all this in a modest way by adding raised footrests and configuring handholds to existing models to make squatting possible over a conventional toilet.[48]

Across industrial Europe, toilets keep their idiosyncratic liabilities and benefits (for those who can handle it, some unspeakable pros and cons of various toilets are listed in the footnote at the end of this sentence).[49] There are indeed some superior features that might serve global needs if there was a way for them to travel. A Swedish toilet separates urine and feces in the plumbing system. Relatively harmless, urine becomes immediately useful as fertilizer (merely diluted 10:1 with water before application). Some Swedish toilets use dry systems to deal with feces. Certain Japanese toilets like the one depicted on the next page are, in effect, combination sink-toilets. Pressing the flush lever simultaneously sends clean water out of the spigot on top, drawn from the building's water supply while releasing the tank water to flush away the waste. The sink water then runs down into the tank ready to flush away the next user's deposit. This means that people can wash their hands before touching anything besides the toilet itself (like the release door lever of a public stall). The toilet's automatic recycle of the water used for hand washing is an ecological gain. Other Japanese toilets (Italian ones, too) have separate controls to unleash a heavier wash for solid excrement than for urine. Some have heated seats or upward sprays that rinse body parts. But none of these advantages can easily move beyond national borders.

Taboo more subtly affects a wider range of products, like the French bidet, which plumbing fixture companies have long tried to transfer to the United States and Britain. Besides their enhancement of women's personal hygiene and use as a contraceptive aid, they are good for rinsing feet, bathing babies, and have their "especial value to the many who suffer from hemorrhoids."[50] New York's Ritz Carlton Hotel installed them at the beginning of the twentieth century, but protesting crusaders, considering them immoral, forced removal. Other goods related to human wastes (toilet paper, wipes) as well as any sex products (whips, vibrators, condoms, and dildoes) also engender circumspection.

Some products are more than mentionable; people may enjoy giving consumer tips to one another on computer equipment or sports gear and feel free to spontaneously comment on a new jacket or sofa. Lots of things are midrange. Washing machines are kept relatively apart—both physically in the utility room and topically out of dinner parties—because they are just not interesting in social life (which is why TV ads with homemakers going on and on about their clean wash seem

Japanese sink-toilet. ©TotoUSA.

comically forced). That likely helps sustain top-loader tub versions within the United States, even though European diagonal axis models are quieter and use less water.

In societies where death is taboo, the specifics of burial products cannot come up. Undertakers thus face challenges when trying to introduce new artifacts like jewelry to hold human ashes (offered by CEI/BACO in Aurora, Illinois) or molten glass sculpture incorporating cremation remains (marketed by Companion Star of Hinsdale, Illinois). But the silences do provide undertakers with special advantages in selling extravagant products that do conform to type form. Goods associated with infirmity and disease are often off-limits for casual banter, making it hard for remedial products to easily respond to changing taste systems or even functional needs. Hence things like wheelchairs and crutches were produced in neutral colors and conservative forms—their applications tinged with the closet. The same is true for the larger array of tools and equipment used by sick people—bedpans, urine flasks, and colostomy pouches (the latter made to be imperceptible on the body). Those who end up needing such goods—often unexpectedly—have little foreknowledge that might influence market demand. The stigma shapes the goods and inhibits them from changing.

Prior Configurations and Tipping Points

Previously established products and physical infrastructure thwart innovation and hold type form. To put a train on U.S. tracks, its wheels need to span the standard 56 and a half inches, a convention that Americans adopted from the British rail system. That standard derived, in turn, from the road ruts inscribed by the Romans two millennia before. The Roman road measurements stemmed from the rear-end widths of the two horses pulling war chariots.[51] Now it turns out the same dimension carries into the solid rocket boosters used to launch the U.S. space shuttle. The boosters had to be shipped from the Thiokol Corporation's Utah factory by rail—which required that they be sized to fit through rail tunnels configured for the standard gauge.[52] There could have been a better railroad—maybe even a better booster rocket. An 84-and-one-quarter-inch-gauge system did come into being at one time in England. It allowed train wheels to be larger, permitting an increase in train speed of about 40 per cent (although it did require a wider swath of land). It was abandoned in the mid-nineteenth century because too many miles of the narrow-gauge track had already been installed in the United Kingdom (274 miles of broad gauge compared with 1,901 of the narrow).

This is a classic case of "tipping point," the moment at which it becomes too hard to switch or go back. Another is the demise of Sony's Betamax in the United States, generally considered the technically superior option to VHS. It lost because too many consumers came to have VHS machines; at a certain point, Sony was locked out.[53] Today, a bathtub with even slightly different dimensions will not fit the place where tubs go in people's houses. Fixture elements would misalign with pipe locations in the wall—or with the skills and habits of plumbers. In a case of very low-cost infrastructure still mattering a lot, a smaller version of paper towel, ScotTowels Junior, failed in the U.S. marketplace because it did not fit on conventional paper-towel holders.[54] A new-model car radio has to contend with how car dashboards (and electrical systems) are configured. In contrast, if the core product itself has an especially fast-turn potential, there is less need to conform to prior types. To market a new razor blade, the company can just tie it in with a new razor.

Taxicabs show still another way—access to spare parts—that prevalence of an existing product can in itself maintain sales momentum. In New York, the Ford Crown Victoria, a fairly old and uncomfortable vehicle, had about 90 percent of the market in the late '90s. The prevalence of Crown Vics banging into each other on the city's streets provides a valuable spare parts supply for fleet owners; this encourages continued use of the model.[55] The British company making the London cab remains in a strong position perhaps for the same reason, but also because it is not worth the while of a new investor to share so small a vehicle market.

Factory tooling, evolving from prior manufacturing activities, massively influences prospective stuff, but it limits some kinds of products more than others. The making of goods like toys, software, clothing, and, to some degree, houses all allow easy entry and agile experimentation because they rely on equipment and skills that small producers can attain for themselves. But to make even a simple can opener, you need a factory with the right equipment. Although furniture and appliances may seem to be similar products, the former permits innovation in ways the latter does not. Hence washing machines stay more nearly the same (and are more uniform) than chairs. In media products, the drop in video equipment costs allowed small operators to create without access to legitimate studio resources; this encouraged pornography—with its own distribution apparatus—to increase its markets and evolve as a genre.

In the rise of any product, the surrounding artifact world often affects the specifics of the new thing. In configuring the Palm Pilot, its designers were creating a product that would interface with personal computers as well as with habits and other physical elements in people's lives. Palm users typically interchange their data with desktop PCs. Besides having a direct effect on the Palm's operating system, such links mean that having multiple Palm Pilots does not make sense. A "wardrobe" of Palm Pilots (or laptop computers) would require repeated downloading and uploading and confusion as to just what information was where. To avoid such problems, the market had to be one unit per customer (no matter how affluent), and this implies, in turn, a conservative design that can "go with" any sort of outfit or occasion. As the Palm V designer at IDEO expalined, it would be "something you'd wear," like eyeglass frames or a man's wallet, a slow-turn wearable for the pocket. Previous set-ups of what a computer is like, a pocket is like, what people wear (and how factories are set up) give rise to this "new" thing.

Lash-up Conspiracies

Some type forms result from corporate strategies, with varying degrees of deliberateness, to lock in a whole system of consumption. The idea is to succeed not just with a particular element but with all the elements that intertwine—the razor and the razor blade that can be used only with one another. To a degree, this resembles creating a monopoly like the ones Rockefeller patched together, but instead of manipulating organizational forms, physical design becomes a key part of the strategy. Rockefeller united scattered businesses—oil companies, refiners, and railroads—into a set of interlocking trusts under his control but did not change the nature of oil, refining, or railroads to do it. In contrast, Edison set up companies, including one to generate electric power, because of the technical qualities of his inventions. No power source means no lightbulb. He needed mechanical complementarity as well as organizational coordination, financing, and popular enthusiasm.

Companies can, at various levels of ambition and scale, try to use physical design to enroll consumers in a larger array of goods than they might otherwise have bargained for. For example, a firm can deliberately create a product inconsistent with competitors' surrounding peripherals to stimulate a complete switch into a new product line.

Harman/Kardon high fidelity broke with prior forms in a way that encourages purchasers of one of its pieces (tape deck, amplifier, or CD changer) to buy all pieces from Harman/Kardon. Until the company's gambit, audio components were almost always done in Bauhaus rectilinear form, allowing buyers to easily mix brands; the stack would still look pretty good. Harman/Kardon's concave fronts not only made its goods distinctive (see the photograph that follows), but did so in a way that inhibits combination with other product brands. There has to be a sizable group of first adopters willing to replace their entire system either to get the "total look" of the new stack or because one item of the ensemble is so superior they will chuck out everything else so they can have it.

The Apple computer, with the high level of confidence its creators had in the core product, displays such a gamble—one that gave Apple a quasi monopoly over the new type form it created. For many years, Apple benefited from the unity of its product elements in terms of color, buttons, and plugs, icons, mouse, sounds, and lights and, of course, the basic operating system (with closed architecture). For its approximate decade of prominence after 1984, the Apple ensemble created barriers for competitors' peripherals as well as for other computer makers. When lacking such a breakthrough element or system of elements, it becomes smarter to design a product as conventionally as possible so users can add it into other systems.

In a still more ambitious and, it seems, more successful effort than that of early Apple, Microsoft has enrolled a world of software and hardware peripherals around its central products. Intensely fought by other corporate actors, some of them huge like Netscape, the Microsoft lash-up aims to keep expanding and intensifying the shared expectation of what all these products should be like: they should look, act, and think like Microsoft. "Outside" inventors are led to create nothing else and consumers come to be in a position to find that nothing else works as well, given their other stuff and personal habits and practices. Perhaps such guided innovation is the heart of hegemony; producers' and consumers' creativity, at every stroke, reinforces the power of the central force.

This becomes a way to recast the meaning of corporate power over consumption. Once corporate stakeholders are in place, they will

Concave front stereo stack. Harmon/Kardon Festival Intelligent Music System.
Photograph courtesy of Ashcraft Design.

indeed act to sustain the array of interconnections that define the way
of doing things that bring them most benefit. Their efforts offer
more than plausible evidence that structures of power are an influence on the dynamics of demand. But they are only part of a story

that ordinarily involves not a single plot, but the intersection of many schemes, dreams, and games to form a particular "fix." And sometimes it is corporation against corporation; the steam car champions were commercial operations in the same way as the fledgling and hyper-competitive gasoline engine advocates. The Beta system lost out to corporate capitalists, but itself arose from Sony Corporation, not some indigenous social movement. How much does a private corporation's capacity to enforce standardization restrain innovation compared to encouraging it? This was a central issue in the federal government's litigation against Microsoft—one that admits of less than obvious answers because sometimes a stable type form at the core, like a standard set of weights and measures, helps stimulate inventiveness at the periphery.

Overcoming Type Form

Against the inertia that sustains type form are forces of change. Some come from within individuals and internal group dynamics and others from outside political and institutional forces. As for internal dynamics, we can start again at the cognitive level. Repeating the past, I repeat, is not easy to do. People find it hard to re-create, in any precise way, what has come before or what others are doing at the same time. In part, it is difficult because so many details need copying, but it is also difficult because group dynamics keep changing what those details are. I once participated in an acting school theater game that provided a lesson in how imitation works. Circling around a large room, the instructor, Bernard Beck, told each person to mimic the gait of the one directly in front. In so doing, as it turned out, each of us had to keep readjusting because the person in front was also changing. Such never-ending adjustment must run through any group of imitators. In terms of production and consumption, these kinds of forces press against type form, perhaps cumulating into something recognizable as clearly different. This can happen in all kinds of ways including efforts to imitate goods and consumption of the past as well as to encapsulate some vision of the future.

Nostalgia

Ironically, nostalgia can make new things happen. In part this is because bringing back the past never brings it back as it was. Retrieving "Ethel" does not carry the connotations accomplished by the parents of Ethel Kennedy, Ethel Waters, or the TV sitcom creators of Ethel Mertz. Some day, "Ethel" may return, but as with present-day revivals of "Max" and "Joshua," it will be a whole new thing. In products, a nostalgic leap backward usually yields, in physical terms, something that had no prior existence. Reinventing the wheel results in a different one.

When set up in organized ways, remembering becomes "heritage," with goods to match. In Britain, the heritage industry has become one of the country's economic mainstays, involving visits to stately homes and affection for associated goods. Based on imaginings of pastoral gentility, these goods and services do not "bring back" the past, which includes suffering and tedium as well as tea parties.[56] Ceramic water pots may be reproduced line for line, but they are now for flowers rather than as the in-house water supply. In the United States, nostalgia helps "rebuild" old city neighborhoods but in ways their earlier inhabitants would likely not recognize. Early colonial town buildings, for example, commonly had advertisements written across their brick facades at every level, something not usually tolerated by later preservationists. Real buildings and their accessories change right after birth and keep doing so,[57] providing not one, but a range of moments for potential imitators to "remember." "Preserved" houses now can have more heritage stuff than was ever present at any of its prior times. In their combination of attributes, these are new things.

Nostalgia goods typically incorporate contemporary technologies and mechanisms of manufacture as well as new uses. "Gas lamps" flicker with electric currents; the tubs on claw feet have mixer taps, maybe even Jacuzzi jets discreetly mounted in the sides. Colossal "Roman" buildings like New York's once proud Penn Station (built to "reproduce" the baths at Caracalla) consist of steel ribbing holding up vast glass domes. Old car models are brought back, sort of. Working to simulate the 1930s Volkswagen Beetle, the 1998 reissue successfully incorporated modern advances in exhaust pollution, engine efficiency, and crash-test durability, reaching still higher levels in some of these

Chrysler "PT" cruiser. ©DaimlerChrysler Corporation. PT Cruiser and Plymouth are trademarks of DaimlerChrysler Corporation.

regards than any prior VW models. After the Beetle's success, Chrysler brought out the PT Cruiser, combining the look of a gangster car (actually the 1937 Ford) with the utility of a modern minivan. Its box-like shape permits more headroom than other contemporary sedans and also allows for more comfortable back seating because there is so much space for springs and cushioning. The back seats are raised above front seats providing a "stadium" configuration—a newly popular feature in car design. The big spaces and big doors also allow easy changes in seat configurations—from one to five passengers. The retro design and trim makes the product aesthetically acceptable—individual fender forms "add voluptuousness," in the words of the car's designer, Jeff Godshall, to what is a simple rectangle.[58] Even as form reaches backward, the mechanical advances are retained—or even furthered—"underneath." Nostalgia transforms the past in the act of recalling it.

Hybridizing

Mergings with the past, however remembered, run parallel to how mergings work with the stuff of contemporary others. As with the spread of names through contacts among different ethnic groups (like American Jews taking on WASP names), so it is that people adopt other people's goods.

The incarceration of so vast a proportion of young African-American males in the late '80s and throughout the '90s yielded the oversized pants of hip-hop, as youths imitated the ill-fitting trousers worn by prison inmates. The style then moved from ghetto to suburbs and across the globe with effects on couture and then adaptations for the likes of The Gap, Banana Republic, and every other major outlet. Beyond clothing, hip-hop influenced sports equipment, electronic goods, and even car models, at least in terms of surface motifs.

In a more politically explicit fashion trend begun in the African-American community, ethnic leaders of the '60s wore the dashiki as a statement of political and cultural identity, engaging in deliberate "messaging"[59] with their goods. But in doing so they also prepared the marketplace for images that otherwise would have faced greater consumer resistance—they play the conventional role of the avant-garde. Dashiki prints spread across larger segments of the African-American community, then to other people's clothing. The adapted dashiki look moved to luggage, rugs, picture frames, furniture, and pillows, "putting the Dark Continent [*sic*] in the spotlight these days as African-inspired products start to enter the mainstream of the marketplace," as the trade publication *Home Furnishings News* offensively announced the trend in the year 2000.[60]

Such meldings take place under all sorts of conditions, benign, authoritarian, and in between. Stuff that today seems intrinsic to ethnic and national movements often can be traced, quite ironically, to contact with alien worlds. Scots' national dress, the kilt, was imposed on them by the hated English industrialists as substitutes for the traditional long dress coats that could catch in machinery. The now classic dress of Hawaiian women, the muumuu, arose from a heavy dose of coercion. Before contact with Europeans and North Americans, Hawaiian women wore little; subtly hued tapa bark cloth covered some of their lower bodies but left most of their breasts exposed, including the nipples. Nineteenth-century missionaries from the American East forced Hawaiian women to cover up, and because they lacked the fanciful tailoring and trims of the day, they created the simple muumuu. Eventually, the missionaries' prim prints (often little flowers) gave way to bright island designs of Hawaiian flora and the motifs of the pre-contact tapa bark. Now something of an "indigenous" tradition, the garment connotes tropical pleasure, worn commonly by Hawaiian women but also as summer clothing across the United States. Popular with locals as well as tourists, the Aloha shirt is similarly an amalgam. The basic tailoring—simple square shape, no taper, no pleats, and worn over the pants—comes from the shirts worn by Japanese laborers working the plantation economy. Japanese women made children's shirts from leftover kimono fabric, which is the source of the bright colors and silky texture. Application of the Hawaiian word "aloha" came from a Chinese clothing merchant in Honolulu who undertook the early commercial runs. Florals and fruit motifs, otherwise appropriate to women's (and children's) clothing, thus invaded menswear.[61]

Some criticize the hybrid process as "simplification" because it abstracts from something otherwise complexly authentic (a dashiki print from the pan-Africanism it represents) into a different style system that lacks those other particulars. The sin compounds when high people are selecting and appropriating for their own purposes, often for entertainment or amusement. But these borrowings go in all directions and under all sorts of auspices, with unpredictably rich results. Just as African music earlier influenced people, white and black, in North America and Europe to create jazz, music flows "back" to Africa in a "hypercreativity," yielding highlife music in Ghana, the new Afro-Arab music in Kenya, Caribbean reggae in the 1950s and ska more recently.[62] Such changes and others of more limited scope do not replace a complex context with a simpler one but substitute one complexity for another. It may personally offend to see a peasant's cultural artifact converted into costume jewelry, a McDonald's arch worked into a Balinese temple motif, or a boy wearing a nose ring at his Bar Mitzvah. But in each case, there is no shortage of meaning or the actor's personal experience of it. To try and enforce separateness would be artificial and authoritarian. It simulates the sumptuary laws of prior epochs. Edward Said commented that the "worst and most paradoxical gift of imperialism" was "to allow people to believe they were only, mainly exclusively, White or black or Western or Oriental" even as it so mixed cultures and identities on a global scale.[63] Combining diverse stuff does not negate authenticity, but is its condition.

Product Mobility

Some products, by their nature, move around, encouraging hybridization. Beads and jeans and sneakers self-advertise as they circulate among the populace; cell phones are not only big enough to be seen, but annoyingly evident as their users speak into them and as they sound off in random locations. Cars are moving billboards, attracting many sets of eyeballs in the process of normal use. Clothing spreads in this way.

For some goods travel helps demonstrate what they can do. Post-its made themselves known on their own steam and spread like a benign virus (there was virtually *no* advertising). People do not just see a Post-it, but put it to use in the process of receiving it (reading its content, raising it up as a "flap," lifting it off the page). The product as it came into one's hands, displayed the new need it could fill and how to work it. Having such intrinsic capacity to spread through contact and then lodge in practice helps overcome type-form resistance. In sharp contrast are the things like shrouded gears of factory equipment that meet the eyes only of the maintenance crew assigned to keep them going. They do not travel, and whatever they give off goes to a small circle. Even more extreme, the underside of the coffin lid could be seen by only the deceased, at least among those who do not do open-casket funerals. For such products, designers have less need to consider a larger public's concept of what it should or should not be like. Innovation comes slowly if at all and whatever works is what continues on.

Art Moves

Given the historic role of art leading to technological advance—to recall Cyril Smith's message—it makes sense to think of art as a way around type form. Art can help people go for things that may not make sense to their practical imaginations or assuage anxiety that change engenders. Sometimes, as with the Wave bathtubs, producers explicitly call upon art to close the sale. By pitching high art, including documentation of the art that went into the process, the designer could reach a crowd of people with eyes for Matisse. Museum shops, of course, trade on such connotations in virtually every sale. Italian designers, particularly those at Olivetti, consciously used major artists to move their goods away from type form—early U.S. computers looked like radio sets or TVs, but Olivetti's looked more like something altogether new.

I came across a designer using art or at least "artiness" to change hi-fi speakers. Resembling postmodern wall sconces, his product runs against type form of what a speaker should be like. By creating a new form, the speakers might overcome consumers' resistance to eight or ten speakers (an emerging high-fidelity vogue) across their living room walls. In the way that people have come to expect lamps to be decorative (many in a room, often beyond practical need), these speakers may redefine the very concept of the product.

Toys—art objects in the expanded sense—also help open up some space. Low up-front costs and high levels of whimsy allow new technologies to come into being; about six thousand new toys appear yearly in the United States.[64] For their part, children—often, but not always the end users—have less personal history or product customs to hold them back. Besides the fact that designers might use toys as inspiration, the toy stimulus can be more direct. A designer adapted a cheap toy voice synthesizer that kids used to "talk like a robot" to make an artificial voice box for cancer patients who must speak without a larynx.[65] Many of the basic products of our era began as recreations and toys for adults—the first railroad "was a London amusement ride, developed exclusive for that purpose."[66] Ford's great underestimation of the fun factor in the appeal of his product has parallels across other industries. The telephone won its greatest following not as its first producers imagined—as a business tool—but from social conversation.[67] The phonograph, imagined by Edison as useful for dictation and other sober applications, gained its audience through music. The developers of the tape recorder, variously held to have been wartime Germans or the U.S. Ampex Corporation, produced it as a piece of business equipment. The company later to become Sony (Tokyo Telecommunications) purchased the rights from Ampex. Only when the Japanese company made the product more user-friendly and marketed it as an entertainment device did sales take off, launching Sony to global prominence.[68] In turning these products toward their own recreational pleasures, consumers made an "end run" around the producers to make the things happen.

Computers are another case where the pleasure aspect caused product take-off. Experts have debated at what point (if any) computers came through to boost efficiency. Much investment took place by financiers, marketers, and consumers before it really made sense. No less an informed historian of technology than George Basalla committed the only howler in his otherwise superb 1988 book, *The Evolution of Technology*, when he concluded the home computer would never amount to much. His suspicions were apparently aroused by the fun people seemed to have been having with it. Basalla writes:

> By the mid-1980s the home computer boom appeared to be nothing more than a short-lived and, for some computer manufacturers, expensive fad. Consumers who were expected to use these machines to maintain their financial records, educate their children, and plan for the family's future ended up playing electronic games on them, an activity that soon lost its novelty, pleasure, and excitement. As a result a device that was initially heralded as the forerunner of a new technological era was a spectacular failure that threatened to bankrupt the firms that had invested billions of dollars in its development.[69]

The fact that consumers "ended up playing electronic games" signaled failure to many besides Basalla; companies like IBM, DEC, and Wang all dismissed the personal computer as "snake oil," as silly or irrelevant.[70] Prejudice against the sensual neutralized the evidence before them that this was a product people desired and could adapt to their taste.

If there is such a thing as true breakthrough, fun seems to be a key source. The people who created programs to make the Internet accessible, Dan Lynch and about two hundred other volunteers, worked for what Lynch calls "fun."[71] They did it without salary or any financial rewards in view. Operating systems like CPM and MS-DOS similarly came through young hackers trying to solve a puzzle that was only remotely connected to the billions in wealth their inventions would generate. The founder of Yahoo! was trying to round up some neat sites for like-minded young people to access—"just fooling around," doing it "just for fun" in his words.[72] As revealed in the aptly titled book *Accidental Empires*, it did not occur to Apple founders Steve Jobs and Steve Wozniak to patent their invention, and hence they made almost nothing on the $100 million in copies first sold. They had fun with the mouse technology and icon-driven interface that brought a gamelike choreography to the computer screen. Hackers today, as in the past, make software available to all at no cost. Because it avoids the "spiritually wasteful" secrecy of proprietary controls, such "freeware" has been praised by no less a market booster than *The Economist*[73] as often superior to its for-profit rivals. In synch with others in the freeware movement, a 21-year-old student in Helsinki, Linus Torvalds, gave away Linux, which has become the fastest-growing computer operating system in the world.

Outside Forces

Against the currently fashionable idea that government strangles innovation, government can be its source. The obvious examples are in research; government sponsorship provides the resources—as well as the agenda—for developments in medicine, the military, aerospace, and high technologies, including the Internet (originally funded as a Defense Department program). Without standardization in things like railroad gauge, electrical amperage, and coins (and, of course, weights and measures) the related artifacts (locomotives, toasters, vending machines) would have been all but impossible. Government, in effect, coordinates the lash-up. Authorities' stabilizing core aspects of a product category can be the prerequisite for product innovation.

Government also creates new stuff by responding to social movements and goods' critics. Nader-inspired government rules altered engines, bumpers, and body frames and led to child seats. Bright chrome knobs can no longer protrude from dashboards, and crisp Bauhaus edges had to disappear from potential contact with passengers' heads. The new safety aesthetic, perhaps once odd to the eyes, became part of the appropriate look, increasingly embedded in type form. U.S. cars also had to become smaller and more aerodynamic to achieve government mandated fuel efficiency. From the regulatory wars now afoot, new versions of hybrid cars and electric vehicles take shape.

Legal reform also finds its way into architecture, including aesthetic preference. The stepped form of the Empire State Building, the classic of all skyscrapers, comes from regulatory rules. New York City building codes, opposed by many developers, aimed at preserving sunlight below by requiring series of setbacks as a building rises in elevation. The Empire State went on, with a little help from King Kong and Fay Wray, to become a preferred style for tall buildings all over the world—including Moscow State University, which stands in a great open lawn. The Empire State defined what a skyscraper should be like, no matter where it is.

Stuff is also shaped by movements not related at all to cars or buildings—like organizations pushing to eliminate stigma on physical impairment. As long as such stigma remains, the goods are closeted, and their unimaginative, unchanging, and tedious design acts as further evidence that people needing them are engaged in something tinged with shame—something apart from normal society. But gear like crutches and wheelchairs are starting to get with it. They now come in bright colors and incorporate other features oriented to specific niche markets— kids, for example. In developing a headgear stick device that enables paraplegics to communicate via an electronic receiving monitor, a team led by Chicago architect Stanley Tigerman made sure it was "cool." The designers styled it in a contemporary way with zippy color schemes, on the reasonable assumption that people with even radical physical impairments share tastes appropriate to their age and culture groups.

The booming sports injury market, itself fueled by a rise in amateur athleticism, works with the other trends to change "medical" products. Unlike old people and others with impairments, hurt snowboarders, to take an extreme example, wear medical appliances as a badge of battle. One company making what it calls "fit and sleek" leg braces,

Innovation Sports, touts its "extensive custom paint program . . . (that) allows patients to express themselves with color and patterns that bring bracing to life."[74] These braces can be worn either under the pant leg or over it. Physicians now prescribe them in post-operative care more generally and for patients with osteoarthritis. Social changes have made what were at one time medical devices into sporting attire.

The Jacuzzi tub's transition from an appliance for the infirm to a sensual hot tub accessory benefited from the '60s licensing of sensuality. In the case of condoms, social trends and social movements converged to increase talkability and hence adoption. Growing acknowledgment of youthful sexuality under the harsh reality of AIDS and other sexual diseases opened up discussion. Under the slogan "Silence = Death," activist groups insisted on making gay sexual practices acceptable as topics of research and public talk. This expanded condom sales, and with it some increase in product quality and variety.

All the social shifts and movements, aristocratic or bottom-up, have product consequences—starting with how they affect idealizations of the body. Early-nineteenth-century English ladies' zeal for milky-porcelain skin led Josiah Wedgwood to produce black jasperware tea sets (a variant on the more common blue) to, in his own words, "show off to better advantage the current feminine vogue for bleached white hands."[75] At the other end of the social map, the 1960s counter-culture, celebrated in the musical and movie *Hair*, bolstered markets for goods like fancy combs, brushes, barrettes, and probably—in a later permutation—blow dryers. When Americans of African descent value straight hair, wigs sell (African-American women were the largest U.S. market); when "Afros" rise, wigs fall—but new kinds of combs and "ethnic" body accessories make gains. Punkers buy stuff that helps their hair stand on end. Makers of peace symbols, organic food, and "hippie furniture" evolved into prestige creators of products for the latter-day "bourgeois bohemians" or "Bobos," as David Brooks calls those trying to manage the ideals of doing good with a thirst for consumption.[76] Volvo, rich in safety, functional good sense, and Swedish welfare statism, became their official car (even if now owned by Ford).

STYLE WARS: NO TIME-OUT

Some who create and consume think they are not participating in fashion at all, but instead are making choices of intrinsic value. "Serious" stylistic movements almost always elevate their members' taste as the fulfillment of the history of taste, loaded with moral finality. The Victorians, later to be so disrespected as advocates of mere clutter, saw accumulation and display of objects as a signal of Christian virtue, a way to show a family's true character through its furnishing cornucopia.[77] In reaction came a series of movements to advocate spare and simple, eventuating in the modernists, of which Bauhaus is the great exemplar. Here was the fashion to end all fashions by providing a universal aesthetic and democratizing moral purity. The catechisms of the new aesthetic are now famous: "ornament as disease,"[78] "form follows function,"[79] and, in the dictum of Mies van der Rohe, "less is more." All this was most explicit among adherents of the "minimalist" or "international style"—so called because its severe geometrics (as in a Mondrian painting, a glass-cube skyscraper, or a rectilinear refrigerator door) bypass any particular national culture or historic context. In celebrating the steel, glass, aluminum, and synthetics of mass production, designers wanted to reveal how the building is held up or the chair held together: what you see is how it works. Both in products and in the factories that produced them—like the open-plan glass-walled "Crystal Palace" Lewis Kahn designed for Ford in 1910—beauty would come from the honest presentation of materials and utility.

Critics of modernism have had a field day showing how the output did not square with the ideals. In retrospect, we can see the appeal of modernism was always its *apparent* practicality (and democratic potential) rather than anything intrinsic. A certain look came to be seen as functional and, in effect, aesthetically valued by that appearance. There is a semiotics of functionality, as with any other aspect of physical appearance. For some people, some groups, some products and at some times, apparent functionality may be in demand, while at other cultural moments, a different signal—romantic charm, perhaps—may help something win out. As biographies and cultures shift, taste changes in terms of the value placed on whether goods "should" be functional and of how functionality is defined. When practicality is in vogue, goods coded as having it—as Bauhaus stuff was both by doctrine and appearance—become attractive to those in the know. Besides talking it up, the intelligentsia—at least the more affluent ones—bought the stuff. The Frankfurt School shopped at Bauhaus.

Unless one accepts the idea of modernism as a fashion, it is hard to understand its advocates' enduring enthusiasm. The goods are not cheap to make or buy; the familiar Mies Barcelona chair (pictured on the next page)—created in 1925 for the Barcelona World's Fair and still on the market at $5,500—requires intensive labor and precision to get the right joins. Nor are they necessarily comfortable, in any conventional sense. An extreme of the genre, the so-called Butterfly chair collapses the body's internal organs and jams the hip joints, no matter how you sit in it.[80] Easy to buy (it is cheap) it is hard to get in and harder to get out of. "All 'well-designed' chairs," Reyner Banham says flatly, "are both uncomfortable and inconvenient."[81] The list of function liabilities of modern styles runs long: sharp metal and glass corners injure soft bodies; finger marks derange a beauty dependent on uncluttered surfaces of mirror and steel; modern houses have nowhere to put heirlooms, children's drawings, or the other evolving paraphernalia of life. Adding a room to a modern house, bumping out a wall, or even just moving a piece of furniture can upset a carefully crafted "composition." For some of these reasons, ordinary folks tended not to buy into it, clinging to period styles —with all their mixed bags of advantages and drawbacks— and loving items like La-Z-Boy chairs, ergonomically wonderful and the epitome of kitsch. Poor people, saddled with modernist taste in public housing, struggle to offset antiseptic surroundings with stuff that renounces the idea of less being more.

The foibles of modernism have become increasingly apparent with the rise of environmentalism—a different kind of functionalism entirely. Modernists sited buildings with no reference to sunlight or fresh air. They showed off control over nature and access to cheap power, as well as the commercial desirability of simplified construction and standardized office-block modules. They put up buildings so tall they made no economic sense because so much of their precious floor plate had to be for elevators. Even in Manhattan, every floor above

Ludwig Mies van der Rohe, Barcelona chair, 1925.
Photograph courtesy of Knoll.

Jorge Ferrari-Hardoy, Butterfly chair, 1938.
Photograph courtesy of Knoll.

about the fiftieth represents a drop in practical efficiency. Only decorative motivations, like putting the corporate logo *über alles*, justifies going higher. New York's Seagram Building, arguably the glory of the international style, albeit at a modest 38 stories, was extravagant in a different way. It used bronze as the exterior metal, not because it has greater strength but because, at great cost, it had a favored luster. Still more revealing, the bronze I-beam flanges that run up the 38-story facade play no structural role. New York fire laws require builders to enclose such load-bearing metal in concrete to prevent buckling under heat. The Seagram's I-beams (shown in the photos on the next page), are thus paste-ons used to "express" the real ones invisible underneath.[82] This is not less. Similarly an expensive ergonomic-looking office chair by Italian designer Emilio Ambasz, the former design curator at MoMA, has a distinctive corrugated plastic tube between the backrest and seat to "express the movement of flexibility of the chair as a visual idea."[83] But the tube plays no functional role. Summing up what must be going on in examples like this, the late architectural historian David Gebhard once spoke to me of the ongoing "tradition of hiding aesthetic decision behind the notion of utility and function."

However true it may be that modernists misinterpreted their movement and moment, the critics—Gebhard was not among them—go too far in dismissing the goods as having too much hypocrisy to be taken seriously as design accomplishments. First, there were some successes within the ambitions of practicality and low-cost. Even Cranz acknowledges the 1928 Corbusier chaise, akin to the La-Z-Boy chair but without the feature of adjustability, as ergonomically excellent; it raises the legs and causes the rear to land just where the back will receive good support. And although the authentic Breuer chair (chrome frame with cane seat and back) remains very expensive, a nice enough knock-off sells in the year 2001 for a mere $79, with replaceable seats going for $29. Across realms, modernism surely lowered costs by sponsoring standardized-module production systems for both buildings and furniture.

In aesthetic terms, appreciation of high modernism remains as appropriate as for any other type of stuff. Designers and others of similar taste can legitimately enjoy "the spare beauty of each part," as one spoke to me of Bauhaus-inspired Braun appliances. All along, there

Seagram Building. New York. Photograph by Jon Ritter.

Seagram Building I-Beam "paste-on" detail. Photograph by Jon Ritter.

Marcel Breuer "Cesca" chair knock-off. Photograph by Jon Ritter.

were modernists who spoke of beauty in an explicit way, acknowledging special measures they took to achieve it. Modernist architect Richard Neutra wanted opening a door to feel like "the thrill of a lover." The prolific Philip Johnson baldly remarked that "comfort is a function of whether you think a chair is good-looking or not."[84] It is, once again, form and function together and fashion all the way down. Styles come and styles go. This does not mean, however, that they are any less worthy.

Whole categories of stuff once celebrated for modern functionality have gone by the wayside. As historian George Kubler calls it, in a more general context of explaining technological change, things can have "intermittent duration."[85] Here is a partial list of things once thought functional that have pretty much disappeared: clock radios that turned on the coffeemaker, cars with internal voices that said when to buckle up, stoves with self-adjusting gas burners (the "burner with a brain"), refrigerators with revolving shelves. In the late '50s, the Hoover "Constellation" vacuum cleaner was the biggest seller because it cleverly floated on the jet exhaust propelled from its base—no wheels needed.

In toaster history, the 1932 Dreyfus-designed pop-up had a see-through side panel, a feature that was not to return to a toaster until the 1990s. A Sunbeam toaster (model T-20) that lowered the bread on its own (took it right out of your hand) was a big hit in 1949[86] and was imitated—but then it and the feature disappeared, apparently as the "convenient living" theme began to wane. Also short-lived was the zeal for built-ins such as home entertainment centers and in-counter kitchen combinations of blender, mixer, sharpener, and more. A problem with multi-tasking—so evident in today's world of VCRs, cameras, and computers—is that one must figure out not just what a particular thing does (a hammer bangs things), but the array of potential functions and how to apply them. So it's a judgment call, one that keeps changing, as to whether such advances increase or decrease functionality.

The judgment differs across cultures. A VCR for Korea would have, according to one of my designers, "lots of buttons in even lines" to signal multiple features in rational array—a configuration given up by U.S. consumers who came to interpret buttons distinctly matched to each feature as the more functional display. The Koreans preferred the more minimalist version of functionality. In the German market, even cheap cameras should look "serious," photography being a serious activity, while in Korea and Malaysia, according to another design authority, "cameras are always considered hobby equipment and intended for pleasure"—hence making use of color or cuteness.[87] Akin to a technology of enchantment, the quality of the cultural match determines the usability of the camera. A good product for Japanese men—but not women—another designer said, contains some apparent challenge to the user that can pridefully be mastered. Whatever the precise empirical correctness of these generalizations, there is variation over time and across groups in terms of what is or is not functional.

Besides modernism, there are other contemporary versions of anti-fashion fashion. Various subgroups of the elite may embrace antiques as evidence they do not participate in the fashion system. But antiques themselves rise and fall as people switch from one period or culture to another—the '90s rise of Craftsman goods being a case in point. At a lower market level, the vogue for "shabby chic" treasured a used and abused look—perhaps boosted by images of the peeling paint on the chapel where the dashing John Kennedy Jr. was married. Merchandisers obliged by manufacturing peeling-paint furniture, complete with factory-produced marks of distress and other faux reminders of what museum conservators call "history of use." In a very different niche, rebellious youth have an alternative way to display their anti-fashion. Whereas skiers follow general canons of good taste with matched colors and textures in their "outfits," young snowboarders contrive grunge combinations that invert proprieties—clothes do not "match," for example. Snowboard equipment companies respond by continuously changing their logo to not look "too corporate" and deploy conspicuous bad taste, like a dissected frog's innards splayed across a full-page advertisement.

AFTERMARKET CHANGE

People change their stuff after they buy it and these changes can enter back into mass production. Designers watch what people, quite on their own, do to alter the stuff they buy. The work of motorcycle and car customizers, most notably in the career of Harley Earl, is often the start of changes in mass production. When Sony first issued the Walkman, it had jacks for two sets of earphones because people were imagined as listening to the same music together. Sony advertised the product with couples sharing, some in romantic pose. But people didn't. So later models dropped the second output jack and a personal listening device became even more so.[88] With pickup trucks, some people (white Anglo adolescent boys, typically) raise the bodies to clear off-road boulders (or to make it appear they drive places where boulders happen); others (Chicano adolescent boys, more typically) lower the same vehicles to enhance machismo glory on Main Street. Either way, and in a million other possible moves, when folks alter stuff they buy, designers pounce. End users' adaptations are a part of the product change dynamic—interactive with the production system in determining the nature of stuff.

Rather than being a generic characteristic of modern times, change in products comes from the details of surrounding lash-ups and is specific to different types of goods, their market niche, and much else. Among this "much else" are the mechanisms, like shops, through which goods get to their end users. To some degree, the distribution medium *is* the merchandise. How this could be true comes up next.

CHAPTER 5
Venues and Middlemen

Standing between maker and end user are a series of intermediaries that include wholesalers, retailers, and people who buy for other's use, like gift shoppers and purchasing agents for businesses and public agencies. The mechanisms of goods' distribution encourage certain products but hinder others. Because attention to goods so often focuses on their means of production (number one) and their consumption (number two), the "middle" can be missed. But an effective lash-up requires the presence of a complementary distribution arrangement.

For many who work in offices, someone else chooses the tape dispensers and paper clips in their hands. If an organization supports only IBM-based operating systems as opposed to Macintosh, there will be fewer Macs in the world, which will limit the variety of Mac peripherals in existence. Community college and school district boards order textbooks, rather than teachers, students, or their parents. Military procurement officers shop for the guns that soldiers will fire and the pants they will wear. Prison authorities choose equipment for the guards and everything the inmates will ever use—an essential characteristic of a "total institution."

With clinical equipment, the medical insurance industry and national health ministries must OK reimbursement for the procedures a piece of equipment involves. Because some medical ware is so expensive, health purveyors in a single country, even the United States, may not form an adequate market. So enrollment may be needed by, say, the British National Health Service and agencies of still a third major medical system. Such goods must thus also work in a bureaucratic sense to be. Even when the product is for home use, like a self-administered test or therapy, the doctor's recommendation may be the key to consumer acceptance. As patients turn to the Internet to directly access medical information, medical goods may more closely conform to other consumer products in form and modes of operation, and also better support non-establishment clinical regimes.

For high-end home building projects, architects influence which products are bought for kitchens and baths. For the more common spec-houses, contractors and developers make the choices. Compared to the end-users, their interests tilt toward ease of installation and generic acceptability as opposed to long-term efficiency or specific preferences of distinctive age or gender groups. They want to avoid the cost and special supervision of various crafts that moving off type form would entail, given conventions in carpentry, plumbing, and building codes. Using a tub like the "Wave," for example, risks trouble.

Such organizational intermediaries aside, the vast majority of goods find their way to consumers through commercial stores. The variations in shops, both in type and over history, affect the goods. A given kind of retail environment responds to the existence of a certain kind of product, but once in place, the store type "demands" that particular stuff come into being. Expensive cosmetics, perfumes, and designer scarves have come to depend on duty-free shops, which concentrate affluent airplane passengers ready to buy expensive goods that fit in an overhead bin (cutbacks in air travel, as happened after the September 11 terrorist attacks, threaten these goods).[1] Because sales of motorcycles depend on a rugged environment, their retailers resist stocking motor scooters, and as a result their distribution outside of Italy and a few other countries has been constrained.[2]

Two elements make retail environments effective in doing their work with a particular kind of stuff. One is the merchant's capacity to entice customers closer to the product, helping them see what the thing can do and otherwise stir up desire to have it. So there needs to be an element of physical allure and enjoyment of the site. The other, less obvious retail resource is the social context—the enthusiasm of others who make up a common shopping audience. Shoppers and bystanders can create a specific buzz for one another over the goods.

This combination of the physical and the social has always been a part of the distribution apparatus. The Greek agora held commercial activities, including goods for sale. Roman grandeur was the backdrop for commercial interactions as well as homage to the gods. In many religious traditions up to the present day, social, artistic, and economic activities merge with the religious, dwelling in the same space or at least in close proximity. Often the central square, piazza, or plaza has the everyday commerce, flanked by major institutions of state, economy, and spirituality. The marketplace in the middle, however regal or primitive, is where it all comes together. In imperial China the markets "were the places where poor women could chat with each other and exchange the gossip that Chinese men condemned so strongly."[3]

The commercial spot is the happening place because people seem to rally around goods and enjoy watching others make their choices—reflecting a process of "collective selection," as sociologist Herbert Blumer said of shopping several generations back.[4] That commerce and community adhere is obvious in the case of establishments like pubs, coffeehouses, cafes, beauty salons, barbershops, and general stores. Such "third places"[5]—something in between home and work—can be the very heart of community. Besides a setting of conviviality, their clerks and keepers are the "public characters" who, as Jane Jacobs says, do the small favors and maintain the vigilant "eyes on the street" that help keep communities secure.[6]

What we today call "marketing" was an intrinsic aspect of the economy of eighteenth-century England and involved integrated ways of making new things, generating allure at points of distribution, and promoting social interaction around them.[7] Josiah Wedgwood's innovations are especially well documented, an important scholarly asset given that ceramics, along with cloth and production of pins, nails, cutlery, buckles, hats, shoes, kettles, and toys—"the adornments of ordinary life"[8]—were the bases of the production regime of the time, indeed of the industrial revolution. To justify the investments and efforts

Wedgwood jasperware with classical motif. Photograph by Jon Ritter.

needed to make his ceramics—including the development of new production tools (kilns, thermometers—"degrees Wedgwood" was once a
standard industrial phrase)—Wedgwood needed tactics for maximizing
a market for the expensive elements of his product lines. Especially significant were the commercially successful jasperware designs, modeled
on pieces unearthed at Pompeii and Herculaneum. The designs, introduced in 1775, layered the white ceramic relief of classical figures on a
(usually) medium-blue background. The technique, called "sprigging,"
is another aspect of the extra expense faced by Wedgwood that he
needed to recoup at retail. The classical taste, especially strong in
France, created a market across the Channel.

To gain access to the French customers, both as buyers and as tastemakers, Wedgwood established elegant London salesrooms that, an innovation at the time, were themselves attractions.[9] With their constantly changing displays of dinner tables laid out with his place settings, they became "one of the sights of London."[10] With some help from changes in British export laws—which he helped forge—the French could have his goods. Wedgwood also engaged in what would later be called market segmentation, niche marketing, product differentiation, money-back guarantees, targeted advertising, point-of-sale displays, and culturally adjusted descriptions of goods in other languages, especially French.[11] He succeeded in having his best pieces purchased by British royalty so as to leverage other sales; he also deliberately set about having artists like Joshua Reynolds put his goods in their paintings (product placement, as it were).

The coming of "obligation-free browsing" by about 1800 in Britain[12] provided a legitimate way for women to be in city streets on their own, encouraging further varieties of female-oriented goods on the market.[13] Adding to the excitement, and functioning as a promotion aid, were the dandy and flâneur male connoisseurs of the social sidewalk and its material appeals, akin to gay shoppers in today's major urban centers. Tearooms for ladies became part of the early department stores, which first opened in 1852 in Paris. These elaborate emporia have been called the "radiant sensual center at the city's heart."[14]

In both Europe and America, the more up-market department stores put on gallery displays of art; in the United States, this helped create acceptance of impressionism while simultaneously selling products carrying high-art motifs. At a more popular level, department stores brought in stunts and attractions, Santa Claus most notably. The invention of Santa as a retail ploy helped make their toy departments a launch base for the industry. Some department stores made their tie-ins with early movies, exploiting, for example, Hollywood's *Garden of Allah* with "Oriental" merchandise, reinforced in window dressing and elaborate aisle displays. With their scale of space, finance, and expertise, department stores could manage the sorts of initiatives unavailable to ordinary retailers. Belasco, the impresario and Broadway lighting expert, did Wanamaker's interiors, window treatments, and store fittings.[15] L. Frank Baum, creator of the *Wizard of Oz*, operated his own retail store and was a consultant to others; he started the trade magazine *Show Window*. Raymond Loewy's first U.S. work, in 1919, was decorating Macy's New York windows.

Part of the social in shopping is buying for others, whether through the routines of family grocery procurement or buying gifts. Noticeable to past armies of anthropologists as well as to some contemporary observers, people court, sustain friendships, and link kin with regular and sometimes extravagant presents, making holidays, birthdays, and weddings the center of many retailers' existence.[16] Giving gifts—like the potlatch or other traditional systems of material display and sharing—holds people together and redistributes some wealth. But it has to be done precisely. As with bringing home the wrong kind of cereal brand for one's child or buying beef for guests who are Hindu vegetarians, error can be gross.[17] At the extreme, one could buy a radio for a deaf person, a war toy for a Quaker child, or just something "you should have known" one simply does not buy for another person. Just the right retail setting, operating with just the right object, can help solve the problem. In modern merchandising, the categories "gift shop" and "gift department" help solve some of these problems by affirming the goods within are more or less appropriate. Someone wanting to buy something for an elderly aunt can go to a different venue from that of a shopper looking for a present to give a teenage boy. The sales clerk in the cosmetic shop can advise what a young woman might like in a compact case; a hip kid-clerk in the snowboard store can guide an out-of-it uncle toward the accessory a boarder might require.

Luxury items like expensive jewelry and some types of luggage and fountain pens are examples of products that likely owe their very existence to gift buying. Responding to a designer who expressed doubts about the utility of his "Pocket Fisherman" product, the inventor said "It's not for using; it's for giving."[18] Gift giving encourages stuff to have evident frivolousness or luxury so as to display affection, respect, or generate reciprocity. This may mean the gift can have conspicuous superfluousness, including being made of an overqualified material (like diamond or gold) or being overbuilt in durability. Affluent men receive wristwatches that "meet the test" for piloting a supersonic plane, diving to 100 meters, and lasting hundreds of years. Selecting just the right gift means determining how the various "extras"—both decorative and the apparently functional—fit into the recipient's life. Appropriately enough, success reaps appreciation for the "thoughtfulness" that went into the selection.

Some types of goods are, by the nature of their end users, always bought by others. Products used by small children have to attract adults—infants, in particular, have no sense of what is or is not "cute," much less an ability to buy it. The CEO of Joe Boxer clothing referred to his company's line of children's clothes as "grandma bait" because "when you sell cat food, you aren't selling to cats."[19] As children grow older, the purchase becomes a joint decision, which is why advertisers pitch to both parent and child. When Sony issued its "My First Sony" Walkman tape players for children, it bought TV ad time when both would likely be watching.[20] Based on type of toy and age of child, toy stores show the merchandise in ways that both adults and their offspring can gain access.

Goods take shape by the way merchandise settings intersect with class and ethnicity. Some shopping districts become ethnically homogenous, making possible goods that otherwise would have a harder time existing. As a practical matter, clustering ethnic shoppers in a single retail district or specific store allows specialty goods to exist, like woks and wood steamers for Chinese people, menorahs for Jews, dashikis for African-Americans. The goods that result are often formed specifically for their setting; they are not just "imports" from an authentic world of cultural goods. I have seen menorahs for sale in California shops that not only have a California appearance, reflecting trends of thin, curling wrought iron of the day, but with a surf-board form holding up each candle. This could not exist just anywhere Jews are found. It came into existence through the particulars of a specific venue.

The presence of such goods, including their sounds and smells, bolsters a social reassurance that loops back to reinforce the product in the market. The reality of "ethnic signature" goods plausibly helps ease the psychological burden of shopping; their very presence signals a surrounding consumer base large enough to warrant a store stocking stuff like that. Along with "signs and symbols that the (store) owners use to proclaim their identity," the result is "to shape the collective definition of an area for residents and outsiders alike."[21] From their contemporary studies of two London shopping malls, Miller and his colleagues conclude that social classes and ethnic groups constitute themselves in part by the kinds of stores their members frequent and consider appropriate. Although there is much overlap in the content of what is being sold in the two major shopping centers, there are also differences—and these differences, beyond any quantitative accounting, signal social markings that become intrinsic to the goods themselves. Miller and his colleagues also describe how contemporary Ghanaians in London (among other immigrant groups) sustain not only family ties, but to some degree their very identity as a distinct ethnic group within Britain, by shopping for goods to send to their relations in Africa.[22] This is, again, still another influence on products. Consumption preferences in Ghana, as interpreted by gift buyers and merchants in London thus helps shape what some stuff will be.

CHAINS AND BIG BOXES

The coming of chain stores has increased retailer influence over goods. Even when they are not directly commissioning stuff (which they increasingly are), retail chains are in the minds of designers and manufacturing executives as they go about their work.[23] In one unhappy lesson, a design principal told me of a retailer's killing off his line of high-fidelity speakers because they were "too good." The designer had set out to rescue a manufacturing client notorious for "big and clunky" wares, stranded at a low price point. The new line was as cheap to produce as the old, and according to the designer, better both technically and aesthetically. But the manufacturer's major retail client rejected the design because it already had "good-looking" speakers; the niche was for goods he agreed were clumsy. What matters in this case is not an optimization of the product in itself, but its fit within the range of goods the retailer offers. This response from a retailer keeps a given producer at a particular point in the product hierarchy and shapes the look and feel of the things themselves.

The switch to self-service merchandising is now responsible, in the United States, for the bulk of sales in many realms—food, clothing, and hardware. An early impact was to foster brand-name packaged goods as a substitute for buying from bins and "famous makes" instead of goods from craftspeople and small-scale manufacturers. In effect, self-service cuts out the merchant as the advice-giving middleman who guides the consumer around otherwise unknown commodities. The small merchant can point out features of products otherwise not obvious or, as has evidently been common, move consumers toward goods with higher profit margins.[24] Absent the merchant's assurances, consumers depend on branded goods in snappy displays to enable them to move expeditiously through the aisles. Compared to bulk products that the customer must bag up and that the cashier must weigh, measure, or count (flour, nails, rope, paper goods, picture hooks), branded goods are set up for scanners and also to withstand the rigors of shipment, stocking, bagging, and the trip home. Self-service thus lashes up with standardized branded goods.

"Big box" stores like Wal-Mart, so called because they often are architecturally configured as huge boxes surrounded by a parking lot, are really department stores set up as supermarkets. The goods have to sell themselves. Stores do cater to basic shopper needs by grouping goods "logically" together—the equivalent of putting the peanut butter with the jelly—but the finer arrangement niceties do not happen. For example, in the "old days" a furniture or department store design person arranged pieces as ensemble in a "room setting," thus helping sell a certain lamp by placing it with mutually complementary goods. This might be particularly important for a background piece that otherwise would seem commonplace. Or it might help sell a particularly strong item, loud even, which might be subdued in the right context. A New York retailer of high-design goods explains that his shop operates as an "advocate" to "illuminate these things, so people actually stop and take the time" to see the "beautiful proposals for living embedded" in the stuff he displays.[25]

But in a big box, the store puts a sample on the shelf, and the stock rests below in sealed cartons. Management typically locates goods by category—all lamps are together, maybe within sight lines of buzz saws. Chain stores are purposefully designed, but for good traffic flow, moving high-profit items, and inhibiting shoplifting rather than helping particular goods with artful juxtapositions. How well the product will sell itself helps determine if it will be given prominent space, such as the end of an aisle (the "end cap") or on a shelf at a height likely to meet shopper's eyes—low for children, high for basketball players. Manufacturers do offer financial payoffs to retailers for "good placement," but the product and its package have to be right for the merchandiser to avoid a dreaded dead space in the store.

Self-service packaging should secure the product against fingering and other sources of damage while still making it visible and accessible to the consumer. Many products now come in clear plastic shrink-wrap, which allows the goods to be seen but discourages physical touch. This is bad for the sale of plush toys, but does no damage to sales of light-bulbs ("nobody touches light bulbs").[26] Some goods are put in "clamshells," rigid clear plastic enclosures, often made oversized to hinder shoplifting small items that are expensive enough to worry about. Products like personal stereos (of the Walkman variety) are frequently sold this way. Because shoppers cannot listen to the product, they are in no position to compare sound quality among competing models and brands. This discourages higher quality and more costly goods from gaining a market—and indeed, personal listening products cluster in the same lower cost range. Telephones and phone answering machines are almost never set up to be heard. Again, this discourages machines with higher sound fidelity, but promotes features that can be appreciated from a list or from display as buttons (e.g., automatic redial or memory).

Self-service environments need products that store in a compact way. Stackability is one solution—something reflected in the omnipresent plastic garden chairs now found around the world and in many other types of furniture. The propelling force behind the design of such goods has at least as much to do with the need to minimize shipping costs and the amount of retail space required to sell them as to convenience for the buyer. Knockdown goods ("K-D" in the trade)—items that come as separate pieces that end users assemble at home—readily stack, sit on a trolley for travel up the aisles, and fit into car trunks for immediate self-delivery. Stores selling bulky pre-built products had to have separate warehouses in less accessible areas, where rents were cheaper than their main retail location. Stores had to have employees whose job was to deliver the items, and customers had to wait for delivery. K-D allows inventory to be in the place where the sale occurs. Also sometimes called "flat-pack," such furniture has specific effects on furniture styles, helping give modernism, in particular, a life in mass markets. Straight lines and flat pieces permit compact packaging as well as clarity for the amateur assemblers. At the front end of production, engineering tolerances actually have to be more rather than less precise since fit cannot be checked or adjusted at the factory; this builds demand for higher quality tooling. Only then can home assembly substitute consumer labor for work at the factory—a last step in the global chain of production activities. This K-D concept has helped Ikea build the world's largest furniture retail business by creating, in terms of look, mode of fabrication, shipping, and delivery, a new kind of stuff.

Self-service stores operate on a smaller profit margin than conventional retailing and this also affects the substance of goods. The postwar appliance discount house stores sold merchandise at cut prices. This was the origin of the big box concept. The stores added in additional products that could compensate for the low profit of the major goods. So a retailer making $20 profit on a $200 television set could make an almost equal amount on a TV stand or on a fancy-looking indoor TV antenna priced at $25. This led to ever more elaborate-appearing antennas—with twisting coils and switches that switched nothing. Because customers knew the value of the television set from comparison shopping and advertised list prices but not of antennas, such peripheral items could provide retailers a major source of profit. The mode of retailing supported a particular type of product's existence.

Self-service also alters the goods by creating substitutes in the product itself for the lost in-store personal service. Directions on and in the box as well as pictures, graphics, and videos that come bound up with the artifact tell how to set it up and use it. These are not separate from the product but intrinsic, often having had an influence on how it was made. One of the Mac's advantages was its superior transparency for customer set-up and use through directions—on the box, in the box, and on the shroud that, matched to the technology, is user-friendly. Everything is menu-organized with words and icons: "Open Me First," along with appropriate tabs and other physical cues with the machine's software taking over for the last steps.

Unless there are such mechanisms—and even with them—self-service does not work well with goods that move off type form. Big box stores thus sell conventional materials and major brand goods whose apparent bona fides are built into the name and packaging. Sometimes producers turn out special variants for big box chains, similar enough to their standard line to assure shoppers they are getting familiar products, but somewhat different so that higher cost retailers will be protected from appearing to price gouge. So Bose, a relatively expensive brand of high-fidelity equipment, makes a distinct—but not very different—line of Bose products for the Cosco store chain.

There can be at least signs of daring at the big box. The Target big box chain boldly hired architect Michael Graves, of the Princeton faculty, to create a line of housewares—serving pieces, scrub buckets, brooms, toilet plungers, light fixtures, and more, to be sold only at Target stores (more than two hundred separate items have been produced). Graves's postmodernist motifs enter directly into ordinary goods but in a way that does not break their type forms. Graves puts his look on goods that are not otherwise new—a disrespected ploy in many professional design circles. But whereas his original teakettles for Alessi, like the bird whistle design shown on the next page, sell in museum and kitchen gourmet shops for well over $100, his Target version (with a somewhat different appearance and a whistle replacing the chirping bird at spout's end) goes for $29.95. The Target kettle is made in China while Alessi uses its factory in Italy, where it claims higher quality standards can be upheld. Whatever the compromise, something new is born. These are not just Target goods or Graves goods; they are Target-Graves, meaning that it is the connection of a particular kind of retailer with a high-style architect that yields them—a big box/big designer product.

OVERCOMING RETAIL BLOCKAGES

Terrance Conran, founder of UK-based Conran Design group, says that retailers (at least in Britain) are the most conservative of any actors in the production-consumption chain, inhibiting manufacturers from

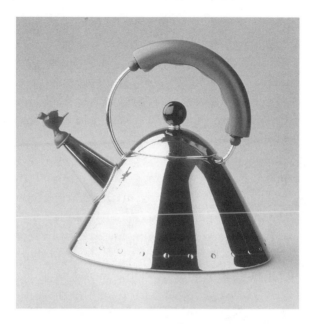

*Bird teakettle, designed by Michael Graves for Alessi.
Photograph ©Alessi.*

Graves' whistle tea kettle for Target. Photograph by Jon Ritter.

producing creative designs. Conran refers to department store buyers, in particular, as "a solid . . . block cutting off a much livelier public on one side from groups of manufacturers—more lively than they are given credit for—on the other." Only by setting up his own retail store chain ("Habitat" and "Conran"), now with operations in five countries, could he find a way to distribute the furniture and fabrics he was designing and manufacturing.

A long-standing method of easing dependence on store policy is to offer free samples—if not in the store itself then through the mail, on the streets, or at point of use. Early instances include Procter and Gamble's blanketing the U.S. in about 1912 with Crisco samples, along with free booklets and recipes encouraging women to replace butter and other fats with the company's new, "modern" product.[27] Gillette circulated detailed instructions to show men how to shave using replaceable razor blades as opposed to straight razors at the barber's. To bring sewing machines into the home, Singer set up its own network of retail stores sponsoring group lessons, instilling a social element into the task of diffusing the technology.

Encyclopedias came to exist, as a mass product, through door-to-door guilt mongering from sales reps who led parents sitting together through the kind of feature-by-feature page turning they would not otherwise endure. Few would buy an encyclopedia set off the shelf at Wal-Mart, and nobody would stand in an aisle for such an unending spiel. Tupperware works the home setting as well, arranging with women "hostesses" to invite their friends for a party at which the goods can be demonstrated. At Tupperware parties, customers can be shown in the home setting and in front of one another just how particular items solve problems, and support one another's enthusiasm for the various remedies. Retail experts do think people shopping together are more likely to buy than when shopping alone.[28] Tupperware makes "backstage" activities like storing leftovers enjoyably topical. The feedback loop provided to the company by the reactions helps shape the products themselves—the parties are an ongoing focus group. The result is the most extensive and elaborate array of plastic ware to hold leftovers—as well as an increasing number of additional kitchen goods.

A realm of toy products lends itself to vending on the streets. All over the world, little gizmos that do things like skittle, jump, crawl, play, chirp, sing and soar find their venue in the informal economy. Such inexpensive items charm on the spot. They work in a retail segment of small investments up front and low prices that casual passersby can pay without worrying about product durability or the merchant's exchange policy. Certain products are harder to market in store environments where narrow enclosures make demonstrations more difficult.

Some kinds of goods appear to need an alternative to the self-service venue, yet still operate through a physical store. Gourmet kitchen shops provide ways for even sophisticated people to learn what a particular product can do. Gaze upon the Starck Alessi juicer; it helps to be told to press a citrus half down on the pointy top with a twisting motion, after sliding a vessel underneath to catch the liquid. Starck juicers are sold in museum shops and expensive kitchen boutiques where sales clerks in "gourmet" smocks walk the aisles to share culinary tips. Such stores commonly offer cooking classes precisely because they make a good base for selling unfamiliar stuff. At the same time, the unfamiliar is what the shops need to differentiate themselves from more routine venues.

Mom and Pop hardware stores may survive by helping people deal with idiosyncratic tasks; rather than mass marketing the "carded" and shrink-wrapped standard items on chain store shelves, these special places keep a more varied batch of parts and tools alive. Small niche clothing stores persist to demonstrate, sell (and make possible) fashions at various ends of the spectrum—for groups as diverse as the avant-garde young to the marginalized elderly. Tattoo parlors, S & M shops, alternative health stores, and ethnic goods outlets not only offer up expertise about their exceptional artifacts, they also provide cultural reassurances on the appropriateness of the merchandise—something especially important when dealing with a type of product that has disapproving adversaries. The unspeakable becomes speakable.

Because the limits on commercial talk were never quite overcome in the United States, gay organizations had to create a quasi underground of condom marketing and distribution through bars, bathhouses, and a gay press. As part of the effort to get them used, these media tried to

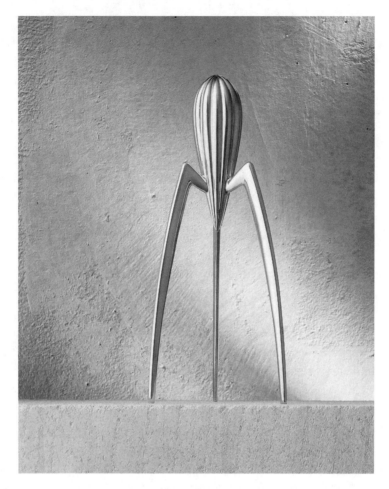

Juicy Salif, designed by Philippe Starck for Alessi.
Photograph © Alessi.

eroticize them, supplanting more establishment depictions of them as ways to be more "socially responsible." Although condoms managed to move from beneath the pharmacist's counter to the racks with other "health aids," they are not sold with recreational, cosmetic, or other lifestyle products. Consumers cannot be instructed on how to get the right fit, precisely when to put them on, which type to use, or the niceties of disposal. This holds back demand for variations in physical texture, taste flavor, add-on padding, bejeweled carry cases, and other

possible accessories. Retail taboo inhibits creation of new drug paraphernalia (perhaps a variety of different kinds of needles tailored to
users' physiology, mood, or application occasion). A rare exception is
the Australian needle packet (mentioned in chapter 2) designed to prevent reuse.

Beyond condoms and needles, there are different kinds of conventions about just what a customer or clerk can do to demonstrate an
artifact's use. In a bedding store, it takes some nerve to lie down on a
mattress, even if the clerk invites one to do it. It takes still additional
courage to use the bed as one would in real life—remaining on it for a
fairly long period, curling up and unfolding as one would actually do,
gyrating in the manner of one's custom. Couples may be reticent to lie
down together, much less check its qualities against the variety of positions they may actually take. In most places, sheets cannot be felt with
the fingers, much less experienced by lying on them in the nude.
Similarly, one does not "try on" bathtubs; tubs might be softer if people had a chance to recline in them before making their selection. Many
people would likely change their toilet choice if they could sit on the
seat and hear the flush—or run still more thorough tests. When shopping for a toaster, it does not seem appropriate to power up the floor
samples and test them on a piece of bread. Women readily apply
makeup at cosmetics counters, but men do not, in part because most
men's cosmetics departments are located adjacent to women's cosmetics—something that holds back the whole industry, in the opinion of
retail consultant Paco Underhill.[29] That the men do not have their own
location—"men's health department," perhaps?—restrains such basics
as sun blocks for those who work outdoors or razors that might work
better on different kinds of skin-beard combinations. Without a way to
even bring up the topic of nose or ear hair clippers, they are bought
through catalogs where reticence keeps a never-ending series of ineffec-
tive devices alive in the ads.

Adults do not jump or perform sweaty activities in conjunction
with even sporting goods. Shop etiquette makes it hard to test shoes by
running in them or kicking against a solid surface. A man is expected
to try on shirts in change rooms rather than exposing his upper body
on the sales floor—an exposure that is perfectly conventional in settings

like the ballpark. Neither men nor women are supposed to take off their lower garments on the sales floor when selecting among pants or skirts, even though their underwear would cover about as much as do some bathing suits. Given that men tend to dislike shopping more than women and to spend significantly less time at it on average,[30] they may buy less than they would if more could be tried on in less time. Less frequent shopping likely nudges them toward slower-turn and hence more conservative products. Dictums against exposure may also induce men to buy without trying things on, and this too may have a substantive effect. What looks good on a mannequin or rack may look less good on one's body.

Some retail environments grant customers special license to try things out and otherwise act differently. Many of these places have qualities that merchandisers refer to as "destination retail"—people do not stop by on their way home for a routine provision; they go to the store for a special kind of experience. So once at the Disney shop, it's easier for an adult to try on a Mickey Mouse hat because the place itself is a bit "silly," compared with a regular hat emporium. Taking a deep drag on a pipe comes more easily in a Berkeley head shop than at Dunhill on London's Bond Street. Nike's new range of NikeTown stores invites customers to measure their fitness and learn about kinetics in connection with products on display. REI sports store in Seattle has a mountain bike test trail and a 65-foot-high climbing structure on which it's OK to sweat. Middle-age women can hold and coo over adult-marketed porcelain dolls at retail stores like "My Little People" in Weathersfield, Connecticut, in a way that would be more difficult in other venues.[31] In some large lighting stores, customers can take the time to reconfigure different combinations of lighting and see them at work. Buyers may switch from light bulbs they like in a box to those they like when lit.

CASE STUDY ON DISTRIBUTION: THE MENDA BOTTLE

Getting goods to end users involves wholesalers as well as retailers. Both are consequential for stuff. The Menda bottle, the kind used by nurses and doctors to pump alcohol into cotton swabs (mentioned in chapter 2), almost perished because, in its first incarnation as a pastel baby oil bottle, there was no way to sell it. Like Starck's juicer, the Menda bottle needed someone to demonstrate how it worked. These bottles broke with type form; their liquids "poured up" via a pump rather than down through gravity. But it is impossible to know this by looking or even touching. There were not then, and still are not today, shops where knowledgeable sales staff demonstrated products used in changing diapers. Stores selling infant goods were around, but these were baby furniture stores offering cribs and bassinets, often staffed by men. Though in some countries (Sweden, as an example), nurses come to the home to instruct new mothers in the latest child-care technologies, this avenue of spreading word on the product also did not exist. "There we were with our inventory of pumps, bottles, top dishes, and no repeat sales from the department stores," recalls David Menkin, the product's inventor. The designer hired by Menkin did his job well enough to attract the retailers' interest, but the product, as a diaper changing aid, died on the shelves.

Menda migrated into medical settings because of how doctors buy their wares—through wholesale medical supply houses. A Menda sales representative peddled the product with personal visits to these wholesalers, demonstrating the new bottle at each stop. The supply houses placed orders; their field reps then took the bottles across the country, making personal visits to doctors within their usual assigned territories. The bottles could be carried by every rep and then easily demonstrated in the places they would actually be used—no special skill necessary. In this way, the bottles indeed seemed to "sell themselves" and within about six months, 90 percent of all physician's offices in the United States—about one hundred thousand at the time—had the device in use.

The organization of the medical supply business, coupled with the nature of the technology and its small scale, helped make the product; in that sense, it did not sell itself at all. Indeed, it was a different product from the original; instead of pink-and-blue plastic, it was made in plain brown plastic or, at a later time, in stainless steel. Rather than have "baby oil" marked on the bottle, the makers silk-screened on the word "alcohol"—it shifted purpose, context, and user group. Exactly

MENDA SCIENTIFIC PRODUCTS, INC.
PASADENA, CALIFORNIA

Menda alcohol bottle in which the liquids pour up.
Photograph courtesy of David Menkin.

what the thing is, we can see, turns on the availability of the kind of distribution apparatus it gains. Indeed, the stainless model came about when medical people started asking their surgical supply reps if they could put other chemicals, like acetone, in their Menda bottles. Because acetone reacts with plastic, the answer was "no." But the need for an all-metal, stainless steel Menda bottle was shown to exist, and that is how the product that was to become the center of the company's business came into existence.

Once part of the wholesalers' distribution network, Menda added lines of other goods to sell to doctors, some never before on the market but involving no technical innovation at all—for example, plastic stor-age cases for tongue depressors. The company also started making standard bottles that doctors could have bought from any number of other providers, but again, once access was established for one Menda product, advantage came to other Menda branded goods. Menda used its "signature" product to gain access to other markets and indeed had some modest success with its "peripherals."

Wholesalers were also Menda's route onto the factory floor and the still bigger market it represented. In about 1960, a direct order came from nearby LA-based Hughes Aircraft for five hundred stainless steel Menda bottles, with more large orders following almost immediately. Apparently having noticed the Menda bottle at his doctor's office, a Hughes employee figured it would be useful in soldering. When solder-ing metal parts together, one appreciates—as with inoculating an arm or dealing with a baby's bottom—not having to use up a hand to hold the bottle. In a soldering operation, one swipes the surfaces clean with a chemical like acetone, applies the flux, makes the join, then wipes again to remove excess acid in the flux. Menda was an obvious help. Following the first two Hughes orders, Menda sent literature to the industrial supply houses which then put the bottles in the hands of its field reps, who sold them to individual industrial clients. The industrial application saved Menda because doctors took up using alcohol satu-rated swabs, a turn of events that greatly depleted the medical market.

Another aspect of the Menda story further instructs how products emerge from interaction with a distribution apparatus. The early fail-ure with the baby oil dispensers saddled Menda with ten thousand pas-tel bottles that languished in a Los Angeles warehouse for eight years. With the warehouse set for a new use, the building's owner ordered the bottles off the premises. Desperate for an application, Menda put a standard spout pump on the top and a decal saying "hand lotion" on the base. Department stores again bought them but different buyers for a different department—this was now "lady's vanity wear." And this time they sold well. Menda followed up its vanity wear triumph with "matching" tissue box, soap dish, and hand mirror. For about a ten-year period from the mid-1950s, Menda was one of the two or three largest U.S. producers of this kind of product. The company added new designs using decorative objects "stuck on" the housing. Tastes were to move away from this sort of bathroom stuff, and it was all to largely disappear. But Menda bathroom accessories had a good run, made possible by the accident of unsold inventory from a failed prior product, a pressing need to move it, and the fact that their original designer— whose presence was something of an afterthought—had done a job good enough to build the company's first retail market. Most relevant to this discussion, the stuff sold because it was appropriate to its distribution setting—a product consistent with type form in ladies vanity goods. Success is all about getting the right combinations, one following the other over Menda's history of product applications:

Lash-up #1—Medical Application: Plain plastic base, the word "alcohol," wholesalers, and a time when inoculations and antiseptics were in but alcohol saturated swabs were not yet around;

Lash-up #2—Vanity Wear Application: Decorative base, the word "lotion," the existence of retail "lady's vanity" departments and a moment of enthusiasm for decorative shrouding of home products.

Lash-up #3—Industrial Application: Stainless steel base, no words on the bottle, factory supply houses, nearby aerospace soldering.

MEDIA SELLING

Print and electronic media help give particular qualities to goods. One of designer Raymond Loewy's early tactics was to convince companies their products needed professional design so they would show better in print.[32] Products sold through catalogs have to be self-evident on a page, at least with a short text explanation. Especially if it is good enough in these regards to go on one of the covers (the equivalent of end-cap placement), it can become a truly mass product.

Television is a good medium for stuff that needs kinetic demonstration (but not touch) to gain market potential. Legendary examples in the United States are the slicers and dicers, kitchen rotisseries and Broil-Quiks of the late 1950s and early '60s pioneering infomercials. TV can connect a product with an audience, even an off-type-form product that "disrupts" how people go about their business in the kitchen. In marketing the Veg-O-Matic—a gizmo that slices and dices fruits and vegetables—TV could "train the camera on the machine and compel viewers to pay total attention to the product you were selling. TV allowed you to do even more effectively what the best pitchmen strove to do in live demonstrations—make the product the star."[33] In regard to the success of its precursor device, the Chop-O-Matic, writer Malcolm Gladwell explains the TV edge: "You have to show them (the prospective customer) exactly how it works and why it works, and make them follow your hands as you chop liver with it, and then tell them precisely how it fits into their routine."[34]

These products were indeed made for TV.

More recently, the U.S. shopping channel QVC started marketing its own brand of non-stick pots and pans, taking advantage of the ability to show off the non-stick feature in real time cooking and clean-up. It can work out well. One product, the Showtime countertop rotisserie, generated $1 billion in sales in year 2000; the version selling at $129.72 racked up sales of more than $1 million in a single QVC hour. In promoting exercise goods, TV displays to audiences what "abs" look like when coupled with the right piece of exercise gear—and then shows, through the movements of fit young people (always smiling), just how to use the equipment. Many people did not even know they had abs, much less what they look like when properly toned. But it would not be "appropriate" for the salesperson (especially a man) in a normal boutique or even sports shop to show off a well-sculpted stomach to contrast with the customer's distended pouch ("OK, now let's compare it to yours"). TV opened new possibilities. TV goods can later drift into bricks-and-mortar retail settings, as ab machines have done, a trend illustrated by a U.S. chain of stores called "As Seen on TV."

The web also helps shape goods. Even compared with TV, including the narrow-casting capacities of cable, the web enables marketers to visually demonstrate products to small niches. Once a company such as Amazon.com develops its basic system of interface, warehousing, and marketing, the cost of adding new products to the site is marginal. So is the added cost of setting up targeted messages for a particular market niche. Some products may not work well on the web; as with TV, goods that require tactile feel, that need to be tried on, or that benefit from the shop as a social setting may not be good web candidates. The web will not replace the physical shop as a place to buy an evening gown or wedding bands, the latter involving a "very personal shopping experience," in the words of an executive at one of the largest U.S. direct marketers.[35]

Sometimes customers need physical contact with goods before their first purchase but can switch to catalog, TV, or web for replacements. Though women trying a new kind of makeup may need to see it on their own skin at a store demo counter, they can later switch to electronic purchase for repeat buying. Men may need to try on their first pair of pants at the store before ordering successive copies of the same model over the Internet. A new line of goods thus needs shops more than later versions of the same or similar thing.

Business-to-business goods that are bought repeatedly and in bulk can be handled over the web and not be changed by that fact. In the case of cement, to take an extreme example, a builder may use e-commerce to place orders because the web does not alter the product itself; the same with Gem paper clips for the office. This plausibly contrasts with books, a fast-turn product already sold in large volumes over the web, but likely changing in substance by virtue of the new sales medium. Some books, because of their design and texture, need physical presence to be appreciated, say, for the quality of their binding or physical feel. There may thus emerge a niche product milieu of design-intensive books with a boutique setting; indeed this may be the future of the store-bought book as electronics otherwise becomes the major means for delivering information content.

The web provides vast potential for customizing products. Nike now has a site that lets consumers configure shoe colors and add a name tag—"an interactive, design-a-shoe experience," the company calls it. Customatix.com permits consumers to select every part of the shoe (laces, tongues, soles, stitching), at least in terms of color and basic configuration, resulting in millions of potential combinations across various styles. Website developers are creating interactive fitting rooms where customers' body dimensions can be translated into the appropriate-size goods, across brands and product types. Once the site "knows" a person's dimensions, it figures out which pair of Levi pants or DK-brand blouse should be sent, perhaps to be custom manufactured based on such data.

Customer design through the web would help bypass one of the current problems with fashion. Constant change creates difficulties for those whose specialized need has been filled by a product that then ceases to exist—or has so changed appearance, model name, and even brand that it cannot be found again. So, for example, a running enthusiast seeking a particular shoe that gave her comfort can no longer find the same model, even if it exists under a different cosmetic layering. A solution proposed by the designer who told me this story (himself a runner) is for users to specify to the factory, via the web, their precise foot configuration and running habit so as to generate "their" shoe. In this way, fashion could change even more rapidly by keeping certain core elements of the shoe constant.

As a way around the impersonality of the web, site organizers can create at least a primitive form of togetherness. Much of the web works through people interacting over a common interest, say tulip growing, '30s vampire movies, or dog breeding. Although much of this activity now happens within list-serves, it also occurs through commercially managed websites related to the common topic (e.g., dog collars for dog lovers). If the company controls access to the website, through "membership" and passwords, it owns not just the website and related software paraphernalia; the company owns the community. And this also can shape the goods. When, for example, site visitors exchange tips on computer performance or the best brush for a dog's coat, the goods themselves may undergo change as the company responds to the social "conversation." Each of the customer's selections—an image, a chat partner, an entertainment, a purchase—simultaneously generates information about the user. Such "transaction-generated information," as it is called, provides the company with information it can use in future pitches as well as to substantively change its products. The company gains a never-ending focus group; the product and a cultural niche can build in tandem.

Analogous to having the right geographic location for a bricks-and-mortar store, virtual retail draws in customers by beaming out the words and images that correspond to customers' prior stock of cognitive tools—their "mental" location. The computer interface has to work with what is already in the minds while doing what is possible to bend them toward the website. The book business, a realm of so many different products, points to the principle. Books sell through the wording of their titles, publisher classifications, and key words assigned to their content—all of which are markings (some directly on the product itself) designed to catch the attention of the right customer base. To help its low-tech products along in the electronic age, Joe Boxer shorts puts the company's interactive website address on the inside band of its underwear as something to read when sitting on the toilet. The idea is to mark the stuff to encourage access to the company's goods via an electronic search. Marketers now emblazon their website on everything anyone might see—shop fronts, delivery trucks, packaging, employee uniforms as well as the goods themselves, in part because it's cool, but also in the belief it will yield direct results.

LEASING

Not as apparently radical as e-shopping, leasing eliminates buying all together and has its own impacts on the nature of the goods. Americans acquire about one-third of their cars through leases. If people think they will only have their cars two or three years (leases contain options to buy, but most lessees do not exercise them), they make less conservative model choices than they otherwise would. In other words, the products become faster-turn by the lease arrangement. Other possible changes appear as leasing moves into other industries. The Carrier Corporation—the largest maker of commercial air conditioners—now contracts with users to cool their buildings to a certain temperature. They do the repairs, replacements, and maintenance as part of the deal. In effect, people contract for "coolth."[36] Having the air conditioner maker retain ownership encourages equipment of greater durability and cheap repair. If the maker is also responsible for utility costs (another variant), the stuff will be more energy efficient. Xerox Corporation now operates much of its copy machine business in a similar way, charging clients for the number of copies they make while retaining ownership of the machines.

Moving from copies to rugs, some carpet providers now lease floor covering. When portions of carpet or tile wear through, the supplier replaces depleted sections to maintain a given standard. The provider has incentive to use long-wearing materials and to install the kind of carpet that will not show where the new and old pieces meet. Carpet tiles are a method to do this or broadloom with the kind of pile (cut, not looped) and coloration (like tweed) that will be more forgiving of seams. Again, the replacement of purchase with a lease affects the goods.

THEATER-IN-STORE

Perhaps the master trend in the retail world, across the media and settings, is the professionalized use of aesthetics in the transaction environment. While not new in its essentials, the rise of entertainment itself as a leading economic sector increases awareness and also provides new resources (techniques, talent, ideas) for retail applications. The new entertainment twist, caught in phrases like "retail theater" and "experiential" selling, gives the old bricks-and-mortar setting an edge. It also gives some edge to goods that align with the new emphasis—sporting goods, "fun stuff," and products with direct entertainment tie-ins, like those licensed by movie studios.

At NikeTown stores, video screen walls use simultaneous projection techniques in ever more complex configurations to depict struggle and thrill. About half the retail space is given over to displays and attractions rather than merchandise. Each store of the women's clothing chain Anthropologie, a high-end purveyor of informal clothing with a hint of expedition, has a "visual manager/stylist" on staff— someone who continually arranges displays and signage. At the very expensive end of retail, the avant-garde Dutch architect Rem Koolhaas designed Prada's New York shop with public space for lectures and performances. One of the Las Vegas hotels (Caesar's Palace) uses complex arrays of timed lighting to simulate "real sky" at its Roman Forum indoor shopping street; another ("The Venetian") has two Koolhaas-designed Guggenheim Museum spaces within its precinct. But even U.S. suburban malls now use fountains, video walls, and art exhibitions. Mall of America, near Minneapolis, includes a seven-acre theme park in its midst with rides, civic events, and musicians—including appearances by major stars. So just as an entertainment company like

Disneyland learned it could sell stuff to those who came for the rides, more conventional merchandisers learned to provide entertainment for those who may have come "just to shop." The two routes converge both as a setting and in the way they fuse into the goods.

For some who denigrate Disney kitsch or Vegas vulgarity, goods sold in heritage spaces offer a fantasy alternative. Mass-produced reproductions and adaptations service those who are rejuvenating houses in old neighborhoods but also reflect the tastes of people moving into new suburban housing. Recently built communities influenced by the so-called "new urbanism" (with its front-porch "howdy neighbor" simulation) typically peg themselves to some past idealized moment, circa 1890–1920. Implicitly at least, gaining the goods associated with those times can bring back some of the admired lives that people are thought to have once lived (iconography and implements related to the 1897 depression, 1918 killer influenza epidemic, or World War I battle deaths are omitted). The stores honor the idea of preserving something worthwhile through the process of acquisition. In the current moment, the U.S. chain "Restoration Hardware" neither restores anything material nor offers hardware in the sense of gaskets or drill bits. Instead it works with the *idea* of restoration, providing a venue for purchasing an old-fashioned watering can or corkscrew, as well as related evocations in furniture, fittings, and towels. The store marks its products not just with price tags, but texts to indicate how the artifact putatively fit into the vanishing life style but can be of contemporary use. Here is the little sign that explains why you should buy a set of tiny-capacity measuring spoons:

> The key to Good Cooking
>> Pinch, Dash, and Smidgen
>> I'll bet you never realized that pinch, dash, and smidgen were actual measurements used in cooking. Well, they are. According to our source, a dash is 1/8th of a teaspoon, a pinch is 1/16th of a teaspoon . . . These diminutive spoons give you the precise amount every time, and they're matte finished stainless steel, so you know they're serious culinary instruments. They're also cute as a bug . . . $6.00.

The store and the goods work each other up.

Uses of the past both at Las Vegas and Restoration parallels the historic borrowing going on in architecture and graphics and then getting into the products. In their commonplace postmodern renditions, retail malls evoke medieval and Renaissance-like curvilinear spaces and alcoves, sometimes with multiple balconies suspended into soaring atria. Departing from the conventional linear shopping malls (a department store anchoring each end, with chain stores linking them up), one may not quite know what will be where—the idea is to make the experience of movement itself a bit of an intrigue. Architects choreograph "the space between" buildings to egg people onward toward new consuming pleasures. Products themselves in the form of real estate commodities, they have been variously condemned as undemocratic, dysfunctional, fraudulently inauthentic, and entrapping.[37] Putting it most severely, Fredric Jameson states that such "postmodern hyperspace has finally transcended the capacities of the individual human body to locate itself, to organize its immediate surroundings perceptually, and cognitively to map its position in a mappable world."[38] In the context of the mall, the consumer is overwhelmed into purchasing acquiescence—putty in the hands of the spatial entrepreneur. What people buy becomes even more superfluous than it otherwise would be; disorientation and delirium cause shoppers to select still shoddier, more alienating merchandise.

The alternative, of course, is to see the latest bend in retail arrangement as corresponding to other changes in fashion, much as has been the case before. "If one can identify any characteristic style of major structures in the Western city since the Renaissance," says planning expert Susan Fainstein, "it is bastardized historical re-creation."[39] The more recent rejection of rectilinear modernism in shopping centers, parallel to the demise of the style in products, came after critiques of modernist malls as devoid of interest, human scale, and a sense of pedestrian surprise. These malls are modernistic in that "at every moment the work itself is wholly manifest."[40] The tedium of the straight path and ersatz Napoleonic boulevard thus gave way to medieval bows and haunts and the central festival space of the current vogue. That spaces can be opaque means people can move into surprise—like hitting upon a piazza after a meander through a Venetian maze. Indeed, the taste for such spaces likely trades on the increased experience with the real Venice, either directly through tourism or indirectly through entertainment media location shoots of medieval and Renaissance streetscapes. However short the new malls may fall in terms of authentic replication, their designers and money-backers want them to be inviting and non-threatening, again parallel to what the creators of products want their goods to accomplish: semiotic handles that *work*. It is this very compatibility with commonplace psychology, sociability, and trends of the moment that make them commercially viable. Most simply put, the shift in retail environment aligns and helps support the shift in goods sold within it—influencing the stuff just as the stuff influences it. Perhaps it is an occupational hazard of the intelligentsia, heads abuzz, to have so much trouble finding their way. Maybe if they just went shopping at the mall, they would have a better experience.

All this does point out that geographic place enters into the goods picture, but as I will explore in the following chapter, not just as part of the retail transaction. At the heart of the production apparatus—even in a world of e-commerce, globalism, and virtual simulations—it's still location, location, location and all the accoutrements of milieu that influence what stuff can be. Local geography—the nature of cities and regions—subtly permeates virtually all aspects of stuff.

CHAPTER 6

Place in Product

Places produce stuff, but not just in the obvious sense that everything has to be made and distributed somewhere. The nature of a place affects what stuff can actually be because locale contains the ingredients, including subtle ones, that go into making up goods. And because, I would argue, places do differ from one another, so does the stuff they produce.

That one can see the same goods and services almost everywhere does not mean, points out geographer Michael Storper, that those same "anywheres" can innovate, initiate, and distribute these increasingly omnipresent things.[1] So although main streets all over the world may end up with a Starbucks, not that many places could originate such stores and their collateral goods (ceramic mugs, audiotapes, coffeepots). Affluent people across the globe may wear Armani suits to their meetings, but only one world region could spawn those specific garments. Even marginal local distinction can generate huge consequence—both for the originating locale and those far afield.

The main question regional and urban experts typically have asked about places is why one of them beats out the other to produce a particular commodity—why Detroit, say, surpassed Toledo, Ohio, to become the center of U.S. car production. To figure out how Detroit came to be, they look for its "competitive advantage" in car production. They take the fact of cars, and of a certain sort, for granted. The alternative is to imagine that there is something about Detroit—and cer-

suits are global, not regional

tainly about the nation that surrounds it—that influenced how cars and the auto transportation paraphernalia would turn out. That is my approach. To gain still another route into seeing how goods happen I look for the ways place qualities influence the nature of stuff. And that means thinking, about how all the realms that do make up a place—aesthetic, social, material, natural, technical and all the rest—interact differently in one spot compared to another.

I can become more exact by drawing on places I know through research and personal experience. This means I emphasize Los Angeles and the Southern California region, which I define as the zone from Santa Barbara (where much of my life has been spent) south to the Mexican border (where I have been a frequent visitor). As I stress the ways places differ, I do not mean to say they are utterly distinct either in their underlying characteristics or in the stuff they produce—just that there are differences that count in tipping goods toward one version and not another. I search for the distinctive nature of places and then trace how those local tendencies yield goods of a certain sort.

PLACE TRADITION AND CHARACTER

Especially at a time when world homogenization supposedly flattens geographic distinction, how does one find the differences that matter? The poets, songwriters, and novelists have long tried to capture the distinctive essences. They can "feel" it. So Paris is the "city of Light," Chicago the place of "broad shoulders," and Reno "the biggest little city on earth." New York is "the city that never sleeps," that has a minute that goes faster than in other places. These notions imply something beyond the statistics of population size or industrial base. Anyone who has been to San Francisco and Houston knows they are not the same, nor are Toledo and Denver for people who have lived in both. These differences, however subtle and largely disregarded by social scientists looking for crisp indicators to count, "are not imaginary, but rather are actual features of the world," as one thoughtful geographer comments.[2] A particular "structure of feeling" comes to somehow permeate.[3] Prescient in his terminology several generations ago, the economist Alfred Marshall used the nicely open term "industrial atmosphere" to suggest that the air people breathe together causes certain productive things to occur and not others.

Dissatisfied with the results of their researches, social scientists have had to continually expand the range of factors needed to explain competitive advantage. So beyond the "hard factors" of location—access to labor, raw materials, and markets—they recognize some "softer" forces at work. Especially as cities shifted out of heavy industry and into service economies, analysts looked at things like local knowledge as important. "Labor" is not just access to hard bodies, but skill and education or "human capital," as the economists say. A further extension goes toward the idea of "social capital" —the connections and knowledge people in a place have of one another's skills and resources, and the capacity to draw on them.[4] Social capital becomes not just a matter of adding up the number of connections, but their quality. Further along, analysts gave weight to "cultural capital"—particularly to knowledge of the fine arts of painting, sculpture, literature, and dance.

Eventually, we start getting to what the poets were after. For something to happen, including a product, a place must forge linkages—fast, easy, and some even humanly pleasurable—across the diverse spheres. Jane Jacobs spoke of something like this, I believe, with her term "co-development webs." She regards them to be as necessary for an economy as they are for biological development and ecosystems.[5] I think of the words "place character" and "place tradition" as summing up the way, for better or worse, such diverse elements manage to cohere and deliver the sometimes ineffable feelings that signify difference. Character represents the mode of lash-up in a given place at a given time—the specifically local way people bring it all together. "Tradition" stands in for that character as it moves across time and gives local character some permanence.[6]

Looking at character and tradition in this way allows a pursuit of the local even in a place like LA—a metropolis often portrayed as mere vacuum. Nobody ever accuses LA of being intellectual like Berkeley, quick-witted like New York, traditional like London, or solid like Boston. It is instead, in the voices of its critics, a place with little substance at all: "The illusion factory," wrote Blaise Cendrars in 1936,[7] a "world of make-believe," said Daniel Bell in 1976,[8] "the world centre of the unauthentic" remarks Jean Baudrillard in 1989.[9] But the flip side of all these lacks is a certain kind of substance that shapes the goods. Some think there is an identifiable LA-region "feel" across the whole range of furniture, appliances, cars, and even medical equipment created there. In *Business Week's* hyped-up version, Southern California designs are distinctively "exuberant, warm, optimistic, and playful . . . part California, part Japanese, a brash expression of Pacific Rim confidence in the 90's. Think myth, metaphor, humor, and color."[10] In a recurring LA refrain, we also learn that "The new rule is no rules,"[11] that California designs have a special "sense of fantasy and wit" and "invented histories."[12]

In reviewing an Oscar ceremony for the *New Yorker*, Harold Brodkey explains LA's "great potency" as arising from its role as "the real home or center of what is worldwide middle-class right now."[13] Because LA's lifestyles are so diverse and its culture industry can incorporate so wide a range, the use of LA in stuff helps goods to be "multidomestic"—local everywhere.[14] This LA combination of deviance and embrace of the middlebrow gives it a lot of business. At this relatively democratic moment of consumption, LA can—as the examples to come will show—get into a lot of things. As I look at how place character plays out in specific industrial sectors in Los Angeles, I have in mind that there are analogous processes of lash-up in other regions as well, even though the substance is different.

CONSUMING MILIEU: TOURISM

People travel, in good part, to experience the character and traditions of other people's places, something that goes a long way back, perhaps to the earliest human communities.[15] Indigenous American peoples would go hundreds of miles to witness another people's ceremony they had not before seen or "just to bring back a hammock."[16] Tourism is now—maybe always has been if you factor in pilgrimage—the world's single largest industry, roughly 6 percent of the global economy.[17] Although a kind of service product, tourism affects durable goods, and this affect obviously depends on the local. Much of tourism is in search of ensembles—nature, artifacts, and residents all in interaction. Travelers then buy reproductions of their experience through videos, postcards, paintings, and merchandise souvenirs. The shape and features of the camera, indeed much of its market, owes a lot to tourism and the premium it places on portability and the need to adapt to long-distance shoots and unpredictable variations in light, subject matter, and vibration.[18] Consumers also buy souvenirs—durables that hold memories of a visited place—more unwittingly when they get home and select furniture and other goods that contain images and ideas they can associate with their visit. U.S.-made coffeepots change after enough Americans return from Italy; at least some British crave mixer taps after using them in the United States or Denmark. It is not just that the foreign trip creates demand for something intrinsically "better"; people gain some of the milieu itself, its feeling, in the goods they later buy and use.

Southern California still attracts tourists looking for novel ways to health and a better soul, routes to the fresh and fantastic, the natural and the wild, rather than the venerated and sanctified. Thus comes the theme park—Disneyland above all others. It treats merchandise access as a core element of its choreography through rides, amusements, and sociability. Besides the stuff sold on site, it brands clothing, food, office equipment, kitchen tools, video, jewelry, and toys sold around the world. LA had the elements that could make Disneyland happen. In terms of physical structures, it had prior experience with fantasy buildings, especially but not only the movie palaces: castles or tepees, temples of the Mayans, Egyptians, and Chinese. Made with light stucco construction, buildings could themselves become "novelty items"; restaurants, shops, and gas stations evoked the product for sale. So merchants sold hot dogs from a structure that was, in stucco, a hot dog; a tamale stand was a tamale, an ice cream store an igloo.

LA as movie capital provided the Disney characters that preceded the parks and the merchandise. Disneyland training materials refer to workers as "actors" and "actresses"; their uniforms as "costumes"; and they are expected to speak from "scripts" that will deliver "the same consistent show."[19] The Disney rides, life-size animations, and other attractions used techniques and personnel from the region's aerospace-military complexes. After replicating theme parks in other countries, Disney Corporation has taken the formula to real estate development, with the quasi "new town" called "Celebration" in Orlando, Florida. There Disney assiduously invokes nostalgic references in every detail of its newly constructed downtown, its public buildings, home subdivisions, and street furniture. Celebration may yield an LA-originated real estate business to export across the world. This may then further expand the repertoire of Disney-related goods into all manner of household appliances and other home products that "go with" the real estate.

Disneyland's toy landscape incubated infrastructure innovations in underground power generation, sanitation, and vehicle guidance systems.[20] Disney also stimulated production of plastic-fiberglass composites in architectural work, based on its originating demand for turrets and towers, "rock" walls, massive "timbers," and pirate dungeons. In part because of the Disney lead, benches, trash cans, and street signs (again, shaped and configured any which way) were manufactured for other markets by the Disney suppliers. Disney's needs fed further experiments using resin systems in decorative construction materials by, among others, William Kreysler, who had begun with racing sailboats and then moved into construction materials. Builders now use the material, impervious to corrosion, rot, and pests, in load-bearing applications, like the 3–D IMAX Theatre dome in Seattle and an increasing number of bridges around the world.[21] Composites open architecture to non-angular forms, making possible such buildings as Gehry's Bilbao Museum and, for better or worse, low-cost knockoffs. LA's recreational and decorative tendencies thus helped develop and hold a technology while the various challenges like building codes and technical problems were worked through.[22]

CONSUMING MILIEU: PLACE LABELS

People often prefer that goods of a particular sort come from a particular distant place, almost as a matter of type form. So perfume should come from Paris not Peoria, watches from Geneva rather than Gdansk. Such "valorization of milieu"[23] is potent. For Paris, fashion centrality has long been self-conscious; Baptiste Colbert, minister to Louis XIV, said that "fashion for France should be what the gold mines of Peru were to Spain."[24] What went on in Paris among designers, clients, and commentators created, in itself, an export market for products attributed to the milieu. Paris continued as "model of enlightened consumption."[25] Whatever superiority French consumption goods might be thought to possess, part of the demand comes from just the fact of the geographic origin, something reflected in the country's fierce battles to control regional wine appellations like "Champagne" or "Burgundy." Such favorable geographical stories create entry barriers for products from other places. Through purchase, consumers in effect cannibalize a distant locale without actually going there, taking in some of its social and cultural power.

Makers often respond by exaggerating the place-theme in the products, using materials and designs that connote the favored geographic spots. Ashcraft Design reissued its JBL speaker series as "Control L.A." for the Japanese market—the packaging was full of LA things on it, including a Western-eyed blonde and her stuff along with surfboards and other Southern California paraphernalia. Government and local boosters work up coordinating sentiments in public works. A redo of the LA airport lined approaches and exit roads with hundreds of mature palms and a vast spectacle of "contextually perfect" 12-story internally lit translucent pylons in "Hollywood colors."[26] By contrast, San Francisco authorities, perhaps disdainful of the tinseltown rival to the south, redesigned their airport in a more restrained albeit inventive manner, expanding an already impressive arts exhibition program (it is the only airport museum officially recognized by the American Association of Museums). Both cities are much more varied than what they use to announce themselves to the world but they work to sustain their stereotypes.

Place images do change and with them the products they help form. Once more known for tomato sauce and marble, "Italy" has become a desired global brand in sophisticated clothing, furniture, ceramics and lighting—fields that now make up 82 percent of its exports.[27] Early in the nineteenth century "the prejudice against American goods" was so great that U.S.-made jellies, jams, and pickles were marketed abroad under a British label.[28] "Made in Japan" was once a stigma for cars and electronics on the American market, but no more.

In realms where it can work, U.S. marketers take advantage of their country's image of exuberance, showy "fun," and athleticism. In the right niche, it can sell durables. U.S.-designed sports utility vehicles manage some sales in Japan, along with US-designed off-road-looking clothes and accessories, akin to stuff from the movie "Raiders of the Lost Ark."[29] In a full-page ad in Germany's *Der Speigel*, Chrysler headlined its Voyager model with the Springsteen lyric "Born in the USA." In contrast, German auto companies push "German engineering" in the United States. In its line of kitchen appliances for Europe, General Electric deliberately used overscaled handles (still smaller than used in the U.S. market) to connote, with bigness, the American origin. GE also marketed a large refrigerator (finished by the Italian company Frigo) with a huge graphic of a passenger plane approaching the World Trade Center—a design that had to end for obvious reasons.

For LA, "Hollywood" sells many things.[30] Celebrities can usefully demonstrate products to make them more acceptable. A star applying makeup in a movie scene shows just how to "take a powder" and run a lipstick, smack the lips, and wipe away excess. Virtually every beauty queen backed up Max Factor's products with her photographs and endorsements, given free of charge and then featured in advertisements around the world with the word "Hollywood" always in evidence. Likewise with clothes, celebrities show just how to wear them, including which strut, smile, and pout goes with what. Like the toga that needs the extended hand, one sits or stands in certain ways with particular types of garments. Without "lessons" from the movies, it would have been harder for certain articles to catch on (recall the Dorothy Lamour sarong). Similarly, entertainers help sell furniture; they can place their limbs in unusual configurations and yet avoid awkward appearance. As an LA designer of unusual furniture told me, "they look great doing it; they know how to use their bodies, even on my pieces." Sometimes the product is never seen, but the movie still sells it. Cleopatra's wavy bangs in the Claudette Colbert 1934 movie depiction boosted demand for curling irons.

Because of the associations people make between Southern California and the outdoor life, sportswear and sporting goods companies rely on Southern California terms; hence brands like "LA Gear"

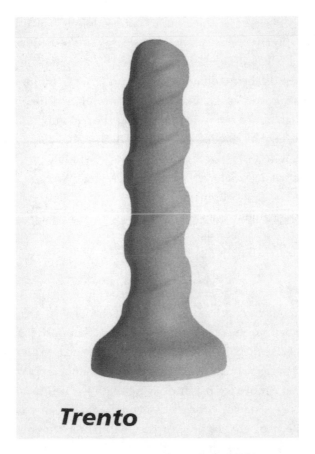

Trento

An Italian city brands a "non-phallic" Dildo.
From Babes' "Kinky Range." (www.babe-n-horny.com)

and "Ocean Pacific" (which also uses palm trees on its signature). Detroit sometimes puts California marques on cars, for example, the Chevrolet Bel Air and Malibu models as well as the Pontiac Ventura. They join favored European spots on the road (Chrysler Cordoba, Buick Riviera). Even when these images are "stolen," they affect the nature of the goods, probably enhancing the market for authentically local products. Using Italy, a California company called "Giati" makes teak and mahogany high-end garden furniture in Asia for the U.S. market. In Manhattan, a residential high-rise developer names his project "L'Isola," which is, in fact, a rather ordinary neighborhood in Milan.

The developer celebrates the tenuous connection with a full-page *New York Times* advertisement that says: "Milan is not just today's fashion center, it's a world design leader. In everything from chairs to coffee machines, from fabrics to bathroom fixtures."[31] The building's Italian looking marble and lamps likely further stimulate demand for more things "Italian" and for travel to Italy to see the real thing. The ultimate compliment may be the one paid by the BCM Babes company operating out of London that names models in its line of high-art "non-phallic" dildoes after Italian locales—e.g., the "Trento," "Murano," "Verona." In contrast, the same company markets its butt plugs (for anal insertion) with the names of central European cities—"Prague," "Tula," and "Bruno."

SELECTIVE MIGRATION

Migration tends to continuously reinforce the local patterns that end up in stuff. Besides the economic deprivations that push people out of one location and the job opportunities that pull them to another, there are other, "softer" pushes and pulls that demographers typically ignore.[32] People move for reasons having to do with ethnicity, religion, sexuality, or less obvious forms of identity—for reasons of aesthetic appeal or perhaps the vague idea they will better "fit in" elsewhere. Repelling, expelling (or annihilating) certain kinds of people similarly shapes milieus. That so many intellectuals and artists fleeing European fascism ended up in New York, Chicago, and Los Angeles affected American culture and goods' substance in each of those cities, most obviously allowing Bauhaus to eventually take hold as part of their design vocabularies. Cultural leanings nudge more ordinary people to different types of destinations. I imagine, for example, that a worker who lost his job when a Detroit factory closed would tend toward Los Angeles if dreaming of stardom, Santa Cruz if a vegetarian, San Francisco if gay, Houston if aspiring to make a killing in real estate. On the other hand, a woman not "at home" in, say, San Francisco will be more likely than her neighbors to accept a job in Houston.

Even when they share the same occupational designation, people are a mixed bag of talents and tendencies that show in their styles of leisure as well as how they vote, what they buy, how they do their work, and what additional work they take on. So even when places look alike in having, say, attracted the same number of "mechanical engineers," they are made different by the habits and personalities of the engineers who come versus the ones who go. Some places are more likely to captivate engineers who hunt (I'll say Idaho in the U.S. context), while others specialize in engineers who paint landscapes (I'll guess Santa Fe). At the neighborhood level, the coming of gay enclaves yields a different kind of market oriented toward wares for home entertaining and other products preferred by people usually without children.[33] The presence of divorced career women with pied-à-terres in London creates a not dissimilar consumption niche.[34] Change in family structure (and stigma systems), conjoined with migration, thus shapes product demand and the nature of some goods.

Beyond the notorities of the film business, the LA sensibility acted as a draw. Those who came to populate the aerospace industry (Glenn Martin, Donald Douglas, John Northrop, and the Lockheed founders) were part of an "early flowering of a culture of amateur aviation in the region,"[35] driven by hobbyists and adventurers. Architect Richard Neutra's exodus from his native Austria began with a poster—a German one, reading "California Calls You." He reported that for several years he repeated the words, "in a kind of commando tone . . . over and over again."[36] Neutra gave credit to Southern California for producing "a people who were more 'mentally footloose' than those elsewhere."[37] One designer told me, "I aimed my car for California," then figured out what to do after he arrived. Another says he "would have turned into a vegetable" had he remained in Detroit.[38]

Each such gesture of movement reinforces the character of a place as site of production, consumption, and the imposition of regulations that also affect product development. In this way, the kinds of cultural distinctions present in a locale's place reputation and emblematic economic sectors like finance, movies, or oil affect those filling the mundane jobs that run parallel and in logistical support. Operating with the economic forces of push and pull, cultural sortings are always at work, refracting back on the economic outcomes. The beat goes on.

Internal Market Base

Localities build products through the support their own populations provide as an initial market; the locals are the proving ground. Besides being a critical mass of consumers who might nurture the initial runs, the local constituency affects the appeal the product will have elsewhere. If makers can satisfy say, style demands of consumers in Milan, they can satisfy comparable locales—parts of the world populated by people of similar tastes and affluence. This helps explain why, as an empirical fact, the richest countries tend to trade together most.[39] They want each other's stuff. A discriminating home market is among the three critical assets that productivity guru Michael Porter uses to explain the wealth of nations, along with advantageous cultural assets and appropriately skilled workers.[40] Michael Storper writes that better "knowledge evolution" exists where "groups of 'dedicated' demanders" are in interaction with their producers.[41]

In the LA case, local consumers keep their producers guessing. LA people will desert Nissan for Toyota, just as they originally led the nation's switch from U.S. car brands to foreign ones. Political party loyalty has always been weak; in religion, there is niche marketing for people who pick and choose a denomination as if dealing with competing brands on the shelves. Local goods, material or symbolic, have a tough test to pass. Variety in employees and residents, along with tourists, business visitors, and other "city users," as Guido Martinotti calls them,[42] provides access to world sensibilities that can get into the goods. In commenting on the fact that Americans "are all foreigners," Alfred Hitchcock once said that "whatever frightens the Americans frightens the Italians, the Rumanians, the Danes, and everyone else from Europe."[43] This is the advantage of having the global in situ.

The local base of outdoors- and sports-oriented people changes clothing; LA is the largest U.S. producer. Southern California tends toward lighter colors and bolder configurations and "comfort styles," which means, for example, elastic waistbands on skirts and pants for easy fit.[44] The head of the California Mart, which is LA's dominant clothing showroom center, describes the Southern California industry as "a little way out, a little kooky."[45] LA does not do couture or tailored suits—New York does.

Southern Californians' propensity for outdoor sports and its athletes' fame also come through in the goods. Individualistic (rather than team-based) sports are big for participating and for watching: surfing, bicycling, swimming, snowboarding, rollerblading, skateboarding, Frisbee throwing. At the Barcelona Olympics, California (and mostly the southern portion, although the data are reported by state) had more than a fourth of all U.S. athletes, and the state produces half the top swimmers in the world.[46] Because athletes in individualistic sports do not usually wear uniforms, there is greater potential for "civilian" spillover into mass products compared to team competition. "Pro" clothing worn by individual competitors translates into lines of general sportswear like tennis shoes, sweats, jackets, socks, and pullovers. Once incubated locally, the stuff moves out to other regions which, while perhaps inappropriate to have worked as an origin point, are receptive as locales of consumption. After Europeans accepted the U.S. tennis shoe as everyday wear, Nike, Reebok, and LA Gear (all based on the sports-oriented West Coast) gained major access to world shoe markets. For both the foreign markets and other U.S. regions, the shoes changed into hybrid sports and street goods.

The local climate and attitude that goes into LA houses and their furnishings also have wider product consequence (the Los Angeles area produces more furniture than any other part of the United States except the state of North Carolina). LA houses use virtually every theme from Polynesia to Poland. Differences show up in the detail: the ubiquitous "Spanish" contains North Africa, Italy, and 1930s industrial USA (as in omnipresent steel casement windows). Southern California tiles used in Craftsman houses incorporated a "freer use of color"[47] than those made elsewhere. The large size of Southern California houses (consistently bigger than the national average) invites big-scale furniture—"works generous in size and spirit," in the words of *House Beautiful*'s 1987 special issue on "Big Style Directions from California."[48] Upholstered chairs and sofas have chair backs and armrests almost as wide as a seat might be in more ordinary goods, and very deep sitting areas. There is obvious contrast with tastes for traditional shapes among, say, the British and those in the U.S. East. Even in the case of modernism, LA's version was distinctive, departing from minimalist rectilinearity and machine-age materials. A Frank Lloyd Wright kind of spirit[49] invoked the outdoors, natural materials, and a capacity for the eclectic. Patrons of the modern were frequently Hollywood intelligentsia and LA nonconformists. *Better Homes and Gardens* and *Ladies Home Journal* distributed Richard Neutra's house plans, in the former case as "Bildcost House." The glass-walled, slider-to-the-patio, single-story knockoff "ranch house" arose in suburbs everywhere, as well as larger-scale "motel modern" emulations. The architecture boosted markets for aluminum, glass, and plastics as well as kindred interior furnishings. Neutra's Lovell House (for the leader of the country's natural foods movement) contained the earliest use of suspended ceilings which, in turn, encouraged built-in ceiling light fixtures.[50]

Orientation toward sports, casualness, and immodesty—as well as the nature of the climate—means "there's more skin," in a designer's phrase, which discourages use of sticky upholstery surfaces or ones that work poorly with sweat, like velvet. Local furniture is thus in interaction with local clothes. Climate does not, we have to remind ourselves, dictate bare skin; in some very hot places folks' sense of modesty or religion keeps them more covered—people in Mexico, India, and the Middle East, for example, do not bare themselves like Southern Californians. LA weather, along with patterns of using the outdoors, does encourage blurring of the indoor-outdoor distinction in furniture. Tables and chairs can be used either in or out and, when kept on a covered veranda, both. In another instance of cross-industry linkage, LA's Brown-Jordan, one of the country's largest makers of outdoor furniture, was the first to use aluminum for commercial furniture—an application borrowed from local war production. The company created pieces that could duplicate classic designs and reflect new ones at lower costs than with iron or steel.[51]

With these LA goods, as with the other local stuff, products can end up where they do not "belong." LA-inspired furniture crowds the small living rooms of New Jersey apartments. Easterners who have captured the

"California look" with "picture windows" overlooking alleys and sliding glass doors to rarely used patios desire California pieces compatible with their imported architecture. Those doing the distant consumption do sometimes lose touch with the fact that the products' specificities "made sense" under circumstances different from their own. But there they are.

Even in the more utilitarian realm of office furniture, California customers have a distinctive preference, favoring, for example, "daring" prints.[52] Again, there is bias against period pieces; it apparently would not do to have pseudo nineteenth-century English furniture in a rock impresario's office or a computer software design studio (except perhaps as irony). In one 1990s trend, furnishings are supposed to encourage working in groups with spontaneous consultation and "connectivity." Each worker has her or his own space (a "cave" in the trade) arrayed around a "common"—an open conference or specialized equipment area. The hardware to support such an office environment includes low and movable partitions configured to permit some visibility of who is doing what and lots of stuff on wheels. It does not matter for my purpose whether this shift works as it is intended or is just a temporary style preference. American Seating Corporation acquired Condi, a high-end LA office furniture manufacturer, specializing in this market.[53]

In the furniture industry, especially at the more expensive levels, there are close relations and frequent contact between a decorator or designer and the factory they use. A good deal of furniture output is in small batches, often for a single client like an institution or large hotel. In some instances, a design may "grow" from a piece on the showroom floor but is modified to a client's specification. Sometimes there must be fast changes; the finished product needs to conform exactly to intent—just the right tucks and fringes, tufts and thickness, levels of gloss and smoothness of texture. When Frank Gehry designed a chair line for Knoll, he insisted Knoll establish a small factory adjacent to his existing architectural practice in Santa Monica so he could "stop in on short notice."[54]

Less important for the upscale Gehry furniture but certainly significant for the production of other goods—especially clothing—are the poorly paid immigrant workers that LA draws. By bringing poor immigrants into the scene, LA-region firms have hardworking, low-cost labor proximate to design professionals and an appropriate consumer base. Producers can make goods of relatively high quality or with fast-turn frequency at a low enough price point to exist in the marketplace.

In the car industry, it was the LA entertainment rich who hired Harley Earl (and others like him) to make their vehicles something special, which then changed car making everywhere. Starting in the late '70s, all the world's auto companies began opening design studios in Southern California, at first to create "advanced design" prototypes but then models for mass production. The designers are clear; being in LA gets the milieu into the product. They take in the fashions of the city's boutiques and high-end junk shops. The shapes and colors of jewelry, the textures and combinations of outfits, all may end up in design details like knobs and fittings, upholstery, and even body outlines. They draw on car customizers, particularly Chicano youth (*Low Rider Magazine* gains half its readership from the Los Angeles area).[55] Other hobbyists preserve old and exotic models, which keeps the history of car design visually available. Chrysler's vice president for design explains his company's presence in Southern California as taking "advantage of the local culture there, even the air they breathe."[56] LA car studio staffs sometimes leave the auto companies and spin off other design offices, prototype suppliers, and computer animation and special effects studios, creating all manner of artifacts.

Cars have within them the fact of LA's pioneering of the American *car system*. Freeways, highways, and their service facilities developed more fully and at an earlier stage in Southern California. The local ensemble included cheap, locally produced oil, drive-ins, and the other appurtenances of America's "auto-mania," as it was termed in the 1920s.[57] LA's entertainment industry has been a rhythm section building up a certain type of car, with cruisin' song lyrics, make-out sequences, and adrenaline-fueled chases. At least some U.S. autos must be able to play music loud, have space for sex, and be powerful enough to squeal out of dead starts.

A consecrated U.S. car feature is the cup holder—and this seemingly incidental element signals the rise, again first in Southern California, of fast food. Americans drink and eat in their cars. Fast food, in turn,

Googie architecture, googie car. ©Petersen Auto Museum

changes the nature of cooking equipment, store fixtures, and other architectural goods linked into the food scene. Restaurant exteriors are meant to attract those who make their choice from behind auto windshields—billboard architecture. During the drive-in heyday, auto fenders and other car parts shared shapes with drive-in overhangs, soaring rooflines, and exuberant signs. The combo, dubbed "googie" style, had help from bombers and space gear, much of it also locally indigenous. Examples include the Ships chain (which featured a toaster on every table), as well as those that took the concept to the national level: Bob's Big Boy, Denny's (the largest coffeeshop chain in the country), Jack-in-the-Box, Sizzler, Taco Bell, and the mother of them all, McDonald Brothers', whose original hamburger stand opened in 1948 in San Bernardino.

LOCAL ART WORLDS

In a way more intense than other production sectors, an area's arts and culture industries press into local stuff. Virtually all places have culture

industries, whether unsung and unprofitable or celebrated and commercially remunerative—galleries, art schools, theater groups, choirs,
local publications, county fairs, craft shows, radio and TV stations, and
more. Art work reverberates through the whole system, whatever the
scale of place or enterprise. But it transfers into goods differently, dep-
nding on the kind of art in the geographic setting and the types of
forces that thwart or facilitate its transfer into products.

Notwithstanding efforts for cosmopolitan reach, the history of art
is also a history of regionalism and local tendencies. In the LA case, the
early 20th century "Eucalyptus School" differed from other versions of
impressionism through its palette of "rose, ocher, and gray of dry ter-
rain and foliage."[58] During the depression, high costs of imported oil
paint hit California especially hard, encouraging new schools of water
color art.[59] In contemporary times, one prominent critic sees in LA art
"a certain cool . . . bemusement at all the self-righteous 'struggling' and
huffing of the New York gallery scene."[60] Mike Kelley's paintings show
a "gleeful use of adolescent metaphors" that simultaneously embrace
and reject "the hot-rodding, anti-intellectual, surfer-boy high jinks
that, in the 1960's, shaped the founding ethos of art in Los Angeles."[61]
It is "hedonism according to a blueprint," says *New Yorker* critic Adam
Gopnik.[62] Some serious Zen is also an element. Just as late impressionism is impossible without Paris, a genre happens through the LA mix.

Part of the nature of any art world is in the way its arts' organizations,
like museums and galleries, operate. New York's Met once promoted its
decorative holdings to help designers put period styles into products,
holding special exhibits and workshops for the purpose. LA had less to
offer in that vein and, given local taste systems, it would probably not have
found much application anyway. But there were other routes from museums into stuff. The Pasadena Art Museum held annual "California
Design" exhibitions in the 1960s and '70s. The curator, Eudorah Moore,
"went round the garages looking for surfers and climbers, the real innovators."[63] These mixed media shows, which included both sculpture and
mass-production pieces, helped launch a number of small companies,
with several focused on surfboards, snowboards, or furniture.

A place's design education centers can influence local production,
at least when the rest of the ensemble is present. In the United

Kingdom, although there are heavy design school enrollments, the effects are limited. Though the schools build a receptive crowd for high-styled goods in sophisticated zones like London's Soho and produce fashion makers who sell in small boutiques or street market racks,[64] there is otherwise little capacity to mobilize the talent. The country that gave rise to the Beatles, Clash, Sex Pistols, and a world of mod has trouble mounting a successful home appliance. In Southern California the training effect—through design programs at Long Beach State, Otis, and most especially the Art Center School of Design in Pasadena—reaches into durables through a functioning industrial base, both locally and nationally.

Architecture often provides a vehicle for art on its way into products. In the contemporary LA case, Frank Gehry's ideas were "certainly grown out of his association with the LA artists, whose casual, funky aesthetic often coincided with his own." Artist Ed Moses says "Frank was a comrade," speaking of the group that also included artist-friends Larry Bell, Jasper Johns, Frank Stella, Billy Al Bengston, and Chuck Arnoldi.[65] Gehry says he saw artists like Stella making art from junk and cheap materials, giving him the idea of using similarly mundane stuff in his underbudgeted remodels and house additions—now landmarks in architectural history.[66] The chain-link scrim across his Santa Monica Place shopping center parking structure morphed into the titanium enclosures of the Guggenheim Museum at Bilbao and the Disney Concert Hall in LA. Once achieving prominence, Gehry and others of his so-called LA school are able to specify the furnishings and fittings for their buildings, sometimes designing the stuff themselves. Still more important, both product designers and shoppers see the structures, adapt to them cognitively, and make them a part of their repertoire.

Culture workers are typically each interdisciplinary and spark one another's energies across genres. The great majority of artists are active in more than one art.[67] But they do still other things as well, mostly out of necessity—only 15 percent of LA union actors, for example, are working at any given time as actors, and that means they take their "creative multipliers"[68] to sectors beyond the arts themselves. As they do so, they work differently than others who perform the same tasks. New York restaurant waiters, as one example, bring a theatrically specific manner into serving food. "The accents and appearance of waiters," Zukin writes, "affirm distinctions between restaurants as surely as menu, price, and location."[69] The consequences magnify when a painter switches to a dot.com, a costume maker develops a line of clothing, a set designer works on industrial products, packaging, or print. When artists build, staff, and service tourist complexes (which they do), they change the nature of the facility.

When they are not on any sort of job (or even when they are), they maintain their identity as artists through the places they hang out, the clothing they wear, how and where they eat.[70] They congregate at "haunts" and in districts that they change by how they act and interact. Their art work relies on such informal contact as people exchange news, ideas, and skills; in the show business world, it helps coordination occur across disparate realms like scripting, music, design, lighting, and so forth if and when the time should come to work together. In part for this reason, arts people relish the diversity that may offend others—they would not move to the suburban "desert." In the process, they increase the desirability of the surrounding real estate as well as of the goods they put in their spaces. They are first adopters.

Expressing it in conventional industrial terms, 15 percent of the U.S. labor force now produces all manufactured goods and agricultural products and provides basic government services like police and fire.[71] That means most of the rest are "taking in everyone else's washing": working in restaurants, movies, theme parks, and tourism—the creative service economy. And even in much of what is classified as manufacturing, the real activity is in fact design, product development, or R&D—making up 60 to 80 percent of costs in one estimate.[72] Even ordinary manufacturing "is becoming," say Lash and Urry, "more and more like the production of culture."[73]

THAT'S ENTERTAINMENT

The entertainment business, especially film and TV, show how the culture industry moves into durables. LA's dominance makes it the obvious place to employ for tracing the process, and clothes are the obvious products to use as starting point. Southern California's mix of patriotism and subversion met at denim. The denim jean got steady movie promotion through the pioneers and cowboy heroes, as well as the "rebels without a cause" and other errant youth in 1950s pictures like *The Wild One* and *Blackboard Jungle*. The tight-fitting "501" jean made San Francisco–based Levi Strauss into the world's largest clothing corporation. In a different part of the spectrum, the Ralph Lauren–designed wardrobe for the film version *The Great Gatsby* set off a '20s revival (as remembered) 50 years later—and became the basis for Lauren's clothing empire.[74] *Details* magazine credits Tom Cruise's 1983 role in *Risky Business* for the Ray-Ban sunglass vogue.[75] To help clothing makers keep abreast, the *Los Angeles Times* ran a "screen style" column through the mid-1990s, describing in detail the clothing, jewelry, and eyeglasses of various stars and characters.

The moral texture of Hollywood, including how it responds to censorship, goes into clothes. Before color, the need for erotic imagery led to women's gowns with lots of sequins, net, and lace to depict sexuality and glamour.[76] Movie clothes cut back on fabric volume to better show movement.[77] As various states enacted censorship codes in the 1920s, Hollywood countered with clingy satins and silks to expose women's breasts, otherwise banished from view. The movie moguls—at once both brazen and timid—found ways to keep scintillation alive. Entertainment styles also come from the local scenes including among the disaffected. The "hip-hop" look of the '90s went from LA youth (where it landed very shortly after its New York inauguration) into video. Designers watch and translate "the next day" what they see, emphasizes design educator Brantley, into new product schemes.[78] Even the Southern California surf wear designers brought inner-city styles into their clothing lines, just as designers elsewhere took the same look into high fashion.[79] LA shifts to incorporate new elements as the city and the world change. Vienna has the opera and a relatively fixed repertoire of reputation and cultural theme to take into goods and services; in contrast, LA adapts to a wider variety of popular trends and has, in the entertainment industry, the art form to transfer trends into mass goods.

As with sequins on gowns, black-and-white movies encouraged black-and-white furniture that, especially in crisp deco style, could imply luxury in furnishings.[80] Fred Astaire's tapping across drawing rooms probably moved a lot of product. In a different mode, Universal Studios furnished the 1927 picture *Arizona* by commissioning the local Mason Furniture Manufacturers to produce a line in the quasi-cowboy "Monterey style." Two other LA-area firms, Jaeger Company and Brown-Saltman, created similar pieces for national markets through the 1940s.[81] Because Universal Studios set designers had a standing contract to buy every piece manufactured by Brown-Saltman, the company gained wide exposure which encouraged new markets for whatever it produced.

LA enters into goods through movie product tie-ins and licensing—in part through clothing manufacture but also as the largest toy making region in the United States. The local Mattel Corporation's tie-ins to Disney help make it the biggest toy maker in the country. With a 50-member Synergy Department, Disney also licenses batteries, linens, and electronic goods, along with many other products.[82] Although the French cinema has had a global cachet, Paris has not had tie-ins, perhaps because market thresholds cannot be met.[83] It is certainly relevant that the subject matter of French movies (and French culture generally) is too highbrow for toy sales and the like. But it may be that the French films would be different (heaven forbid) if the local licensing opportunities were better.

It is an entertainment-industrial agglomeration,[84] with LA interactions going in multiple directions. Architects do movie projects and movie designers become architects. Product designer Syd Mead (once with the Ford styling department) created the space ships and other futuristic elements of the film *Blade Runner*. *Blade Runner*'s brooding futuristic imagery then affected all kinds of goods, including cars; today's boom boxes probably owe their look more to that film than any other single source. On the movie front, not only do costumers go into clothes design, manufacturer Carole Little went into the movie business (with at least one film grossing $100 million.)[85] The makeup industry was invented for the movies when it was learned that Technicolor caused surrounding color to be reflected on white people's faces—intensified by the shiny greasepaint then in use. So Max Factor, the LA immigrant wig maker from Estonia, developed "pancake"—the now commonplace cosmetic applied by dabbing moist sponges on solid, caked-up "dull" product. Max Factor's Hollywood factory, making beauty goods of all sorts as part of the Max Factor system of layering hues and colors, became the world's largest cosmetics producer. In a very different product realm, it was Walt Disney who, in connection with developing the *Fantasia* soundtrack, gave Hewlett-Packard its first significant order—for an audio oscillator.[86] Today, Disney animators' "artificial life" computer simulations (as used in the movie *Ants*, for example) are used by the San Diego–based biotech company Natural Selection to search for "genetic algorithms" that "match" the vulnerabilities of the AIDS virus.[87] Such ventures work off and contribute to the constellation of biotech firms that cluster around UC-San Diego and the Salk Institute.

The careers of Charles and Rae Eames help display the interactions in goods we all know. With backgrounds in furniture and ceramic design, they moved to LA from Detroit to develop a film technique they called "multivision" and went on to complete dozens of movie projects, mostly for corporate clients and public exhibitions. Working with LA's Zenith Fabricators, which had used fiberglass during World War II to reinforce plastic on airplane radar domes, Eames and Eames created in 1949 their fiberglass chair, in continuous production until it finally ended in the late 1990s. With the Plyformed Wood Company of LA they produced wartime molded plywood leg splints for the military,[88] which also helped shape their classic shown on the next page. The more commodious plywood-based but leather upholstered recliner and ottoman was first made as a gift for movie producer Billy Wilder, whose house Charles Eames also created. Eames's designs for airports and other institutions have hit the half-billion dollar mark in world sales.[89]

Even the modest Menda bottle, albeit with lower dollar volume, partook of LA, including—in at least an indirect way—the movie business. Its inventor, David Menkin, had been production engineer at Mattel, with its many direct and indirect links to the film industry. Before that, he had been in LA aerospace, another source of useful connections in making his bottle product work. From such prior experiences, Menkin knew how the metal in his screw caps would respond to the stress of being stamped, bent, and extruded in the unusual ways he

Eames fiberglass chair, 1949. Photograph courtesy of Herman Miller, Inc.

Eames plywood side chair (DCM) 1946. Photograph courtesy of Herman Miller, Inc.

needed. Because of a prior good relationship, the cap maker was "nice enough," Menkin says, to create some special tooling to generate early versions of what he needed.

In all these cases—whether for mundane products or esoteric biotech—things come into being because connection potentials are made real. Various spheres come together not because they are intrinsically related, but because the nature of the place *causes them to be related*. Place gets into stuff by the way its elements manage to combine.

THE WRONG TIME AND THE WRONG PLACE

The need for cross-fertilization becomes evident when the local fit is wrong—a round product peg in a square location hole. In the case of Detroit cars, as we have seen, some adjustments had to be made because Detroit's character was increasingly inappropriate given taste shifts and foreign competition. Having early on brought in a Californian to Detroit, the U.S. auto companies later had to export some significant activity to LA—and not just design. Lincoln-Mercury eventually moved its headquarters to Southern California. Silicon Valley's replacement of Boston as the high-tech U.S. center forms the most famous case. The Boston-Cambridge Route 126 science-engineering corridor, based in MIT and Harvard, could not sustain its technological preeminence. Even when East Coast corporations had direct access to California technical innovations, they failed to absorb them. Xerox operated the think tank in Palo Alto called "XeroxPARC" that developed the mouse, on-screen icons, and critical elements of the Ethernet. But the officials at headquarters in Rochester and Stamford, Connecticut, ignored the innovations. "There was no one to receive the vision," according to a XeroxPARC veteran.[90] So the inventors had to go off site and yielded up Apple, Adobe, and other major companies in California. Silicon Valley's advantage had nothing to do with conventional location factors—raw material access and such—but everything to do with the aesthetic-social context of the nerds who were there initially or who, frustrated with the eastern ways, went west. Compared to the more rigid Boston-area corporate world, business practice was much more casual—and effective: customers, suppliers, former and future employees all hung out in a way that allowed quick movements and fast exchange of information, hunches, and glimmers.[91] As most famously at IBM, eastern style meant working one's life within the corporation; the "organization man" was the ideal and the practice. In California, by contrast, there were social "salons," and regular "cybersuds" get-togethers in local bars of people from various companies, with lines blurred between whether people were in cooperation or competition. One venture capitalist I talked with from New York's Silicon Alley, another place that self-designates as hip and communicative, called the social scene the "glue ware" that held the business and technological energy together.

Whether to launch a software innovation or a world empire, the right places must be there. Columbus went to Spain to outfit his ships, which cost Italians a new world but also gave shape to the way vast numbers of people would live (and rapidly die) as well as produce in the so-called Americas. Marconi had to go to the British to launch radio, giving them a first-mover advantage that instilled English conventions and standards over early radio sets and broadcasting service and—through the mystique of the product and the worldwide voice of the BBC—a reinforcement for things British. In Turin, Giuseppe Ravizza created the typewriter in 1855 (a "writing piano" he called it), but the takers turned out, after a delay and no remuneration for the Italians, to be the American Remington Company in 1873.

Against the idea that where there is a will there is a place and that artifacts whose time has come somehow always do, I assume it does not always work out. First is the fact that part of the "will"—the substance of a creative notion—itself needs the right local fertility. Second, sometimes no amount of inspiration, perspiration, or wanderlust can turn a good idea into an artifact—being in the wrong place at the wrong time trumps it all. When the moment of lash-up is lost, the thing may be gone forever. If the first typewriter had been Italian, it would have been different than the U.S. version (no QWERTY keyboard, for one thing). There must be an infinite array of goods that never come into being because they have no right place and time (an effective auto steam engine may be one candidate). Some of this non-stuff, as I will elaborate in the final chapter, would have been better, at least by the light of many people's values, than what has come to be.

City as Itself Artifact

In its buildings, infrastructure, and iconography, the physical city supports certain kinds of goods production. The configuration of public spaces may encourage one type of productive interaction as opposed to another (artists "run into" engineers, dress designers come across hiphoppers), as well as affecting the sorts of migrants who come in or who depart (people who want a piazza "scene" versus those who prefer separate paths that do not cross). The look and functionality of the city influences designers as they do their work, producers as they figure out what to make, and consumers as they develop their wants. The built environment and its accessories—directional signs, shop design, advertising regulations, window displays, street hardware—provide durable evidence to people of the kind of place they are in, of how things are done, of what is appreciated and what is devalued.

The history of city building parallels the history of goods, with similar comings and goings of style preferences. Sometimes this happens through direct correspondence; a taste for rococo palaces stimulates rococo dishware. The use of classical Greek and Roman styles found in northern Europe and North America helped foster enthusiasm for Wedgwood's jasperware. At least in recent times, it appears that the activities of leftist regimes rather than those of traditional business groups—or imperial authorities—are most consequential on goods through their influence on public space. The sophisticated goods of the so-called Third Italy (Tuscany and areas contiguous to Bologna and Venice) arise from a locale that includes, among its prominent components, consistently communist-led local governments.[92] In the United States, the left regime that took over Santa Monica, California, in the 1980s—denounced by the local right as "The People's Republic of Santa Monica"—generated a rebirth of the city center of this ocean-side town near LA, with vastly higher commercial real estate prices. The intelligentsia, even as its members complain about the fashion system, carries advanced tastes into design. Their preferences in landscaping, public art, architectural controls, coffee brews, consumer goods, and farmers' markets revive places. The "latte towns" they dominate, as American cities like Boulder, Santa Fe, and Santa Barbara have been termed,[93] attract the creative industries, including the high-technology sectors, and their employees draw upon and reinforce milieu in making up their stuff.

NATIONS AND REGIONS: THEY, TOO, HAVE CHARACTER

It is impossible not to notice how national stylistic variations affect stuff. In the context of their nation's success as the first accomplished industrial society and greatest imperial power, British producers gained advantage of favorable trade terms with the colonies as well as symbolic panache almost everywhere. British products, by dint of exploitative relations, administrative rules (including those governing weights and measures and railway gauge), or just by being first, became type form—the standard for what further stuff could and should be no matter where it came from. Into all this was fed the sentiments favoring things associated with the crown, gentry, and other venerated traditions—invented or otherwise—of English manners, breeding, power, even the language itself. In a look back at global cultures, Martin Gannon says that in the nineteenth century, "the adoption of British ways was so universal that it was unquestioned. People automatically chose the best and the best was British"[94]

British romantic attachment to classical design and zeal for the picturesque got into the major industries, including textiles covered in landscape and floral prints. When foreign manufacturers successfully imported British machinery—despite domestic producers' efforts to prevent it—new challenges arose. Foreigners could, for example, emboss "English designs" on ceramics. But drawing on expanded design repertoires and the ability to invoke place pedigree, the British makers successfully adapted by producing new patterns tailored to smaller, more high-end markets.[95] Alas, countryside romance and a penchant for the cozy held on a wee too long, even into the era of electronic goods. The popular Russell Hobbs electric teakettle of the 1980s says "country style" on the sides and even into the '90s bears a flowery illustration. With its affection for "rural ideas," Britain lagged behind trends on the continent and North America. In the 1930s, the British Lamp Company advertised its product (made by Best and Lloyd) as "modern but

Russell Hobbs electric teapot. From Jonathan Woodham,
The Kettle: An Appreciation. *Aurm Press; The Ivy Press, 1997, p. 27.*
Photo courtesy of The Ivy Press Limited

British."[96] Saying "modern but American" (or "but Italian" or "but German") would have made no sense. According to Ikea's research on the British market, "two-thirds of consumers like the flowery, somewhat overblown style." At least among the industrial countries, the British "probably have the most entrenched views about home styling in the world,"[97] led by an "extremely conservative" upper class.[98]

Maybe something like this is what leads the British into tubs rather than showers. Showers use one-fourth the hot water of tubs, are more sanitary (one does not sit in one's own dirt), take virtually no time to prepare, and do not need to be cleaned as often (less water down the drain). They also take up less space. But there is also a heritage of using showers as a medical device and, when cold, as a test of school-boy courage.[99] In contrast, a warm soak—ideally with an Edwardian look and feel—is lovely. Leaving room for debate on the case specifics, modes of national sensuality have consequence on goods and economies. Even when as close in language, income, and history as the Brits and Yanks, cultural differences feed back into what people make and consume.

When the United States replaced Britain as dominant in world affairs, starting at about the turn into the twentieth century, its makers could sell their wares anywhere there was money to buy them. Especially in the immediate years after World War II, when United States consumers made up almost three-fourths of the world's market for manufactured goods, there was little payoff for introspecting on how to design goods to have greater appeal elsewhere. But when European and Japanese producers recovered from the war, other design traditions that more consciously acknowledged aesthetic goals regained their significance and, in some product realms, put U.S. goods at a disadvantage. Reflecting on his move to the United States, Raymond Loewy recalls the U.S. industrialists as "rough, antagonistic, often resentful," making him think his French accent was "not so helpful outside the fashion world."[100] The U.S. industrial designer Charles Pelly, who has many foreign clients, spoke to me of a "discomfort" he sometimes sensed in U.S. executives with regard to aesthetic aspects of design. European executives have, by contrast, "been going to museums since they were a kid. . . . They've traveled; they're not so intimidated, and they're comfortable" working with aesthetic issues. In Italy, reports a designer with work experience in both countries, "Italians considered designers/architects with extreme respect and often referred to them as "maestro."[101] It has been more common for European companies to be headed by a designer compared with their U.S. counterparts, making it more likely for au courant design to be "integrated into the heart of management" on the Continent.[102] The differences seem to run down the hierarchy. An Italian architect overheard two Milan brick masons ruminating while on a construction job about how they prefer to work.

One explained he liked a straight vertical surface to build against so the brickwork would also be straight and even. His colleague demurred, saying he made a habit of creating a slight void behind his brickwork so that irregular courses could allow a play of light. Such conversations, I think, would be less likely to occur in other countries. Many observers notice, sometimes in "astonishment," how seriously design functions as part of the "normal way of acting and behaving in Italy."[103]

In the product arena, Italy leads the world in total export value of clothing, textiles, and fashion leather goods by producing so much at the high end of the market. Advanced Italian style is a part, but only part of what makes it happen. Highly accomplished craftspeople work through family-based small businesses that exist in dense networks of mutual knowledge and familiarity with one another's habits, competencies, and expectations.[104] Wages are high, about double textile pay in the United States and fourfold rates in Third World factories.[105] In leather goods production, tougher pollution laws in the 1980s encouraged a turn toward high-end finished products like expensive purses and away from lower level enterprises like tanning.[106] Through high-fashion, manufacturing thus grew "at the heart of the postindustrial core."[107] It is a high-wage, environment-friendly mode of production made possible by specific social configurations of aesthetics, family, and politics. The Third Italy thus suffuses the world market with products that, in their precise details of style, materials, and craft, would not otherwise be.

An arena that the United States has no problem dominating is the various means of violence and repression, including personal arms, military gear, and prison-ware. High crime rates in the United States and tendencies toward street disorder make goods like public telephones, vending machines, and street furniture more robust than they need to be, for example, in Japan. Such exposed public goods in the United States (toilets included) are thus more expensive and perhaps, in part for that reason, less frequently available. In the redesign of one of its major public spaces, Pershing Square, the city of Los Angeles made defense from vagrants and criminals a key aspect.[108] It would not do, as in the parks of Paris, to have lightweight and movable chairs or, as in London, wooden benches in little garden enclosures. Concrete rules.

The Relative Uniqueness of Place

Products depend on just how the expressive, the material, and the organizational elements, in all their bewildering facets, connect in a given place at a given time. Even as borders lose some of their traditional meanings, locality does not become irrelevant. Because local character, tradition, and difference arise from face-to-face interaction and *in situ* cultural absorption, place differences endure. Indeed, precisely because of the relative homogeneity in what can be consumed across the world, the distinct tendencies to launch different stuff adds significance to place difference. The local has more consequence because it can so vastly move out through the goods to so many other settings. Even if everything being consumed is the same across the earth (which, of couse, it is not), the local production systems that yields it would not be made the same by that fact.

Somehow people get it together to work as an ensemble, leaving a place-specific mark on what they create. Social scientists have struggled for generations to specify how, to put it simply, people can do things together[109]—how social organization is possible. But some speak in a way I find vague and difficult to follow; they talk of "norms," meaning that individuals share a given belief system or subscribe to particular rules, formal and informal, that "guide" them. There must be stone tablets or mission statements up on walls or at least in people's minds that supposedly tell them how to conduct themselves.

Yet social scientists, albeit not usually the same as the "rules-guide-life" ones, also think that actual human activity is far too complex, idiosyncratic, and ad hoc for there to be any such guides or norms that could be of much use—a point I previously belabored (see chapter 3). People continuously meet with intensely perplexing inconsistencies that arise across situations and even from moment to moment in the same situations. How can rules do their ruling when there are always so many that seem to apply and when human activity itself keeps changing what even the "same" rule means, when it applies, and to whom? People need some method other than looking for rules that supposedly apply across time and circumstance.

Here is the method they actually use: they are—in ways spelled out in Chapter 3—"artful." In terms used by the social science school of "ethnomethodology,"[110] people are always taking in the myriad details of context; interpreting and figuring out what must be done by virtue of all that goes on. They sop it all up as non-linear gestalts, configuring and reconfiguring all in their purview. Their busy brains do even better than the vaunted "lateral thinking" of the designers; they see sideways, forwards, in the past and toward the future, and all at once. We're built that way.

Some content of this artfulness—not all of it, as we will see in the next chapter—has a geographically *local* quality, generating styles of activity particular to a place. The mode of this local artfulness is in the air. People breathe it in through the stories, jokes, manners, architectures, street styles, sounds, odors, and modes of maintenance that surround, as well as what they remember and what they anticipate. They enroll in particular projects with special attention and even gusto because they have the local means to "get it," to fit in, to function as more or less reliable members. Whether among Italian cloth cutters, Silicon Valley dot-commers, Hollywood producers, or convenience store workers setting up the shelves, the ability to do this in particular ways and at just the right time are economic assets, however difficult to measure or model. It is the source of the taken-for-granteds that inform—sometimes loudly and sometimes only with the vaguest whisper—how to do something together. Even if only barely noticed, and however much the outside world also plays a role—something to take up in the next chapter—the creative capacity that arises from milieu gets into the stuff.

CHAPTER 7

Corporate Organization and the Design Big Thing

As everyone knows, "outside" trends in world trade, global power, and corporate organization affect goods in no small way. Actors in different parts of the world participate in producing a given commodity—design in one place, raw materials from another, assembly happening somewhere else, and so forth.[1] The goal of this chapter is to show just how the details of stuff exist through these and other aspects of macro-organization, including the changing forms of corporations, the attitudes of investors, and relations across nations.

Those who made the pyramids are the iconic case of the slaves and near slaves who have made possible many artifacts, from great wonders to small nothings. Tithes and natural ruin over a vast hinterland built the grandeur of Rome. Similar modes of domestic and foreign exploitation produced the Renaissance glories still on view in Siena and Florence as well as within the world's great museum collections.[2] Belgium's colonial exploitation of Congolese laborers, forcing the harvest of wild rubber vines, provided the basis for the bicycle tires I earlier celebrated.[3] The manner of imperial departure also can have an indelible effect on products. The Portuguese exit from Angola left in its wake a still continuing brutal civil war, so devastating that Angola ended up with virtually no productive industries except artificial limb factories.[4] In that niche, Angola apparently leads, but with products specific to the low levels of technology in the region—U.S. hospitals, for example, do not import them. This Angolan success comes from a chaotic colonial past, one sustained by collusion of U.S. oil companies and diamond merchants, combined with brutal African regimes in continuous conflict. Postcolonial apartheid in South Africa also yielded up distinctive goods, some for the rich and others special in the way they were formed for the poor. For the affluent, the combination of apartheid and an equable climate led to the Aquanaut home swimming pool cleaner appliance—one of the few South African designs of renown.[5] On the other side of the color line, the workers in the diamond and gold mines used equipment unsafe by world standards. After apartheid, the pool equipment excellence remained (so far as I know), but new strategies of national development and regulation improved mining equipment. They also led to creation of some consumer goods with lower energy costs and easier maintenance that are more accessible to poor people.

In any kind of society, the existence of wide disparities between rich and poor brings into being more luxurious types of goods than would otherwise exist, like jewel encrusted watches and cars such as the Rolls-Royce. The latter vehicle came out of England, rather than the richer but more egalitarian twentieth century Sweden. The mechanical heart now under development in the United States (the AbioCor) requires not only the country's high level of medical technology but the kind of unequal access to medical care that makes such a costly product feasible. For the great majority of the world's peoples, including probably most Americans, the artificial heart will be only fantasy.

Goods' democratization changes what they are. Before the nineteenth century, European peasants typically owned little more clothing than they had on their backs and no more than a stool and a few pots as domestic goods.[6] Even people in poor countries now have more utensils, artifacts, and items of clothing. Having multiples means the objects become more specialized; one kind of knife for cutting bread, another for peeling potatoes. At the same time, democratization can yield standardization, at least as a first stage in mass production. Ford's production system created a cheap car by making it simple and spare. When Atari and other video game companies made product in Silicon Valley, high costs meant they were slower-turn durables sold to older children and adults. When Atari moved production offshore, the far cheaper versions—some produced by competitors— could be made into an inexpensive toy, using less durable materials, for a wider age range, and in a variety of models geared to niche tastes. It became a different thing, many different things.

At a later time, PDAs—the handheld data organizing devices of which the Palm Pilot was the original—recapitulated some of this pattern. Made to be sold more cheaply (around $150 compared to the palm Pilot's $500 retail price), the subsequent "Handspring" models came in a variety of styles and colors that could be spread across a wider and more varied consumer base. But to be sold so cheaply, the designer explained to me, production could not employ the more expensive and sophisticated annealing process used in a Utah factory to put a Palm Pilot together. So the manufacturer has the new product made in Malaysia with more conventional nuts and bolts technology. The factory used about three-fold the number of assembly line workers than would be needed in a comparable U.S. facility. From the beginning, its designers knew it would be unlike the Palm Pilot in how and where it would be made.

Pressing garlic also takes in global shifts. A garlic press cannot be sold above a certain price point but even a low priced model needs to look decent, and this means having an appropriate production apparatus. In the late '90s, Levien Associates in the United Kingdom designed a garlic press with a breakthrough feature, a flip out mesh screen for easy cleaning, as shown unfurled on the next page. An earlier prototype had come through with a visible flaw in the plastic caused by the factory mold. To avoid the problem and to take advantage of an evolved Chinese manufacturing capability in metal fabrication, circa 2000, the designers switched to metal. The factory that produced it, established by an Austrian entrepreneur, makes not only housewares but also fabricates garments and shoes, supplying Nike and other brands. Reflecting a new mode of production organization, the producer just makes things in general, switching among materials and applications as the need arises. At prior times in history and organizational structures, there would have been no place where cheap labor, the selection of materials, and the requisite technology came together. The Levien

Ready-for-market garlic press as produced in metal. Tala Different Garlic Press.
©Robin Levien and Anthony Harrison-Griffin.

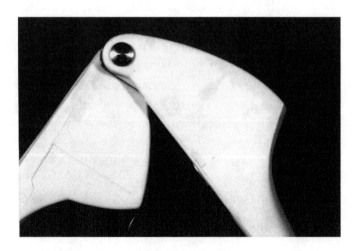

Levien-design garlic press, plastic prototype with mold flaw.
Photograph by Jon Ritter.

garlic press, selling in UK department stores under the Tala brand at about $15, shows there now is.

Producers in poorer parts of the world copy, with varying degrees of fidelity, goods from rich regions often illegally. This also creates distinctive types of stuff. In poorer parts of Asia, factories turn out watches, clothing, and luggage with logos of elite goods made in Britain, France, Italy, and Switzerland. It is easy enough to make facsimiles of such artifacts and stamp them with words like "Rolex," "Gucci," and "Dunhill." But these products, being made without benefit of quality control and at wages even lower than normal for poor country factories, are shoddy. Global relations can be felt in the lower weight of the so-called Rolex and seen, eventually, in the fading away of the "gold" on the surface. The thin fabric of a phony Izod alligator-logo shirt made in Thailand for sale to Europeans becomes thinner still if it's going to be smuggled across the border to more desperate consumers in Burma. Counterfeiting also takes place in depressed zones of rich countries; Leicester, England is said to be "the clothing counterfeiting capital of Europe."[7] All over the world, but especially its poorer places, entrepreneurs knock off music, video, and software with aplomb. Entry costs are low, production easy to manage, and legal crackdown unlikely, especially when national regimes sympathize with the offenders.

The alternative to importing cheap goods from abroad is to bring in cheap labor and make the goods at home. This works well for stuff that needs proximity between designers and production workers. Furniture designers stress the need to "control"; having the factory nearby, as in the Gehry example, yields up products that, although more expensive than they would be if made elsewhere, would not be the same stuff if made elsewhere. One reason goods can change so frequently and be differentiated in subtle ways is that corporations can indeed produce them where sophisticated equipment, advanced-taste designers, and access to cutting-edge technologies all concentrate. Hence some firms do not go offshore at all but maintain production in expensive places like LA or even Santa Barbara. The stuff shows it—in the detail and in the frequency with which the detail can be changed. This points to still another reason why the bulk of transnational investment and trade occur among the rich countries themselves;[8] producers want these kinds of conditions no matter what country they are operating in.

These cross-border relations also show up in products, hybrid artifacts in their own way. Ford and GM put some U.S. convenience and "features" into their models for European markets while making the cars smaller, with less chrome and more stick shifts than their U.S. counterparts. Inadvertant cross-national complications can also get into goods. A home appliance designer (for one of the world's largest producers) complained to me that his company's last-minute decision to manufacture his product in a UK factory rather than at his home U.S. base altered the product, and not for the good. The company wanted to curry political favor with UK authorities, it was said, to gain tax concessions for an unrelated UK plant. To keep the obsolete factory going, it was given over to the new product. But the British plant failed to follow machining specifications, requiring a U.S. redesign to accommodate the UK tooling—weakening the product in the designer's eyes. The fanfare in the business press that greeted the product's release made no mention of the change in manufacturing site, the need for redesign, or the mismatch between operations. Instead, it was handled as still another triumph in transnational production integration, a cover-up of the more haphazard realities that probably increase when production involves complex arrangements across distances and national borders. Indeed, when a trade-press reporter came to interview him, the designer was ordered to keep quiet about the actual events (I was asked by the designer not to reveal his name or that of the company).

CROSS-NATIONAL STANDARDS

Products vary in the degree they require international coherence in the ways of producing or using them; sometimes, a global standard is intrinsic to success. Before general adoption of the Morse system through international agreement, a telegraph employee of one country sometimes had to walk across the border to hand messages to the telegraph employee of the other country.[9] Similar, if less comical, difficulties beset other communication and transportation technologies (as well as legal, financial, and trade arrangements). The standards that countries come to agree upon are not necessarily based on some clear criterion of merit—aesthetic, functional, social, or ecological. These criteria do matter, but so do the whole range of factors that influence and constrain decisions on goods, including dynamics of power and influence among corporations and nations. Every producer wants its technology to become the national and, if possible, world standard. Every national government wants its producers' goods to win out over the producers of other countries.

Sometimes there is not much of a contest. Two U.S. companies, Boeing and Douglas, developed and produce the preponderance of aircraft equipment used in the world. Working with the fact of such equipment, over which it had some prior influence of its own, the U.S. Federal Aviation Authority (FAA) requires all components of any airplane to meet U.S. standards as a criterion for American landing rights. Even more far reaching, FAA listing of a foreign airline as falling short means, in effect, that its planes cannot land in the many other places in the world which have, out of practical or political need, adopted the American standard. Any subcontractor, whether producing for aircraft or airport equipment, must thus work under the U.S. corporate conditions, generating a high degree of worldwide conformity in all aspects of plane and airport production and maintenance.[10]

Corporations operate through their trade associations or, especially in the case of U.S. firms, directly pressure international organizations to encourage rules that serve their interests. If they sense they can't win, they may block standards altogether.[11] In part to fend off Japanese competition, European and U.S. companies thwarted global agreements for a standard code for television, VCRs, and videotapes. This is why a videotape recorded off a TV set in Chicago cannot be shown on a TV in France. Instead the world now has three different systems ("NTSC" for the United States). The game repeated with the coming of high definition television (HDTV). The giant Japanese conglomerate NHK first developed the new TV technology, called "Hi-Vision," in the mid-1980s. The EU and U.S. operatives prevented the International Telecommunication Union from approving Hi-Vision, resulting today in one standard for Europe, one for North America, and still another for Japan. A production and marketing inefficiency, inconsistency can be tolerated in a way aircraft or telegraph variation could not be.

It is a wonder, given the complexity of interests and technologies, that there ever come to be standards at all even within countries, much less across them. But they do—in realms like shipping, telephone, and areas of contract law, to mention a few examples. Sometimes, a dramatic crisis induces agreement. The United States initially refused to join other countries in creating a world standard for radio broadcasting, which meant, among other things, that ships at sea could not be assured of being able to communicate with ships nearby. When the Titanic went down, other vessels were only 30 miles away but could not hear its distress calls, likely increasing the loss of life that so shocked the world.[12] The resulting outcry, within the United States and United Kingdom especially, helped make these countries a force for global radio regulation. Increasingly, non-governmental agencies play a role in such areas as the environment, labor conditions, and product safety.

Especially where there is competition across companies and a nation (unlike the aircraft industry), coordinating toward some kind of standard becomes deeply problematic. The scholars John Braithwaite and Peter Drahos, from whose indispensable book[13] on global regulations this discussion heavily draws, stress that actors must go through much plotting and effort to knit together the needed enrollments. They engage in an "entrepreneurship of linkage,"[14] in Braithwaite and Drahos's phrase, striving to make it all happen in a timely way given technical circumstances, public opinion, and other elements that structure the opportunities of the moment. Groups and individuals around the world and within countries are not equal in their ability to make these linkages happen. Even a huge Japanese conglomerate backed by Japanese ministries—no minor set of players—could not mount sufficient social or economic capital to bring home the HDTV standard, one it arguably had "earned" through long-term investment, national commitment, and success at product innovation. One can only imagine the kind of disadvantage that inventors, investors, and designers operating from still more disadvantaged settings must face. At least when adoption requires acceptance of standards, their ways do not easily get into the goods. And it is sobering to realize that problems like global warming may, because of their gradual and cumulative nature, never have a "Titanic moment" that might induce the agreements necessary for a new fix.[15]

CORPORATE TRANSFORMATIONS

Changes in corporate form affect goods. The merging of firms across borders and within them knocks out competitors, sometimes yielding oligopolies that then influence what products can be. Oligopolies tend to limit variety, conventionalizing what is on offer. The now defunct Kaiser Motors, a relatively small car producer, was the first post-war U.S. carmaker to offer a significantly smaller and more economic vehicle. Modestly sized Studebaker Corporation created the daring post-war car shape that influenced the design of automobiles and much else, for a generation. The demise of Studebaker and all the other smaller companies (Kaiser, Nash, Hudson, and Packard) plausibly decreased opportunities for innovation. A multiplicity of firms can yield up idiosyncratic product ideas that prove successful later on and for others, operating like toys in that regard. In rigid contrast, mergers and bankruptcies allowed the Big Three to so dominate the American market that they became impervious to technology potentials and taste changes—a mark of oligopoly. This made them vulnerable to new competitors from Europe and Japan. Globalism, in this case, did not induce conformity, but variety. The U.S. oligopoly was an illusion fed by the taken-for-granted permanence of U.S. domination.

One of the consequences of bigness, whether oligopolistic or competitive, is that some things are not worth doing because potential markets are too small to warrant start-up costs of design, production, and distribution. Menda could hold its share of bottle markets not just because it had a strong patent, but because its product had limited sales potential—big enough for a family business, but too small for an expanding conglomerate—like London cabs in that regard. If a big company had somehow got hold of Menda, the specific product line would likely have evolved differently. The hustling it took to develop applications (and product redesign) with small potential markets—Menda also developed a market in nail polishing salons, for example—would likely not have occurred. The ability to generate distinctive products for small markets remains, despite so much talk about flexible production, a challenge for the large corporation because its managers are directing their attention toward bigger prizes.

Large companies are less and less about making something for a specific market and increasingly about manipulating the arrangements behind such makings. This shift even further away from the Menda (or Edison) inventor-maker model has its own way of affecting products. Executives concern themselves with mergers, buyouts, and outsourcing, rather than with what goods their own people can create. The trend toward outsourcing—companies buying parts, services, and even wholly assembled products from outsiders, including those in other countries—changes the very nature of what a corporation means in relation to products. Henry Ford's legendary River Rouge plant put a Ford stamp on everything, even the raw materials, that ended up in a car. Because it actually made the cars, Ford's reputation not only sold the vehicle but also stood as the essence of the firm and indeed of a whole way of organizing systems of production and consumption. We use the word "Fordist" to denote mass production of this sort.

Less and less is Ford—or any company—like this. The "master corporation" exploits subcontractors' cheaper operating tactics and intimate local knowledge of distant sites. The master corporation offloads threats to reputation from lousy labor and environmental practices. Outsourcing permits quick response to product change (like battery-lit heels in teens' tennis shoes); the corporation does not have to know all the suppliers, materials, and design tricks to deal with such shifts. With limited sunk investments anywhere, it can keep shopping for better supplier deals that result from political and economic changes that occur across the world.

The master company becomes a collection of arrangements with other companies if not simply a holding company or "portfolio" of brands that have their own network of sub-contractors. U.S.-based companies like Motorola, Memorex, Smith Corona, Dual, and RCA now market products mostly made elsewhere and by other firms. The once proud Italian manufacturing giant Olivetti also makes little. The master corporation stays loose; one business adage captures a current wisdom: "Make nothing, but command everything."[16]

There is a price to be paid for this departure from Mr. Ford's program. At least potentially, all the outsourcing and cross-dealings challenge coherence across a company's products and operations. In some cases, the same source provides identical or near-identical elements for many purveyors. "Intel's Inside" a lot of different products that compete with one another but which get their chip from the same producer—Intel. Sometimes the entire product may have been designed, engineered, manufactured, and even distributed by a single outsourcing agent. The company called Flextronics, for example, can make almost any kind of consumer product; it has almost 50,000 employees to draw upon in factories and distribution facilities in 27 countries. It sticks whatever brand a client wishes on the goods, like a "Tala" on the garlic press. All this erodes shoppers' capacities to treat a product as actually coming from a particular producer who might be worthy of trust and repeated purchases. Besides customers' perceptions, dissolution and dispersion threatens the corporation as something people will invest in. A corporation is itself a product,[17] bought and sold on stock exchanges, talked about among traders, loaned money by creditors and deferred to or declaimed by politicians. As with durable goods, its rise or fall turns on how these various groups act toward it and whether or not they "believe in" it. For there to be products at all, but also of a specific sort, money needs to go to the companies that will make them. An image of corporate coherence is the beginning of what it takes to sell the corporation, however diverse its activities or locational spread.

BRANDING TO THE RESCUE

Branding becomes intrinsic to the reorganization of the corporate world and the goods that come out of it—a way to orient insiders and outsiders alike. The brand imagery and apparatus unites products even when they are in diverse fields and produced in varied and changing ways and across the face of the earth.

For sophisticated producers, brand consists not just in surface aspects like logos, advertisements, press releases, or accompanying product literature (although those count plenty) but in a consistent look, feel, and functional integration of the product line. The goods themselves physically tell the corporate story, one that reinforces the more symbolic materials. The details of bells and whistles, levers and readouts, shapes and interlocks make up another kind of semiotic handle for consumers. By seeing them as an ensemble and having prior experience with their functioning, one senses what one is getting into. The brand instructs, both in a general way and in terms of the details of how things likely work, how they should probably be cared for, and how the service and backup support likely operate. People assimilate these styles of action and, especially if they involve somewhat complex maneuvers (as with computer equipment) become hooked into the ensemble. An effective brand works with what people are already like, but then affects what they come to be.

The brand also tells what kind of people the stuff is for, providing a come-on that allows the company to herd a constituency of a certain sensibility and then arrange the goods to match. Consumers will then, the marketers hope, recognize a given corporation as "theirs"—taking the brand name to signal that the appropriate pre-selection of form and function has indeed been done. I think customers themselves presume certain policies, fill in what is not always explicit, about what the brand represents in terms, for example, of warranties and return policy. They identify not only with the goods and the brand but also with the other customers, their niche-mates. Land's End customers assume other Land's End types will act in a Land's End kind of way. Land's End people do not, the surmise is made, abuse return privileges. This means the company can and will honor requests for refunds if they are made. By seeing the company as a community of consumers like themselves, buyers actively strengthen the power of the brand.

The brand story has a portability that Henry Ford's operations did not. Mr. Ford actually had to open factories at diverse locations he wanted to serve, or at least have his company directly arrange relations with a multitude of suppliers of raw materials and other inputs. Modern brands do not have these limitations; they easily move from place to place and across product realms. The name "Eddie Bauer," once associated with camping gear, now marks a line of clothing, a chain of retail home furnishings shops, a separate line of Lane furniture, and a Ford sports utility vehicle (a competing brand, L.L. Bean, is on a Subaru). The company tries to serve an envisioned audience that wants "Eddie Bauer-ness" in its lamps and shoes. The Canadian company Roots has a parallel history and includes under the brand canopy a Roots resort hotel where it displays its furniture and other goods.

Fueled perhaps by the vague yearning for the authentic and "natural" that arose toward the end of the last century, the outdoor sports–themed companies seem to have led this branding genre. But others are also taking a stand. So clothing makers Jhane Barnes, Nautica and Tommy Hilfiger do furniture, bedding, wallpaper and, in the case of Benetton, also a full line of house paint. The U.S. homemaking guru Martha Stewart moved from garden advice into a similarly wide-range of goods culminating in a line of housewares sold through Kmart. These "lifestyle companies," in effect, do some of the style work—fitting the pieces together—that customers once did for themselves. Rather than consumers deciding what goes with what within their own subculture, the corporations at least nominate: put these dishes with this overcoat with this vacation. "Style" becomes not just professionalized, as with hiring a home decorator, but corporatized. Old-line companies do it, too, but primarily through licensing rather than production or outsourcing. Harley-Davidson now comes in cigarettes, lighters, clothing, watches, wallets, beer, and eyeglasses. Chrysler Corporation uses its Jeep division to license toys, a portable stereo system, and other stuff. Caterpillar tractors has a line of men's "urban" clothing under the "Cat" logo.[18]

In some ways, the strategy of finding a consumption community and serving it has long been a retailing staple; department stores were built on fashioning a "way of life" or series of ways of life across their various departments. In retrospect, these seem unsophisticated compared to national and global firms' current efforts to discern a taste community and consciously cater to its distinctive sensibilities. The challenge, not a small one, is to use every nuance to create and maintain continuities across goods that a particular constituency will approvingly recognize. Where once this was done primarily at the retail level, now the corporation, even while sloughing off the actual manufacturing dirty work, controls and integrates production and sales strategy.

Branding is not always a corporate panacea; even some very big "power brands" cannot go far. "Coca-Cola" can go on beverage coolers which can be made with Coke-appropriate dimensions. But Coke is not relevant to the wide range of hardware and soft goods whose shape and function a brand like Disney can alter. And even with Eddie Bauer ready to deal with everything, people still do some style work on their own. Folks combine things from Eddie Bauer with stuff they get from Roots or the Starbucks Internet store (which includes furniture inspired by the coffee store interiors), or from their mother's attic or the junk shop up the street. They also still utilize conventional retailers, who may or may not prepare ensembles for them. Home magazines and real estate model houses also offer up ideas on what goes with what. And friends and neighbors are there for emulation, along with the unending commentaries of compliments and innuendo they routinely provide.

Consumers also hear one another judge the purveyors, criticizing them for making a product they think transgresses the brand: "What is *that thing* doing here?" they might ask in the store. Such moral outrage, or at least annoyance, signals corporate success in forming an attentive constituency but also the possibility that a company has made a wrong move. Enough such mistakes will threaten the entire enterprise. In a continuously moving stream of changing goods and altering preferences, consumers discipline the brand even as the brand acts upon them. Not every entrepreneur, regardless of which pieces of the spectrum they strive to serve, will be able to get it right through these complex vicissitudes. Robust as they may seem at any given moment, some will blunder and cause desertions, lose a lot of money, and fold. As a group, they are no more invincible than the once gigantic Montgomery Ward retailer-licenser or now defunct manufacturers like carmaker Packard or the long-triumphant Levi Strauss (given a terrible fall after hip-hop came from nowhere to loosen all jeans).

One group of merchandisers has an edge in generating a loyal consumption community. Non-profit organizations increasingly take their own merchandising potential seriously. Environmental organizations, museums, preservation groups and universities increasingly treat goods as part of what they are all about rather than as merely incidental. They started small, putting their emblems on mugs and tote bags as a way for members to show enthusiasm for the organization's mission—and probably display to one another a mutual moral worthiness. But charity branding has more potential than that. The "cause" already stands for something, without a lot of PR hype needed to convince that the organization has good intentions. Further, the charity already has something of a real community at hand—niche-mates who have respect for both the organization and its members. And supporters likely have high overlap in products they might prefer; *Audubon* magazine readers want binoculars and maybe even toasters with flying geese and—given the average age of birders—easy-grip kitchen tools. Colonial Williamsburg has long been a mass licenser, collecting annual fees of about $10 million (based on $100 million in gross sales) for products like furniture, wallpaper, paint, and house plans. The Sierra Club has developed a full line of clothes, furnishings, and housewares it intends to market.

At the opposite pole from organizations that start off the branding with a widely recognized meaning, some corporations stand for nothing at all except that they acquire brands that have some such recognition. They thus can end up with brand divisions that, while well coordinated within themselves, have little in common with one another. NYSE-listed Fortune Brands boasts on its website of being a "portfolio of premier consumer brands"[19] that include—with little apparent rhyme or reason—Jim Beam bourbon, Footjoy golf shoes, Master Locks, Day Timer personal organizers, Cobra consumer electronics, Moen plumbing fixtures, Swingline office tools, and Kensington computer accessories. Brandness itself is the corporate activity. It must use each brand to inflect as many products as possible under each logo to justify the acquisition. Rather than a given product building up its brand image (a former pattern), these become brand images looking for products to put under their representation.

Besides their use in marketing their goods and the firm itself—their external relations—the brand stories influence work within the company. Especially when goods cover a wide range of products, and particularly when they are fast-turn products, the brand helps tell the various corporate actors what they are trying to do in common. Flexible production across scattered geographic sites provides a distinctive internal coordination challenge. People in even mundane manufacture increasingly work, as in Hollywood, on "projects"; new groups assemble and then break up. Workers must rely on unspoken, shared understandings of what the common enterprise, across occasions, is all about.[20]

Firms require stories that lessen the need for explicit instructions or conversations each time they set out to create an object, enroll a supplier, hire an executive, motivate a worker, make a sale, raise cash, or fight a regulation. The brand, as it works itself out in media and object, tells the corporate participants what is going on and hence helps coordinate a common sensibility across a range of goods and functions. The brand simulates local community where both "local" and "community" are otherwise problematic.

The advent of electronic systems of distribution adds in still another basis for needing meaningful corporate identity. A purchaser on the Internet must believe not just that a product will indeed be delivered as ordered (and paid for), but also that it will have the qualities for which it has been touted. As in the move from family-owned local retail to Big Box warehouse sales, brand is a way to provide assurances in an otherwise impersonal realm of e-commerce. Absent direct human contact from someone whose touch, voice, or gesture can reassure, brand must substitute. Rightly or wrongly, the public trusts some of its brands—Volvo, Apple, Procter and Gamble, and Amazon.com to name a few of the well respected—more than organizations like the police, the government, or the church.[21] They believe more in a brand of bottled water than in what comes out of the New York tap, even though the legal standards are higher for the latter than for the former. Some companies that marketed through mail order catalog now have the advantage of a history of trust that can be exploited in internet sales—like the sporting goods companies now so assiduously spreading across the lifestyle.

DESIGN RISING

Branding, it should now be clear, means design made corporate—an evolved state of taking design seriously at all levels of an enterprise. This way of thinking came only after business itself came to see design as counting and that something had to be done to reverse the "low level of design awareness" once held responsible for "America's comparative lack of competitiveness in the international trade in manufactured goods, cars in particular."[22] In 1989, *Marketing News* said U.S. companies, in ignoring the potential of design, had been "resting on dead laurels."[23] In the same year, *Purchasing Magazine* ran a more upbeat "Quality in Design" piece observing that "companies are discovering" how much design matters.[24] *Business Week* prefaced its 1989 "Innovation Issue" with a bold call for better design (providing examples of just such accomplishments), recognizing that "more and more companies are emphasizing good design," the importance of which it says, "U.S. companies lost sight of."[25] At about the same time, other prominent articles appeared in diverse publications: the *New York Times* ran "Design Gap—Not a Trade Gap," implying that design should be treated as a serious national issue.

The critiques seem to have brought results, both in a rise of design status as well as changes in the stuff. When design becomes something people talk about during production and consumption, stuff changes in particular ways. Demand for designers grew rapidly in the United States in the late '90s, in numbers that go beyond any upturn in the overall economy.[26] In the United Kingdom, design issues began to suffuse British business journals and mass media, in part following government emphasis on design as central to the United Kingdom's economic future.[27] Writing in 1997, *Business Week* editor and longtime design commentator Bruce Nussbaum heralded a "golden era of design."[28]

The business press now recognizes design as the basis for saving whole companies—Apple, for example. After scraping bottom, both in the stock market and store sales, Apple came back in the late 1990s with its I-Mac series. While perhaps marginally superior to its competitors in technical capacities—it was not revolutionary in the manner of the first Macintosh machines—it was clearly off type form in shape, color, and physical configuration. Rounded translucent bodies and candy colors gave it a '50s retro look quite foreign to prior office or high-tech products. As with Starck's juicer, where a different way of working yields a different kind of appearance, the I-Mac's strongest image feature came from a change in physical configuration—combining monitor and computer into a single unit.

Apple pushed its I-Macs with the tag line, "Think Different" in ads and billboards carrying the faces of personages like Gandhi and Einstein. In announcing free modems and zip drives, a series of ads headlined, "Even the offer is well-designed."[29] In other products, the "design" word replaces terms like "powerful," "well crafted," "good taste" or "in fashion"—phrases once commonly used to promote merchandise. "Fashion," in particular, has become an "F word," the victim of too many denunciations in undergraduate courses and in the higher-end media. But "design," replete with upstanding Bauhaus connotations, remains an appropriate aspiration, and makers make sure it's evident in the goods.

Advertisements graphically depict goods as design accomplishments. In the early history of advertisements, artists made line drawings of objects. The product stood alone, context-free.[30] When other forms of art and photography came into use, advertisers decorated the object with people using or admiring it, usually glamorous people whose presence suggested that buying the product would help the consumer toward a more enviable social life. But starting in the late 1990s, marketers cut back on social context, showing cars instead as sculpture, a shift that became apparent to me after I compared hundreds of automobile print advertisements across time (several of which are reproduced on the next pages). Rather than "the whole family" around the car or a sexy woman slouched against the hood, the hood (or a partial fender curve) itself became the sensual come-on. Lexus ads began to show the car on a plinth, with the car-as-art then spreading to adverts for more modestly priced models. A New Zealand and Australian ad on TV and in magazines, headlined "Art in Motion," shows a Holden car surrounded by sculpture. The people-out, art-in trend has spread to other goods, including vacuum cleaners and high-fidelity equipment.

Design is whole-city big. Boosters now sell their cities as sculpture; places advertise themselves not in terms of their entertainments or their people's folkways, but the look and texture of their built environments. Glasgow uses the phrase "City of Architecture and Design" as its omnipresent slogan, capitalizing on the work of native son Charles

Better ideas make a better wagon. A man's wagon.

A man shouldn't have to treat people like baggage, Mercury figures.

So we put a Dual-Action Tailgate on our Mercury wagons. It swings open like a door for people. Down like a platform for easy cargo handling. Crafty.

So are the side panels on the Colony Park, above, that look like yacht deck walnut—but there's the strength of steel underneath.

And the choice of third-seat options, either rear-facing or dual center-facing (see left) so kids get their own built-in playroom and aren't breathing down your neck.

A man needs man-sized room. The Colony Park takes 4-ft.-wide loads without scraping either side. The 2-seat model neatly hides

11.7 cu. ft. of gear in below-decks storage space that's lockable.

Other man-pampering features: power rear window. Power front disc brakes. See your Mercury Man, your Mercury dealer.

Mercury, the Man's Car.

Car as "family" (Mercury ad) ©Ford Motor Company

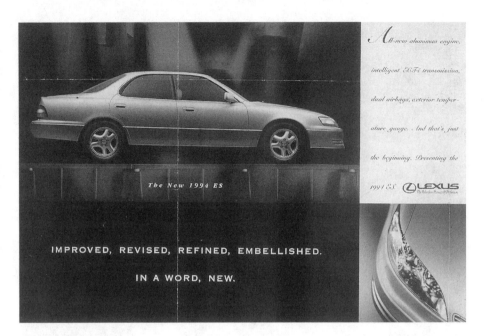

Car on plinth. 1994 Lexus ES 300 print ad. Created by: Team One Advertising and RJ Muna Pictures. Photograph courtesy of Team One Advertising and RJ Muna Pictures.

Rennie Mackintosh. Chicago touts itself in Europe as "the city with architecture that blows your mind."[31] The Los Angeles Convention and Visitors Bureau runs magazine ads under the headline "Art and Architecture in LA." Madison, Wisconsin, which long harbored an ambivalent attitude toward native son Frank Lloyd Wright, now invokes Wright's name and motifs everywhere. In Phoenix, Arizona operators of the dining room at the Wright-looking Arizona Biltmore changed its name, in 1995, from the "Orangerie" to the "Wright Room" to indicate a lineage with the Great One (au revoir, French aristocrats). Wanting to cash in on the reputation of Addison Mizner, designer of the Palm Beach Biltmore built in the 1920s, Florida developers gave the name "Mizner Village" to the ersatz Tuscan shopping streets that replaced the car-centered shopping mall they tore down. Exploiting more contemporary design names, property developers ostentatiously put up "a Michael Graves" or "Norman Foster," hoping such architec- tural branding will bring better rents and maybe enroll some sympathy from zoning boards.[32] These beliefs in star architects modify the nature of the real estate product as well as the materials used in fittings and furniture. As per the course, the featured designs then travel down-market to mini-malls and tract housing, with greatly expanded impact on goods.

By the time this book comes out, all this may have faded; the rage for design, per se, may be "unmasked" as just another form of capitalist manipulation or self-serving hypocrisy. Or people may just be bored with it completely. But if it does wither away, some other discourse will have taken its place as the way to make some goods exceptionally appropriate.

DESIGNER AS LOGO

Not just real estate developers, but product makers also reach for designer names to sell their wares. But because product designers lack usable celebrity, marketers typically use clothing designers and architects as their glamour figures, even for goods well outside those realms. At this moment, it is doubtful very many people—at least American—could provide the name of a single living product designer. But apparel marketers have made clothing designers famous, in part by putting their names conspicuously on the product itself. Yves Saint-Laurent repeats his logo ("YSL") as an all-over pattern on luggage. Gucci shapes handbag clasps to form his logo in metal, thus changing the hardware that the leather must then work around. Designers' product lines take on specific tendencies in looks (tailored or exuberant), materials typically used (natural or synthetic), and the finish (shiny or nubby, hard or soft). The stuff "rounds off" toward the designer's consistent themes that are also carried into store architecture as shop displays, store windows, and fixtures, all keyed to the major design concept created by the designers' staff.

As with some retailers, clothing designers now enter the realm of lifestyle goods, licensing their name to various producers—"licensing heaven," as one designer called it.[33] The designer may or may not have had a hand in creating the goods. Ralph Lauren's "Polo" lines now attach to home furnishings, in part promoted through a joint venture with NBC for "lifestyle programming." Calvin Klein and Versace sell fabrics, furniture, linens, and decorative items. The couturier Prada also has a line of home furnishings, as do Bill Blass (including a collection at Pennsylvania House furniture) and Alexander Julian (who has a 150–piece line for Universal furniture).

Some producers use high-end designers' names on some of their goods to create a halo effect for other products they make—usually more profitably. The fashion industry has evolved in this way; couture houses make dresses for the rich but make their profits by producing for rack sales.[34] In the realm of durables, this "leveraging" goes back at least as far as Josiah Wedgwood's use of his elite jasperware to reinforce markets for his more pedestrian "Queensware"—one of his products that the Royals did not, in fact, acquire. In contemporary times, the Italian housewares maker Alessi uses its designs from the famous architects and figures like Starck to leverage sales of mass-level goods, in the way the Wave bathtub was to help the more ordinary tubs at American Standard.

The use of designer names further reinforces among the public the idea of designers as indeed a big deal. In using architect Michael Graves to position the chain as a cut above the other big-box operations, the Target stores promote not just the Graves products, but the whole concept that there are great designers and that one of them, at least, does dustpans. The head of merchandising at Target acknowledged before the Graves campaign began that "the average Target guest [sic] doesn't even know who Michael Graves is. But they will."[35] The follow-up Target-Graves crusade included eight-page inserts in major U.S. newspapers featuring a half-page picture of Michael Graves along with depictions of several dozen Graves-Target artifacts.[36] A small essay explains how the Graves product arises from "a whole process that involves problem solving, innovative thinking and collaboration." The result is a distinct kind of stuff arising from the celebration of design in general and Graves in particular.

Once again, we need to be aware that the tide could turn on designers, their logos—and brands. The boom in art museum and gallery attendance perhaps fed the rise of the designer "auteur," and the museum craze is itself not necessarily a permanent change in the avocation landscape. Deeper than high art and stronger than capitalism, fashion spares nothing. Just as the major consumption critiques—Veblen's was only one earlier example—sent the self-aware to the likes of Bean, Bauer, and Roots for their Better Way, another turn in the discursive screw could move consumption taste into a still different pattern. David Brooks's *Bobos in Paradise*, a best seller in the year 2000, charged that the Bourgeois Bohemians who use these stores are merely status seeking under a different cover story, but still up to the same show-off tricks. Buying 100 percent high-thread-count cotton sheets may get you to dinner parties where the food was prepared with a superior garlic press, but it neither saves the earth nor gains entry to ascetic heaven. This too shall pass.

More caustic than the *Bobo* critique, Naomi Klein's *No Logo* depicts brand as the source of evil in the world, and hence consumption of brand products as an act of complicity. Branded goods are "the celebrity face of global capitalism"[37] that hides social and ecological exploitation. If her story catches on (and it seems to be), the fact of logo (or designer name) could change its meaning, becoming a marketing stigma rather than resource. At the end of the '90s, high-flying Nike lost market share, and its stock dramatically declined—perhaps because of exposés of Nike subcontractors' labor practices, but more likely because, as Klein pithily remarks,[38] it "outswooshed itself." Its cool could not withstand ubiquity; even the physically fit got tired of "just do it." Consumers may do brand avoidance out of leftist or environmental sympathies, or just because they do not want to be *Bobo* patsies. Whatever the truth of the evils Klein elaborates or the conformity ridiculed by Brooks, word will be out and this next batch of consumers will join those who, like the snowboarders before them, want nothing to do with "the image thing." In that eventuality, the texture of marketing and mass goods, perhaps replicating the snowboard industry's consciously no-logo strategies, will again change to suit.

ELECTRONIC ARRANGEMENTS

Some of the new goods, those involving advances in electronic communication in particular, change the organization of production itself and in that way are beyond at least some of the shifts in fashion, including the rise and fall in the idea of fashion itself. It will take more than new critiques and send-ups to do them in. So design professionals sit at computers to construct models and prototypes, altering the nature of goods and the speed of innovation. The web gathers up information about consumers, including how they communicate with one another as they consider what to buy or merely as they go about looking for fun. To the degree that product turns on what makers know of consumers' habits and preferences, the web can change things. We have all met this capacity of the web when noticing it "remembers us"—a simple convenience when ordering, say, a book or toy online. One does not have to repeat from screen to screen and from ordering occasion to ordering occasion the item selected or the delivery address best to use. These "cookies," as they are called, move the commercial operator to offer up goods tailored to the individual consumer—in effect, a niche of one.

The interactive technologies, and this raises serious issues, allow a vast record to cumulate what individuals buy, think, and do, potentially constituting legal proof of alleged wrong-doing. Such capacity would threaten democratic values at their heart. Just thinking that others might be privy to one's choices in information, art, graphics, and social contacts may have a chilling effect on expression and participation. Electronic search mechanisms could yield profiles of specific individuals, tracking their activities. Private corporations, as well as government agencies, might be able to discover the kinds of individuals most likely to oppose their operations and, using the Internet or other techniques, set actions in motion to frustrate their routines. Disinformation could be sent to the targeted persons and groups; they could be spammed into chaos.

Leaving aside such fears, not to be lightly dismissed, the more commonly expressed worry is that this more advanced form of consumer surveillance will take over minds and encourage more false needs and worthless stuff. We are back in old territory. The rejoinder is also at hand; profiling based on actual consumer behavior creates better information about who is out there and what they want. The speeded up response to such preferences arguably increases consumer control through the simple act of signaling preferences as they are felt. If corporations know more and sooner, they will have less need to entrap consumers into buying what they have inadvertently overproduced. For a number of years even after it became a volume leader, Dell computers made every unit after it had been ordered; there was no stock and hence no overstock. They just produced on command—literally. This changes goods by individualizing output and also by changing goods faster. New models, in effect, arise out of changing needs and activities of consumers.

Other kinds of electronic developments imply still more radical possibilities for change. Just as new technologies have made access so much easier for producing music, video, and graphics, the price of entry for designing and creating physical objects may undergo a similar shift. Rather than needing a complex factory to machine-make an object—something necessary at present for even the simplest artifact—making things with factorylike precision may become so much cheaper that millions of ordinary people will be doing it. Think in terms of the desktop inkjet principle but in three dimensions. Product designers now have a crude form of this in the machine they use to make solid models and prototypes—stereolithography. In emerging versions, computer specifications deposit micro-thin layers of material like molten plastic to form any shapes whatever. There can be hollows and holes; the computer layers-in water-soluble wax to fill-in what will be eventual voids. Orthodontics is on the cusp of this trend; after a computer model is made of a patient's mouth, a series of plastic aligners comes out of the machine. As the patient's mouth changes, the next product comes off the line, tailored to the progress already made. The patient's teeth gradually move into desired position.[39]

At the time I write, machines have come into being to extrude the first artifacts with moving parts, including plastic ball bearings that spin within channels and sockets. Micro-motors built with the same technique are in development. A Stanford research group has built a tiny "helicopter" device (it flies) out of ceramic components, not much bigger than a penny and weighing only 1.7 grams.[40] They form as a whole, emerging from the machine like a baby from the womb. This system portends fundamental changes in the nature of stuff. A jet engine, instead of being one huge contraption arising from the factory floor, could be made of hundreds of micro-engines spilled out from a modestly scaled device. There might even be such a "factory" in the airplane cockpits (and certainly in the space satellite) making the craft ready for repair while in flight.

Eventually there could be personal factories in most U.S. homes— or at least shared neighborhood facilities, maybe at the local Kinko's. People could pull down designs from the web and instruct their computers to produce the result in situ, perhaps with the capacity for custom design adjustments (a topic for the next chapter). The nature of artifacts would no doubt change to make them more amenable to this kind of production process, like in the way a big engine made up of many tiny ones is different from a giant one made on the factory floor. The orthodontic device could come off a home machine rather than the dentist's or the lab's, specified directly from the orthodontist's web-based prescription as part of a treatment regimen that changes daily.

Any such developments of personal factories would involve consumers in an increasingly complex set of tasks. Even now, goods have been expanding—certainly changing—the knowledge they contain and the knowledge needed to operate them. This creates new problems for producers. It is already hard for people to figure out how to use the mobile phone, copy machine, microwave, and the VCR. As individuals move through the appliances of life there are only seconds to discern how to make each of them work. So many features, so little time. The features can easily go to waste. Human proclivity has to be built into the stuff, rather than the stuff depending on books of documentation and training classes. A sturdy principle of much (but not all) design looms large: make the complexities of underlying processes invisible. Hidden complexity discourages self-repair—a downside—and can create mayhem when things go awry, as the crisis at the Three Mile Island nuclear reactor made evident. People have no idea what to do. But from the beginning, as electronics began replacing mechanics, it was necessary to find a way to deal with the invisibility of how things work. Even if you could see the inside of your computer, you would not see much.

To make products understandable, "a new form," as the designer Ettore Sottsass put it in reference to his early designs at Olivetti, "had to be found which, by its nature, had to be more symbolic and less descriptive"[41] This means using color, shapes, and icons to allay apprehension and guide people through applications. As development of the

Web now makes clear, people must be spared the need to know much about what makes possible the little miracles of access. Supplanting geographic location as key, the value of the product comes from the quality of the virtual route to reach it. Now it's portal, portal, portal. If the route is fun, people will make efforts they otherwise would avoid. Representing a continuation of patterns that go back to the earliest marketplaces, but more carefully plotted than before, "merchants" put amusement and purchase opportunity adjacent in time and space— within the same visual frame and within reach of the same fingers. Moment to moment feelings become enormously consequential for determining which stuff will be acquired and hence, given the rapid-fire feedback into the corporation and its production lines, what comes to be made.

All the hullabaloo about the culture industries and particularly entertainment helps smooth the way for these developments. A *Business Week* cover story in 1994 proclaimed the coming of "the entertainment economy." The magazine touted the entertainment industry "as now the driving force for new technology, as defense used to be."[42] Perhaps responding to the message, some CEOs have become performers to reinforce their companies' presence in the fun economy. Richard Branson, whose collection of companies under the Virgin logo spans airlines, financial consulting, computer peripherals, and the record business, authors best-selling books, including one carrying the CEO's nude photo on the cover. Although his attempt to break global bal-looning records ended in failure, the effort gained worldwide coverage for himself and his logo. Branson's compatriot Nick Graham, CEO of Joe Boxer shorts, appears in drag with an assortment of unusual social types in his company's commercials. Joe Boxer produces more than five hundred different underwear designs each year for men, "Joe Boxer girl-friend" clothing for women along with bedding, ceramics, fragrance, toys, textiles, and one hundred watch models annually (for Timex). In a prescient observation, Graham remarks, "We're an entertainment com-pany. The brand is an amusement park, and the products are souvenirs of the brand."[43] Here we have an explicit recapitulation of the Disney route but in reverse order; Joe Boxer and Disney meet at the juncture of goods and entertainment.

Mobilizing fun into product and distribution is part of the larger mobilization to integrate a wider array of elements into the production process. More ambitiously than efforts like concurrent design and engineering, companies come from different start points to arrive at a similar integrative format. Design offices like Smart Design (New York) and Lunar (Palo Alto) emerge as entities that spin off new goods and new companies. Other entrepreneurs move from non-product realms toward product development, like organizational consultant Doblin Group (Chicago), Refac Design, with a background in licensing and patents (New Jersey), and the venture capitalists, Vulcan (Seattle)—created by Paul Allen (the "other guy" who founded Microsoft). Razorfish, a celebrity Internet company, hired the head of New York's frogdesign office as part of the team that would develop hardware and software simultaneously as a single, coherent process. These are linkages that have a certain logic; more ambitious or complicated projects can be launched without waiting for the right combination of client, funders, and design to coalesce yet without losing the creative juice that also must be part of the lash-up.

Some business gurus—most famously the management expert Tom Peters—have come around to endorsing the new approach. For Peters at least, this required a switch; he had originally become a hit by telling corporate captains, in his first big book called *In Search of Excellence*, to "stick to their knitting." He meant they should settle on a central and basic product or sector and keep with it rather than diversify or fall for new fads. It was no-nonsense advice. But later Peters preached sensitivity to change, including fashion; fixed anything is a wrong-headed vision of the future. In his 1992 book, *Liberation Management*, he came out for an "entertainizing of everything," a theme he continues in a more recent work, *The Pursuit of Wow*. The wows have it—a different story line than his previous one about where successful stuff comes from.

THE STORY EFFECT

In a way it doesn't matter if Peters is right or wrong; his stories carry their own weight into the economy and into goods. Investors, consumers, and regulators act on such tales. They could in the late '90s, under the wow tutelage of people like Peters, legitimately "listen" to their own exhilaration—even thinking of it as part of due diligence—when determining where to put their money. But the latest Peters line may go the way of other influential stories, along with defunct products like the Studebaker car and the Hoover Constellation. It has been stories all the way back and all the way down, the manic seventeenth century Dutch speculation in tulip bulbs being only among the more colorful instances of "madness of crowds."[44] Stories of the mid-1960s and '70s depicted conglomerates as exciting forms of synergism that were here to stay, only to be later described as "irrational" hydras that took down well-recognized branded products like Litton and Raytheon ovens, for example. Zealous diversification also ended some stalwart products; Ford acquired TV maker Philco, only to sell it off to conglomerate GTE, which folded it into its acquired Sylvania brand, but then hived it off to a real consumer electronics company, Dutch-based Phillips, which pretty much killed it as a redundant competitor.[45] In the more recent festival of going Internet, company after company went for broke and some disappeared in the effort.

The stories are the art form, after all is said and done, that make the worlds go around. The business corporation grew out of the sociability of London coffeehouses in the first place, establishments of slightly suspect repute where some of the more daring traded the first stock shares. It was only later that places of business and places of amusement were supposed to be sharply demarcated spatially and physically. The issue for products' market success (financial and otherwise) is not whether they are "right" in some absolute and essential sense but who comes to believe in them and how—the Aramis challenge of gaining and holding enrollments. And even when the markets "go crazy" something very real can come about. I would suppose that new tulip varieties did result from the tulip investment craze, just as some of the e-companies of the late '90s created strong products that would not have come into existence without the wild enthusiasm created around them. Most everyone joins in. The economists tell their tales about how it all supposedly works, macro and micro, and the banks and corporations—adding some stories of their own—act one way and not another as a result. The sales clerk explains why one VCR makes more sense than a different VCR; the proto-industrialist pitches to the venture capitalist; the politicians justify to the voters (and campaign contributors) that they know how to make the economy right and put the cornucopia within reach. When these narratives are good ones, emotionally rich and exciting, people act on them. New goods come into being, but so do a changing series of organizational forms through which to produce them.

The stories are as much a force as the so-called economic fundamentals of which they are supposedly only an account. So here we have still another instance of mutuality across the disparate realms. The story and the underlying "hard" reality are inseparable, mutually the cause and effect of one another. And part of it all is fashion: in tastes about economic organization, about best corporate practices, about products, and in how to have fun and when. Also involved in determining goods, although not always in the way or extent they should be, are stories about collective decency and ecological responsibility. These are matters, finally, for the next chapter.

CHAPTER 8
Moral Rules

Given the way creativity in production and consumption actually works, including the nature of the people who design and the routines of their practice, there can be openings for reform. Even if people need to make material fun, do status, and otherwise live through their stuff, they can do it in less damaging ways. The problem is not the will to produce and make life through artifacts, but doing it with such radical inequalities and severe ecological consequences.

Nor is the difficulty simply a matter of capitalist greed. Identifying the source of the trouble in just one kind of regime misses the underlying human proclivities that any solution must address. Modern industries did not invent severe inequalities. Slavery has ancient roots and widespread practice. Faith-based sects and regimes, some fervently anti-capitalist, visit death and destruction upon one another all over the world and right up to the present. On the ecological front, North American peoples ate their way through almost all large animals, sending 30 species of mammal into extinction thirteen thousand years before European contact.[1] Humans created almost all the deserts in the world well before capitalists started taking water away. In Hawaii, making a single feather cloak for a chief required the capture of eighty thousand birds—a practice that helps explain the extinction of a third of indigenous Hawaiian species before Captain Cook entered local harbors.

Crises can cumulate from small events, one bird feather at a time. In the present day, goods production and consumption has some of this quality, creating troubles through successive acts of normality. It is hard to notice the crisis, in part because of some real success. The average life of a car nearly doubled in the United States between 1970 and 2000, just as repair rates went down in most all product categories.[2] But better production in the sense of higher quality at lower price does not necessarily lower environmental damage or amount of waste. The Menda bottle's lifetime guarantee has no effect because users would rather pay the $8 for a new one than rinse the pump every few months to keep residues from gunking it up. Prices have declined for almost all products, especially the most exciting goods in electronics and computers—so old ones are tossed out. Rather than being recalcitrant, the production system responds with hyperspeed to technical capacity and taste change, including the cultural hybridizing that now engulfs the world. It is a mistake to perceive in this revving up of creative destruction some special malice or devious cunning.

Blaming capitalism for everything obscures the room for positive actions made possible by deviations and splits among the top dogs. The exceptions to capitalist unity do not so much prove the rule of their hegemonic power as provide a tactic for dealing with it. If even a small number of allies are won over from the business world (or some "parts" of the same person), an apparent monolith starts to fragment. Where would Marx have been without his Engels?

Sometimes concrete economic interests help corporate figures see some light. Unsafe products and weak environmental policies hurt insurance companies, for example.[3] That is why the insurance industry advocated international standards for ship construction, equipment, and personnel training. Fear of oil spills, often involving huge single-event losses, leads the industry to favor double-hull versus single-hull ship construction. Automobile insurers formed the National Insurance Institute for Highway Safety to support, albeit quietly, Ralph Nader's successful U.S. campaign for mandatory car air bags. At the Kyoto Climate Change negotiations, insurers threatened disinvestment in firms failing to achieve better environmental practices- no small thing given that insurance companies own about a third of the value of world stock markets. Floods and other large-scale "natural" disasters caused by global warming could wipe some insurance companies out of business.

Raging against capital—and this is the most damaging potential consequence for progressive politics—can spill into blaming ordinary people for buying the output. If goods are bads, then those who value them become as much the problem as those who produce. But it is counter-productive to treat drivers and smokers as naïve victims of ideological manipulation. A lot is wrong with the U.S. way of building suburbs, but criticizing returning GIs for their dreams of a suburban tract house furnished with modern appliances borders on arrogance. Rather than being a way to achieve some authentic, non-commercial community, attacks on such goods, infused as they are with social affections and aspirations, threaten the communities people do have—another fundamental reason why intellectuals' proscriptions meet so much resistance.

SUMPTUARIES: PUTTING NOSES IN OTHER PEOPLE'S STUFF

There is a long history, general or very specific, of telling people what to buy and use. Welfare moms should not have lipstick, funeral directors loud suits, a recent widow a red convertible. Some people can put legal or moral authority behind their opinions. The Romans forbade slaves to wear togas. Those who wrote the Bible loaded it with goods do's and dont's—men should cover their heads, women their bodies. The early church father Clement of Alexandria (ca. A.D. 150–220) forbade purple veils because colors "inflame lusts."[4] After the Fire of London, in 1666, the king and court renounced fineries from France as a national atonement.[5] Until the twentieth century, French law required women to have special permission from the police to wear pants.[6] The condo board makes everyone have the same draperies. Institutions and agencies prescribe uniforms in clothing and gear for their inmates, soldiers, and pupils. Social philosophers have deduced elaborate dicta of how much and of what type consumption should be. Marx and Christ were mostly for simple utility, but Voltaire praised private luxury. David Hume, presaging much contemporary economic thought, considered it economically helpful (and socially constructive) for people to be animated "with a spirit of avarice and industry, art and luxury."[7]

Such talk goes on; governments and elites at least try to instruct. In part to raise the taste of British citizens and producers, such luminaries as Gainsborough, Joshua Reynolds, and Josiah Wedgwood helped establish the Royal Society for the Encouragement of Arts, Manufactures and Commerce—in existence still today after its founding in 1754 (similar units were set up in other countries). London's Victoria and Albert Museum was established in 1852 for the same purpose. Still at it in the early 1920s, a V & A show, "Examples of False Principles in Decoration," denounced "direct imitation of nature," as in chair legs or lampshades shaped into leaf or flower motifs. "Landscapes and pictures are almost always out of place in pottery," museum visitors were told, with decadent examples on view to prove the point. More subtly today, museums canonize certain schools of design, particularly Bauhaus, and favor some types of objects over others (chairs more than sinks, for example). Steam iron holes do not count for much compared to the goods with direct links to high art, like the minimalist Movado that, based on its representation in the MoMA collection, advertises itself as "the museum watch." At a different price point, each $20 Makio Hasuike toilet-cleaning brush has a sticker that also attests to its presence in the MoMA.

During emergencies, like war, democratic states move into a more authoritarian mode. They may ban goods using materials needed for military ware or which seem to display too much frivolity. During World War I, the U.S. government pressured tire producers to decrease the number of tire variations from 287 to 9. The French government urged Paris designers to use less fabric to lower demand for textiles.[8] During World War II, the British government exempted simply styled "utility scheme" lines of furniture from the consumption tax, thus cutting their prices by as much as two-thirds. Although justified as a means to conserve resources, the furniture's "good design aspect," says art historian Jules Lubbock, was at least in one respect "quite extravagant, since only expensive hardwoods such as oak and mahogany were used."[9] Perhaps the elevation of mass tastes rather than military austerity was the source of the furniture.

An example of "utility scheme" furniture.

Government more routinely affects goods through import-export rules. India banned the import of gold and gold jewelry to hold down the amount of wealth going into the dowry system. The U.S. boycott of Cuba meant that the particular twist that Cuban culture might have provided its potential exports never saw the light of day. Import and export restrictions constrain product development in guns, plutonium, and biotoxins. Public health and moral crusades encouraged filter brand cigarettes into being; domestic anti-drug measures, including heavy policing of imports, spur local marijuana cultivation, decreasing the quality but raising the price of what sells on the U.S. market. To the degree government restricts marijuana, it spurs imports of cocaine because cocaine's much higher value by weight (and smaller volume) justifies the risks.[10] Greater cocaine availability lowered its street price, helping to usher in retail crack—a simple mixture of cocaine and baking soda. All along, the laws make impurities for all these drugs (including heroin) more common and the demimonde the only available retail setting. As always, there are interests among the moral entrepreneurs of consumption, including those based in class, race, and gender, that keep all of this going.

The British government still tries to influence the design of goods, in part by supporting huge student enrollments in design programs. Prime Minister Tony Blair staged many design-intensive public events, including finance for millennium art projects all over the country, such as the Tate Modern and the Greenwich Dome. Labor strategists are said to have instructed members of the government to never be photographed or videotaped in front of "anything old," so as to boost imagery befitting the "New Britain," or "Cool Britannia." Some blamed the mixed results, symbolized by the Dome disaster (artistically denounced and financially ruinous), on the design establishment itself. *Guardian* newspaper critic Jonathan Glancey singled out the country's "geriatric Design Council, staffed by time-serving men in two-button, polyester suits sporting wide lapels, kipper ties and slip-on casual shoes"[11] for giving its annual awards to all the wrong projects. The UK case at least implies that support for the high arts with money, prizes, and review boards may indeed influence stuff, but not in ways necessarily consistent with desired goals.

On a more positive note, governments can adopt the stance of "model client", using public building programs and goods procurement to encourage preferred products into being. Inaugurated by Washington and Jefferson in the United States, the results endure in many admired structures. European design competitions for public buildings remain common, with competitions open to non-nationals, many of whom win. This does not happen as much in the United States, where ersatz patriotism disallows foreigners; such jingoism takes priority over other bases for judging design, influencing in another way the nature of stuff.

SOVIETS IN THE KITCHEN

More than with most modern regimes, even fascist, the Soviet commissars specified the people's goods.[12] In its buoyant post-revolutionary modern art movements, the USSR had a fervent avant-garde

(Kandinsky was a leader) with a conscious orientation to graphic design, housewares, and other consumer products. The Hungarian-born ceramist Eva Zeisel headed up, in the 1930s, the largest dishware design and production center in the world. But the USSR did not just have a command economy; it had a command aesthetics—an oxymoron if there ever was one. The regime put Zeisel in solitary confinement for 16 months on trumped-up charges of planning Stalin's assassination; she later built a celebrated design career in the United States.

Despite such blunders, the Soviet economic system performed adequately for several generations, especially considering the demographic and material devastation of the two world wars. But it operated by imitating the West, taking apart European and North American goods and then reconstructing them under Soviet conditions (reverse engineering). The first engine designed specifically for the Moskvitch-408 automobile in 1967 was literally copied from the blueprints of the BMW-1500 engine.[13] Imitations never precisely duplicate, in part because they arrive at a later time and are outdated the moment they come off the line. Especially when information and culture industries grew in significance, the USSR's calcified and opportunistic structure of privilege became especially incongruous.[14] There could be no indigenous rise of hackers, or couture, a Soviet equivalent of hip-hop or an effective consumption base.[15] The industrial atmosphere was made ashen.

In their famous 1956 "kitchen debate," Khrushchev told Richard Nixon the USSR would bury the United States in a coming era of "unheard of abundance and equality."[16] In reality USSR stuff remained chronically in short supply, limited in variety, and shoddily made. Palpable evidence of national incapacity, most of it collapsed with the Soviet fall. The Zil limousine that once was the hallmark of status among the apparatchiks lost out to Mercedes and even more ordinary brands from the West.

We presume in the histories of, say, Renaissance rulers that obtaining jewelry, tableware, textiles, palaces, and frescoes was a historical force—indeed that is why much of the stuff came to exist. As with Polynesian chiefs who decorated their boats and houses to signal might, such displays of wealth implied power, including the capacity to attract allies. Keeping up with the Hapsburgs influenced marriage, resource use, and political alliances. I presume the same remains the case under modern conditions. The travels of the Gorbachevs created "profound shock"[17] that villagers in a poor country defeated in the war, like Italy, lived in some ways better than the Soviet elite.[18] Commentators noted that the Gorbachevs dressed and ate well; the *New York Times* referred to Raisa Gorbachev as "chic" in its obituary of her life.[19] People with increasingly world-class sensibilities sat astride a system unable to produce for such a niche—to understate the case. The Soviet collapse was thus as much a case of a taste culture rising as an economy crumbling (the "numbers" were never all that bad). The precise mix of goods now available in capitalist Russia—imported Western products, artifacts made locally but in conjunction with Western investment, and some surviving remnants of the prior system—derives from this amalgamation of biographies and historic currents.

CHALLENGES AND OPPORTUNITIES: LASH-UPS DON'T GO EASY

However flawed, the liabilities of the Soviet system do not imply that market freedom leads to a successful goods system. When ways of having fun and making profitable products endanger the earth, the challenge looms large to find new ways of doing things. Getting off the way we routinely operate—the great type form of wasteful production and consumption—will not be simple. As I have tried to show, something exists because of its lash-up with other somethings. Making change means dealing not with one element alone but with all the others—material, emotional, and political—with which it has come to be bound. The private car, the heart of so many U.S. urban and environmental woes, is intimately bound up with an aesthetics of movement, technologies of rolled steel, a teen's rite of passage, drive-in malls, insurance provisions, freeway maps, tract houses, cup holders, the Beach Boys, first dates, traffic courts, strings of gas stations, and informal norms for sharing cars, roads, and parking lots. The original "cause" of car dependence is long lost in the process of gradual, mutually reinforcing events and enrollments. Any challenge to auto dominance takes on more than the power of the Big Three. Even if it is a system they helped bring into being—and the highway lobby still indeed counts for plenty—the enterprise has grown bigger than they are. The whole economy, in sector after sector, results from iterative buildups that increasingly merge as a single global system of sentiments, institutions, and physical material. A corporate conspiracy would be better news.

People have found their satisfactions, such as they are, in the way of the links. While some indeed have higher stakes in maintaining those links than do others, the hegemony of their advantage rests on the willful participation of so many. For their part, designers thus find not just their livelihoods but also their excitements in ways that mostly sustain the status quo. Creating a better road tollbooth or drive-up window enhances car use, thereby discouraging a better train or bicycle. Each innovation contributes not only to instituting a particular product, but also to the regime of interrelated objects and social practices within which the product is embedded. Designers use what is out there to yield new objects that themselves become part of the conditions under which designers do their next work—a blend of personal freedom and constraint. The beauty and utility of the result, along with the sexism, waste-ism, and racism in the making, reflects and sustains the larger ensembles. To transform such a product *system* requires lateral thinking even beyond the range of the most advanced design project. It means working back over the whole texture of auto-culture lash-ups to conjure a substitute. In transportation terms, it means figuring out ways of getting people from place to place that fulfill their erotic and social dreams as much as their practical mobility needs. Revolutionaries, whether dealing with systems of consumption or political regimes of power, must reconstruct linkages for new ensembles.[20]

Lessons Learned: Change Happens

The good news is that besides the inertia of type form, the other half of the production-consumption tension is the persistence of change. Though there are obvious dangers from the ever-increasing yield of new stuff, the incessant zeal for innovation means there is also a chance to replace something nefarious with something more benign.

Tastes do shift. There are always different ways to get the same job done, whether opening a can or showing off or—as is not an infrequent occurrence—doing both at once. The dynamics of fashion mean that miserable ways of doing things are at least somewhat vulnerable. So the desire for "pure" whiteness in sliced bread and paper goods gave way to brownish whole wheat and gift stationary with visible residues of organic processing. In the early '90s, *California Apparel News* called "non-toxic muted colors" derived from berries and herbs, along with natural fibers, the fashion "hot news."[21] While conventional wisdom of the '50s and '60s was that Americans were addicted to the "status symbol" of big cars, many switched—not away from status symbols, but toward better-crafted and more durable small cars. It was, in terms of air quality and landfill issues, a good move (reversed, alas, by the coming of SUVs). Companies now developing the electric automobile are relying on fashion to suggest that less metal, weight, and noise signals more intelligence and status. Whereas consumers once paid to get the most nature embodied into their products, they now—at least in some realms—pay more to have less of it. The miniaturization aesthetic, reflected in bonsai and palm pilots, taps a disposition applicable to other types of stuff.

Human pleasures similarly embrace both things that last and things that do not, another basis for reform if the tendency can be deftly worked. Across a lifetime, the presence of both, in a yin-yang complementarity, seems to operate. Part of enjoying architectural foods at a bistro or the "fighting kites" in Thailand or China is anticipation of their inevitable demise. Some contemporary art has rapid decay as an intrinsic aspect of its aesthetic. On the other hand, the pleasure of diamonds and tabernacles is in their presumed permanence. Between these two extremes is the stuff of mundane manufacture that has taken up most of this book.

We need for fast-turn things to decompose in a timely way. If better designed, computers and the coming generation of smart appliances might end themselves graciously, indeed as part of the aesthetic of the consumption itself—like the way a sand castle goes from its maker as the tide rolls in. Alternatively, the pleasure of "forever" should be built into those materials that truly are slow-turn, where natural resistance or even exotic compounds might be put to appropriate social application. For the great bulk of stuff, the answer is to make it in a way that uses less of nature up in the first place, under decent social conditions, and with earth-friendly obsolescence.

People will help. Consumers now massively recycle in the United States and other countries, taking the time to sort their wastes. Such efforts, running counter to economists' expectations of individual selfishness, display a commitment to be helpful in a way that gains people no financial profit or even community acknowledgment—it's mostly done anonymously. Consumers also at times take an interest in the conditions under which their goods are produced. Early campaigns against child labor, at least helped along by organized women shoppers,[22] raised the age of factory workers, and through that effort caused more efficient (and safer) machinery to be put into use. Buyers followed Nader, demanding and buying products that increased safety and decreased ecological damge. Consumer-group efforts opposing sweatshop garment production, including university-based campaigns to alter production of campus-logo gear, appear to have brought about reforms in the late 1990s. Consumer anxieties over deaths in factories—and outside them—changed the content of furniture and carpet, with growing use of recycled plastics and new techniques to produce CFC-free, water-emulsified, and air-cushioned materials.

What consumers have been less able to affect is the recycling of producers' waste, a major problem given that, according to the U.S. Environmental Protection Agency (EPA), *only about 2 percent* of all waste comes from households, offices, institutions, and retail in the first place—"Municipal Solid Waste," in the official terminology. Given that hazardous waste makes up about 6 percent of the total, much of it indeed controlled in various ways across the jurisdictions,[23] 92 percent of U.S. waste is unaccounted for; there are almost no data on what makes it up. Most is apparently disposed of on site, beyond prying eyes. Perhaps, as Samantha MacBride reasons, political fear of corporate power encourages this emphasis on management of individuals' wastes versus that of corporations.[24] There are some ways, as I will later explain, to find an approach that might redirect environmental concerns toward the producers.

Serendipitous Improvement

Better stuff and production systems can happen "on their own." In terms of reuse of raw materials, some of the biggest successes have had nothing to do with outside agitation. The big Chicago meatpackers gained their fortunes in part by reprocessing bones, horns, hair, fat and blood into soaps, candles, fertilizers, drugs, explosives, and cosmetics.[25] Indeed a compulsion toward industrial resource recovery—using waste of one production process as input for another—was well understood and used in the nineteenth century. There were several dozen book-length U.S. guides and texts, from about 1850 through 1910, instructing industrialists how to recycle a variety of outputs—like chimney heat, wood pulp, and tomato seeds.[26] This now emerges as the field of "industrial ecology," with an MIT-based journal of that name.

Even the internal combustion engine, for all its faults, was a mechanism that cleaned up some problems on the way to making profits. It eliminated vile levels of pollution from urban horses that carried disease through direct contact as well as through runoff. A product like the modern toilet, woeful in some regards, helped lessen people's connection with their own and others' waste. It eliminated the odious job of the "night soil men," those paid to carry household excrement off to the cesspits. This was surely a gain in human dignity. In the same way, contemporary public sidewalk toilets of the French design eliminate people having to clean the toilet itself. The toilet units within these closetlike structures retract into a spray and scrub chamber that cleanses and sanitizes between users. This spares mostly poor and female workers from going on their hands and knees to wipe away the stray wastes of the more privileged.

Some car models have been better for society than others, merely by feeding on consumer tendencies already in place. Ford used "sporty" and powerful looks to turn a low-powered Ford Falcon into the hot and racy Mustang.[27] A style deceit meant less mineral exploitation and atmospheric fouling. In the big-cargo contest between minivans and SUVs, the minivan uses less fuel, pollutes less, and lowers collision danger for passengers in ordinary cars. Chrysler boosted minivans, in which it dominates the world market, by dressing them with a more "aggressive" appearance[28]—another case of cosmetics potentially yielding a social gain. This suggests there are some normal processes to be worked with.

The Gillette razor history provides an instructive case in ecological backslide and improvement. Gillette first did something environmentally regressive when it developed and marketed throwaway blades to supplant the permanent straight razor about 70 years ago. More was lost when the entire razor was made throwaway. But in 1999, its Mach 3 "permanent" razor, superior in fabrication and appearance, substantially reduced the market for throwaways. A next step would be for the "permanent" razor to be biodegradable, something accomplished by the Danish company Kay Barberhøvl.

Another sign of hope as well as a model to encourage is the fact that there are products that perform multiple functions with minimal mass. The Swiss Army Knife is one happy example. At one time, people owned motors that had attachments that turned them into a vacuum cleaner, sewing machine, or any number of other appliances. Multipurpose motors fell victim to the ever declining costs (and size) of motors, but the goal is for products that adjust to different functions in an open-ended manner. The computer works this way; changing software creates a variety of applications and entertainments with no need for more hardware.

In capital goods, computer technology allows all sorts of different stuff to come from the same equipment. The distance grows ever further from Henry Ford's array of one-function permanent pieces. In contrast to the way Ford had to toss out so much equipment to deal with style shifts, new generations of tooling readily adapt to new applications. Indeed, the whole idea of tooling can be going by the wayside, replaced by computer-driven forming machines that can switch to make any shape of anything by manipulating its program rather than the hardware. This may make for less mass and less waste within the production system.

As always, one should not get too carried away with optimism. That motors got so cheap it made sense to have many of them signals the larger problem; improvements happen, prices go down, and then there are so many new widgets the total mass—and the pollution to create it—increases rather than shrinks. In the current era, the computer did not yield the heralded "paperless office," but instead people's insecurity led them to make hard-copy backups and their creativity led them into desktop publishing to inform or amuse. Paper production pollutes severely. High tech, like the middle and low techs before them, guarantees nothing. But knowing more about the social as well as material dynamics might better exploit the positive potentials.

One possibility is for people to gain satisfaction not by having a product at all, but by gaining an experience equal to the benefits the product would deliver. Sometimes the equivalence is obvious. When a computerlike device downloads music from a website, it eliminates the need for the physical record/tape/disk and its packaging.[29] One gains the same music, possibly of superior quality, off the web. There are ways that such "dematerialization" can work when the equivalencies are less simple. So for example, longer car warranties can substitute for more frequent trade-ins. Expanding on the concept and making use of newer technologies, one could buy a service contract that includes continuous electronic monitoring of the car's movements so that immediate assistance can be sent should the driver have a problem. This might lessen the need for fail-safe redundant automobile mechanisms as well as for buying new cars quite so often. These are thus different types of backups to deal with a similar risk, with one not clearly superior to the other in functional terms. One uses less mass than the other to implement the same goal.[30]

Ever expanding communication capacities can generate new goods that take up little material but which could improve life. Passengers might walk into an airport and read out on their hand-held devices the flight gate, possible delays, as well as content of the movie and meal. As a way to enhance mass transit, one should be able to "hail" a van through mutual tracking; as you walk toward it, the van comes nearer to you. This kind of mutual surveillance through a new set of devices could help mass transportation toward a breakthrough—one that the Aramis project aimed to achieve, alas before the time and place was right. In various ways, consumers might in general dematerialize the economy by paying for experiences and services instead of durable objects. This takes us back, in a very modest way, to humanists' vision that feelings, relationships, and encounters mean more than physical things. The more that pleasures can be delivered directly as experience rather than indirectly as durables, the lighter the ecological load.

Nice Capitalism

Some corporate people at least talk green and articulate social responsibility. Mail order (now Internet) houses like REI and L.L. Bean make high demands of their suppliers.[31] Starbucks, Levi Strauss, and Reebok, arising from a consumer base more youthful and perhaps politically progressive, are said to now insist on compliance with relatively strict labor and production standards among their suppliers.[32] In the camping and sportswear industries, firms continuously trade on their environmental friendliness. Patagonia, which is among the companies making the strongest efforts, donates 1 percent of gross revenues to environmental programs—some of them politically aggressive campaigns. Most of its goods come from natural materials (organic when possible), but it also produces jackets from recycled plastic bottles. Helped by the Patagonia imprimatur, consumers otherwise at the heart of the natural fiber market evidently accept a garment's shiny artificial look because of the cause it serves—showing how powerfully moral preferences can inform what is or is not good-looking. Markets have also grown for organic farm products, and wares of artisan cooperatives and non-extractive rainforest products, with their "imperfections" a signal of value. Taste seems to be growing for renewables like hemp, bamboo, and other plentiful grasses and timber. Even the environmentally ravenous McDonald's abandoned glossy cardboard and Styrofoam on the assumption that customers were ready to see plain brown wrappers as worth having. Concern for the environment fuses with an affection for Third World folkways to make new things possible.

The unorthodox entrepreneurs Anita and Gordon Roddick built the multibillion-dollar Body Shop company on such an appeal; corporate programs support environmental and social change programs around the world. Body Shop advertisements eschew sexist portrayals and stress sustainable production techniques, even while selling sensual goods. In the clothing industry, Benetton mounts worldwide promotional campaigns pushing diversity across race, ethnicity, and sexuality, both as a general ethical mission as well as in regard to the style influences that go into its lines of products. In the high-technology realm, companies like Apple and Hewlett-Packard have ambitious programs to produce in environmentally friendly ways and to maximize consumer recycling of spent goods. Even major critics of the pollution created by high-tech industries in Silicon Valley acknowledge the big companies' strong efforts at reform and cleanup of sites poisoned by their prior activities.[33] That such "morality trips" could prove effective in brand building gives some hope.

No doubt from a mix of motives, major transnational corporations have formed the World Business Council for Sustainable Development. However misleading the "greenwash" PR campaigns that some corporations so deviously wage—U.S. oil companies being masters at the craft—some firms break rank. BP Petroleum parted company with the rest of the oil industry on global warming. Liggett broke allegiance with the tobacco industry's united stance. Smith and Wesson agreed to gun safety design regulation, engendering boycotts from gun wholesalers, dealers, and users. In class dynamic terms, leaders in the U.S. entertainment industry weigh in to the left of where they "should" be—both on environmental and social issues—following big retailers of a prior generation in this regard.

Wisdom Economics

There are at least symptoms of shift toward what economist Herman Daly calls "wisdom economics." Daly, who spent years at the World Bank trying to reverse conventional economic thinking, argued against confusing aggregate growth with "development." Development means, Daly says, refining technique to enhance satisfaction; growth merely piles more on—a greater city by adding more people or buildings, a greater economy by increasing its material scale. A statistic like gross domestic product merely measures the pile and implies that bigger is better. Development, in contrast, means reconfiguration—or, in Daly's words, "the embodiment of more information in a product."[34] Substituting performance for mass is an example of development without growth.

Although Daly's thinking was oriented toward macro-levels of societies and the whole world, the lessons are applicable (and have been applied) at the level of individual firms and households. Across many industrial spheres, motivated by a combination of cost savings, regulation, or fear of regulation, stunning advances have been made in simplifying production and using less mass—a more important accomplishment than recycling unnecessarily huge amount of trash. Some examples: over the course of a single decade, U.S. aluminum cans lost 40 percent of their weight; European yogurt containers dropped 67 percent of their bulk between 1960 and 1990; over roughly the same period, U.S. office buildings decreased the amount of steel required to build them by two-thirds.[35]

The major prospect for further gains turns on the capacity to imagine production in ever-larger visions. A fundamental step is to reconstruct the lash-ups among at least proximate elements. Installing windows with better insulation may yield only minor declines in what it takes to feed the furnace, but taking that action in conjunction with others, like wrapping the furnace, can yield bigger results. More dramatically, properly siting the house and building it out of insulating materials, can eliminate the need for a furnace altogether. For cooling it works the same way but with a somewhat different list: upgrade the windows, retrofit the lighting, open the roof (if possible) to allow hot air to rise away and then maybe the air-conditioning system does not need to be there at all. While conventional economics would likely cost out each additional improvement as approaching a point of diminishing returns, in fact the increments—once they reach a critical point—transform the entire system. So-called passive houses achieve energy savings of about 90 percent.[36] One has tunneled through the cost barrier, as the natural capitalists put it; "synergies and felicities" come about by changing how elements cooperate.[37] This movement toward green technology represents an application, at least in part, of lash-up theory to improve the physical world.

Certain changes in modes of distribution already under way show other aspects of this larger systems approach. Internet merchants, in effect, scheme the entire transaction process as a series of automated connections, minimizing the physical events in between. Besides the increases in productivity and profits, it also saves the energy used to physically move goods from manufacturer to wholesaler to retailer, and it cuts the number of consumer search trips. Leasing portends greener pastures as well, especially as it loses its former stigma as being for people too poor to buy. The natural capitalists like the fact that a firm such as Carrier, by leasing cooling instead of selling units, has incentive to minimize the scale of its equipment and the power it uses rather than trying to sell a customer the biggest thing possible. Similarly, a company providing floor covering under an ongoing contract can leave the material alone that is outside the traffic paths and replace only the worn-out stuff. That means less mass out of nature and less mass for recycling or the landfill.

Designers' Good Vibes

Compared to others in the production process, new rules on ecology or factory conditions become for designers still another element to take into account—additions to their task bundle that make them more rather than less necessary. Just as trial lawyers do not complain about increasing numbers of laws and regulations—to the chagrin of free-market enthusiasts—new controls bring designers new business. This points to possibilities for self-seeking and communal values to coincide. Unlike those in, say, copper mining or suburban real estate development, designers do not gain from increasing the use of earthly resources; they can at least as easily work by manipulating what is there rather than figuring out how to use more of it. The design instinct—based in ideology, artistic sensibility and, often, pecuniary interest—is to do more with less. And because designers typically own no production equipment, they do not have to concern themselves with amortizing past investments. In this they are prototypically the new corporation, ready to create anything because they have few prior material stakes.

The designers' moral stance comes across in many realms. One IDSA convention's theme was "Natural Resources" with the printed program, bound in conspicuously brown-bag recycled paper, listing session topics like "materials, processing, and ecology," "solar cooking," and workshops on ecological awareness. The program chairs and main speakers at the meetings, held in Santa Fe, wore red AIDS ribbons during a time the epidemic was intense in the United States. At a field trip to the nearby Los Alamos weapons labs, designers on my bus felt comfortable ridiculing nuclear work and cynically joked about the wildlife ponds our guide proudly pointed out on the site. In a loud voice, one cracked that the local deer glowed in the dark. A "highway safety feature," another called out to appreciative laughter.

The IDSA lists ecological responsibility as one of the five criteria for its annual awards; one of the three Industrie Forum Design Awards (based in Hanover, Germany) is on ecology alone. Design leaders say things like "industrial design is landfill" at an IDSA plenary session, and even urge in the same forum that design decrease, not increase, demand. Prestigious frogdesign calls for, in its publication that circulates to clients, an end to "the Age of R & D without respect for nature, the Age of Finance without respect for people, and the Age of Marketing without respect for the product."[38] Such considerations and sentiments contrast with what would be found in other industrial realms—the National Association of Manufacturers, say, or the U.S. Chamber of Commerce. An IDSA audience seemed to agree with a speaker who said that industrial designers were the only voice for social responsibility in the production process. One stated from the audience, "I've never heard anyone but the industrial designer raise a question about the social effects" of a product—referring to what goes on "when the doors are closed." He got some disagreement, but not that much. Given the nature of their vested interests, I think that if the circumstances permitted, designers would learn more about recyclability, self-repair, spontaneous decomposition, material substitutability, energy conservation, and probably better social conditions of production, including how to make others' work less dangerous or tedious.

Designers even hint at ways to eliminate themselves completely. One earnestly laid out, as part of an IDSA program on high-tech visions, a happy future in which personal factories, maybe like web-driven stereolithography, would allow anyone to design. Such dreams of professional self-destruction do not, it is safe to say, occupy the fantasy lives of people in most other sectors of the business world. I doubt if Realtors, bankers, or market traders, all of whom by some lights do work that is either immoral or superfluous or both, speak of such "goals" at their annual meetings.

Regulate Smart

However benign the intentions of the designers or their corporate clients, there need to be rules from above to create a playing field that does not put the good guys at disadvantage. The trick is to regulate in ways that respect the underlying social processes of production and consumption including the system's hyper-dynamism. This means changing the envelope within which markets and consumption operate, but in a manner that does not make war on the social and emotional nature of either. The challenges are formidable enough without exacerbating the political and social difficulties.

That gains sometimes inadvertently happen—as with Ford's Mustang or Gillette's erosion of throwaway razors—might lead some to think that government interference is not necessary; the hidden hand of the market takes care if we just leave it be. But corporate chicanery aside, it is amazing how long it can take for firms to institute no-brainer changes that do well for the society while saving them big money—energy-efficient lighting, for example. This means there are impediments rising from within corporate culture that need external and sometimes repeated prompting to overcome. And there is indeed also chicanery—corporate creativity in working with changing taste to bolster devious outcomes. An example is the SUV. Because U.S. automakers have to meet separate fuel efficiency standards for cars and trucks, it was in their interests to create vehicles that people would buy as cars but which could be classified as trucks—the SUV was the result. The success of SUVs allowed the corporations to show lower average fuel emissions in both categories—SUVs pollute more than most cars, but less than most trucks. So the SUV with its outdoorsy-rugged visual appeal is rightly seen as, among other things, a "loophole-riding vehicle."[39] The PT Cruiser, for all its other design solutions, also used a raised chassis (and additional features) to come in as a legal "truck"—setting in motion the creation of still more "tall wagons" by other companies, like the Toyota Matrix and Cadillac SRX. New rules need to stop this. It is a Tom and Jerry game between the companies and the regulators, but one very much worth engaging. U.S. fuel efficiency rules did lower overall emissions, even taking into account the auto companies' maneuvers. And the regulations did not undermine mobility, the

American way of life, or corporate prosperity. Relatively modest measures, in terms of the costs of doing business, can sometimes tip production systems toward more benign outcomes, especially if done mindfully.

Sometimes the market needs some help not because the options for reform are too few, but rather because they are so numerous. New technologies, including benign ones, can require some method of coordination and standardization in order to take hold. As with train track gauge and typewriter keyboards, even suboptimal standardizations can be better than none at all. As I write, various technologies are available to replace the internal combustion engine, including fuel cells based on hydrogen, electrical batteries, and hybrid engines using both electricity and gasoline. The problem is that without a choice being made among them, adoption of any one of them is held back. Making a choice would open up a trajectory of technological refinements and begin the process of installing fuel stations (either in homes, at service stations, or both). Ford estimates there need to be ten thousand fuel stations around the country to make hydrogen as convenient as present-day gasoline. So the lash-up problem comes down to finding a way to coordinate it all: to select a technology and bring the engines and the fuel stations (and public attitudes) into harmony more or less at the same time. The national government is uniquely equipped to stimulate the right technologies (through grants and sponsored research, for example), to move the process forward.

Another role for government is to once again act as model client, but this time on social and ecological as opposed to just aesthetic criteria. Government can use its vast buying power to create a critical mass that would offset development costs; it could sponsor charettes in which design consultancies publicly compete to prototype superior goods. Often used in awarding architectural commissions, charettes sometimes put competing design firms to work in a large hall with members of the public observing the design process firsthand. Not all design tasks lead themselves to such displays, but where possible they usefully expand design intelligence beyond the professionals.

Regulating at point of design is best. Design determines about 80–90 percent of an artifact's life-cycle economic and ecological costs, in an almost irreversible way—what raw materials will be used, gasses emitted, who will get hurt, how much will go to the landfill.[40] If regulating after the fact, governments have to tell people what to use, where, and when and how to manage disposal. It massively interferes to dictate who can use a car, how many miles before it gets tested, or where and when one can drive (downtowns or certain highway lanes). Reducing pollution or saving fuel by legislating the 55 mph limit, as happened during the 1970s U.S. fuel shortage, intruded into billions of human acts. Better to require a clean and efficient car engine (or safer and recyclable toy, sofa, battery, or thermometer) through negotiations between government and corporations about what the artifact can be. By influencing the design rather than users' behavior, the state (or the global organization of states) minimizes its presence, making for better lives with less unhappiness and resentment—always the appropriate way to go.[41]

Another principle of smart regulation, one derived from basic design strategy, is that the best instruction specifies goals, not methods. Designers fervently believe from concrete experience that better outcomes happen when clients indicate overall objectives rather than offering a version of how to achieve them. To be a good client, the state needs to set out the problem (cleaning the river, lowering emphysema rates, setting up appliance efficiency standards) rather than detailing the technology. Experts in regulation law sometimes refer to this kind of goal specification as "open state" regulation[42] because producers compete to attain the desired outcome, rather than being entangled in a thicket of rules and specifications. Form and function can float in the marketplace of sentiment and utility; the task is to put unecological behavior at a disadvantage without slowing down overall dynamism.[43]

There are already good examples of this. First in Germany and now in at least a dozen other countries, there are "take back" laws that hold the product maker responsible for ultimate disposal—"extended product responsibility" and "product stewardship" are the going phrases. How companies manage it is their business. One adaptation is to build in disassembly of used-up goods so that pieces can be easily sent back to the producer or a recycling location the producer designates. Easy disassembly has also lowered repair costs, as in the case of German automobiles. The BMW Z-1 sports car's recyclable all-thermoplastic skin strips from its metal chassis in 20 minutes. There are more ambitious possibilities. To make even goods of diverse materials infinitely recyclable, molecular content information could be encoded in each of a product's elements—designing in a kind of "upcycling passport"[44] to be read by factory scanners and used to sort for immediate re-use, ideally on-site. Take-back laws help solve problems of consumers evading requirements by buying or discarding in adjacent jurisdictions. The solution is in the product, not their behavior.

Not necessarily inconsistent with other forms of regulation, so-called "eco-taxing" attempts to capture true public costs (including harm to nature) by taxing goods according to the damage done through their production, consumption, and disposal. Polluting goods pay more. Governments not only can thereby encourage shifts toward more benign existing technologies, but also—especially if coupled with appropriate product standards and public expenditures on research and supporting infrastructure—stimulate new technologies into existence.

Any scheme of regulation comes with the potential for co-optation of the regulators by the regulated. The more frequent the interaction between authorities and producers, the greater the risk of such "capture."[45] Corporate players can seduce underpaid bureaucrats with prospects of a better job; corporate personnel, sometimes past regulators themselves, often know the technical issues better than hapless bureaucrats. Companies can invoke campaign contributions to pressure legislators; they can threaten (or use) litigation, with its attendant public costs, to win in court what they might lose over the counter. Again, design control has some advantage. At least compared to controls that require continuous surveillance (like restaurant sanitation), design regulation is built into the stuff rather than into inspection schedules. Once off the factory floor (or integrated into the company's tooling and distribution system) better stuff makes its own benign way through the world. Enforcement also becomes easier because evidence of infraction goes everywhere the product goes. At least in the United States, litigation based on product failure can take over as well, providing backup to imposition of fines or prison.

Of course, even design standards carry risk; they require, for each type of product, intense negotiations, and this implies capture potential. But controlling through design does bring in the designers, which means people whose biographies and career routes, perhaps even personalities, run counter to that of the lawyers and MBAs who usually do the work. A field with low visibility, at least when current designers entered it, the profession has many searchers, or perhaps just those prone to accidentally landing in an unconventional place. Some of their heroes pursued exceptional lives as painters, sculptors or radical thinkers—communists, anarchists, bohemians, homosexuals, nihilists, and drug users. There is some justification in clients' and corporate employers' suspicion of designers as not quite fitting in, which is why the designers often have to sell themselves as hard-nosed, loyal, and true. That designers so commonly operate as external consultants—perhaps resulting from corporate need to tap creativity that would die if kept in-house—furthers the potential for autonomous political work. In terms of the capture danger, this is all wholesome.

For their part, consumers are at the ready. In a German survey, about half the population expressed a desire to have more information about companies' environmental commitment as a guide for their purchasing behavior.[46] Producers and retailers could be required to present information on the actual social and ecological conditions of their product's origins—"production audits"[47] akin to the environmental impact reports now mandated for land-use development. The reality of Third World sweatshops or arsenic entering far-off rivers just might dull the magic of a new negligee or video cam. Experts working for non-profits, consulting with designers and engineers, could assign specific products a ranking—Michelin-type star points on the basis of their social and ecological value. A U.S. green building rating system now exists through LEED (Leadership in Energy and Environmental Design).[48] Other models include the "Dolphin-safe" stamp on tuna cans, organic produce certifications, and "Fair Trade Association" endorsement of food stuffs and handicrafts as meeting social justice criteria. Such systems, greatly expanded and properly designed, could become a generic aspect of consumption. The web could provide not just the summary ranking for each product, but full detail as desired on various social and ecological dimensions, as well as links to news stories and analyses that served as the basis for the ranking. Every e-retailer could be required to provide easy click access to such rankings before a transaction could be executed. Or Mr. Gates could just build decency-info access into his next platform and "Voila!"—a good use of monopoly power if there ever was one.

Nothing can exist unless the authorities who control the local industrial geography permit it to be made on their turf; this provides still another mechanism for government to influence stuff. To at least some degree, producers need access to particular places—sometimes because of the distinctive character they can add into the goods. Several generations ago the social critic Paul Goodman, writing with his architect brother Percival Goodman, argued that citizens had a right and duty to judge machines in terms of their social worth, including the production process they implied and the social value of what they produced.[49] If this were applied at the local level—and to some extent it has been with regard to such goods as poisons, pornography, and nuclear devices—there would be still another mechanism for regulating the nature of products.

There are good reasons for local governments to expand their concern beyond this narrow list. Localities could step into the regulation void over producers' waste by demanding to know what will go into the local production process, what will come out, and where it will end up. Over time, knowledge would build on the nature of the waste various production processes generate, providing a handle on how to regulate it and do better design. In this way, the NIMBY system ("not in my backyard") could be leveraged to improve ecology overall. It would also divert attention from consumers as the problem—more blaming of the shopper—and shift responsibility to the producers who create the bulk of the mess.

Once open to local examination, dimensions beyond ecological ones could enter into weighing pros and cons of production. The usual premise has been that new production will bring jobs and boost prosperity all around and thus should be received sympathetically. But a generation of urban and economic research shows this a very dubious assumption.[50] New jobs bring more migrants and the migrants may get the jobs, especially the good ones, at the expense of the locals who most need them. Similarly, the prospects of increasing the tax base also often turn out to be an illusion; the tax base may grow but so do the expenses created by the new migrants and the infrastructure costs to service the growth. Localities need to critically examine proposals for economic expansion and closely question the "growth machines" that otherwise dominate U.S. cities and regions. Rather than competing against one another for more growth, those with power in cities and regions could act to repel production that brings ecological or social disadvantage.

The Global Aspirants

Intervening at point of design may also benefit poor countries and improve relations between rich and poor regions of the world. A billion Chinese do want to drive automobiles, ecologists' nightmares not withstanding. Struggling peoples resist U.S. and European demands that they forgo the wasteful lifestyle so long enjoyed in the rich countries. Short of rank coercion or patronizing sermons, a partial answer can again come from changing the nature of new stuff. In some cases, at least, pressing for better design solutions in the rich world also benefits the poorer one. An alternative to the internal combustion engine solves problems everywhere, not just for Cadillacs in Chicago but for mopeds in Shanghai. Rather than rationing vehicle permits across countries or policing tons of emission within each place, a better engine design solves problems that people never get to know they have. A better production system in the North for making such goods can mean that when production goes offshore, even when compromised, it is less deadly and demeaning than it otherwise would be.

There tends to be a global domino effect of better technology. Because California, for example, is the world's largest single car market, its emission laws can cause companies to make technical changes in engine performance. The improved technology then moves to other jurisdictions, including those that have not (yet) tightened their standards.[56] Even if more expensive—and sometimes they turn out cheaper once the breakthrough investments are made—companies may produce their entire run based on the less polluting version because it is uneconomic to make different versions of the same product for different markets. Global agreements, along with national legislation, can encourage the process.

Besides playing a role in improving world technologies, design expertise might be used to help producers in poor countries better cope with the more recent changes in global capitalism that have put the culture industries and intellectual property at the center of wealth production. Since so many of the images that power the power brands, for example, are packaged (and copyrighted) in the rich countries—the United States especially—all other places are at a disadvantage. Whereas it once might have been that engineers, geologists, or agriculturists held the skills most needed in the poor countries, now the culture workers have information to make development work. Sometimes in their enthusiasm for Western goods, people elsewhere pass over opportunities arising from their own technologies, materials, and motifs. Somehow sympathetic design experts, including those from outside, might help mobilize a local advantage, including the particular ways local people themselves do design. There are some precedents, albeit mostly at the handicraft level. What we take to be Navajo-design rugs originated when Yankee entrepreneurs, wanting a cheaper rug than the kilims coming in from Turkey, showed Navajo people Middle Eastern designs to copy. This resulted in designs more complex than the simple bands of color in the native product but still less intricate than the imported versions. With a distinctive look and feel (a fine weave), the Navajo rugs eventually brought in far higher prices than the versions on which they were "imperfectly" modeled. I am not suggesting at this stage in history that survival can occur through craft production, only that melding can yield strong results. Post-war Japanese products both improved and fell short of the originals, depending on product type and the aspect of a given artifact, but created a platform for development.

One consequence of hybridization is also that products, deliberately or inadvertently, become sufficiently different from patented versions to insulate them from international litigation. By adapting products to different local conditions, including their craft styles and traditions, there may be the chance to make a better product or at least one that bypasses legal strictures. As with recent efforts to put Asia-produced generic medical drugs in the hands of people who cannot afford to pay U.S. and European prices, local versions of Western products could at least help replace imports.

But sometimes indeed ways of doing things can be superior in "unsophisticated places," at least when conjoined with elements and ideas brought in from the rich regions. It is a blunder to consider the rich countries as "developed" and poor places as "underdeveloped." The rich countries have huge economies that keep on growing, but since this growth is utterly unsustainable, it is more reasonable to speak of these economies—following Herman Daly's distinction between "development" and "growth"—as in a state of intensifying development deficit. In contrast, the so-called underdeveloped regions, with experience in composting their waste, use of production by-products, diversified agriculture, and squatting (!), have something to teach. Some products coming on line in poor countries, like simple solar-powered cooking devices and compost toilets, have potential applicability everywhere. Seed and plant varieties, not nearly so richly varied in the northern regions of the world, continue to yield up bases for new kinds of medical, chemical, and cosmetic applications.

This raises the possibility of creating mechanisms in which two-way teaching can occur, and in ways that commercially benefit those who usually get only the short end of the stick. Perhaps operating through some kind of design aid from the rich countries (a designer peace corps?) as well as legal and marketing assistance, the licensing and global distribution of newly developed Third World goods might result. Poor countries, rather than simply losing raw materials (with no compensation for resource depletion or environmental and social costs), would participate in the more lucrative phases of processing, product development, and patents. As is, the 130 poorest countries that make up the bulk of world societies constitute just 3.6 percent of world exports; if this figure is to rise new bases for adding local value are necessary.[52] This also would require changes in rules on world trade. Whereas the European Union imposes no duties on raw materials from poorer nations, processed goods—deemed potentially competitive with European-made products—are met with tariffs and many specific regulations and special conditions (the U.S. has its own way of penalizing poor countries' exports). Ways need to be found to keep the bounties of local cultures from ending up as intellectual property in Europe and America from whence they will be sold back to the poor regions.

Interventions would go seriously astray if disadvantaged places were forced to emulate the currently fashionable schemes of economic growth—high technology and the culture industries—found in the rich world. Something like this has been the historic pattern as ideas like heavy industry, dam construction, nuclear power, conventional Western medicine, and mechanized agriculture were once laid on unsuitable settings. Not every place can be the center of global technology and entertainment, or at least not in the same way, and authorities who inappropriately invest in such goals will gain only deeper immiseration for their people. Just as American city governments overbuilt, at various historical stages, canals, railroad depots, convention centers, and now ballparks and culture palaces, development hucksters remain at the ready with the magic growth pill. Governments from the rich world may lay on conditions that ignore local strengths to better serve multinational corporate interests. Internally, corrupt oligarchs find ways to transmute new resources into luxury cars and guns. Perhaps international non-governmental organizations, with some small added strengths and know-how from the design world, will succeed as counterbalance to lousy regimes within both the rich and poor worlds.

Into the Streets

In contrast to their good talk, the designers do not much engage in the political hardball of reform even locally much less on a global scale. Some designers do, as individuals, donate their services pro bono to charities and political movements—for posters and invitations to benefit events. But these are conventional business approaches to "giving something back." Neither in my interviews nor on the agenda of IDSA meetings does one find discussions over whether to lobby for this regulation or that, meet with legislators to push for one kind of reform or another, ban a product from the market. Instead, there is mutual hectoring and urging that designers themselves make better things—in a way almost oblivious to the structures that hem them in at so many turns. If even a minority of designers were to join movements or political efforts for reform, they would at least help break the knowledge monopolies within industries that so frustrate outsiders. It might make a wonderful difference for those who know just what they are talking about to join the public conversation. The IDSA should take the lead in lobbying for regulations that would foster the better lash-ups its members so often proclaim they desire to see. IDSA sponsorship would help avoid blacklisting of outspoken designers.

At one of the IDSA annual conventions, *Business Week*'s Nussbaum, of all people, warned designers that after years of telling them to play down their "strangling moralizations," they had perhaps heeded his advice a little too well. He hoped they would not leave behind the notions of social responsibility that had been so evident: "Remember where you came from," Nussbaum appealed. He did not urge it, but I will: Designers should use their unique role in the production apparatus to forge changes through political action—a "fifth column" from within the business world. Other professional groups, such as those representing medicine, law, and teaching, have not been reticent in pursuit of their moral and professional goals. Just as the American Dental Association led the movement for prophylactic care—even probably at costs to their aggregate income take—so it might be that the design profession could help right some wrongs. Designers could risk some of their recently acquired cachet; the corporations now know they need them.

Having worked so assiduously to build corporate brands, designers created a new kind of vulnerability for their business clients. The subtlety of their methods in constructing these consistent identities carries with it a capacity for aesthetically skilled insurrectionaries to undermine the very same structures. The power of the global identity can be turned, jujitsu/aikido-like, against the corporations. When oats and soap powder were sold out of big bins in grocery stores, the maker could operate with little or no public awareness of the conditions of production. Once it became a matter of Quaker or Kellogg's, the opportunity arose for public action against the brand. A few bottles of Coke that go bad in France forces down the stock value. An environmentalist campaign against Shell Oil undermined gasoline sales at the company's retail sites across Europe, causing Shell to give in to protests against dumping defunct drilling platforms into the ocean. Organized opposition to genetic-engineered food products ("Frankenfoods," as the British tabloids called them) not only kept such goods off the shelves of European shops, but by focusing on the Monsanto name, greatly eroded the corporation's equity. A Greenpeace campaign caused 3-M, Kinko's, Hallmark, and other big companies to forswear use of old-growth products. Pepsi, Texaco, Heineken, and almost every other brand-name company pulled completely out of Burma (a small market, to be sure) in response to consumer agitation over human rights abuses.

Some activists engage in anti-logo "culture jamming." Vancouver-based "Adbusters," a skilled group of wits, make acerbic print ads and video spots that usually are more interesting and entertaining than the advertisements they ridicule. A corporate logo with blood skillfully oozing from its crevices can be a more effective weapon than a long white paper documenting the company's complicity in acts of social mayhem. Associating Hitler with khakis as in one Adbusters campaign aimed at The Gap's promotion of khaki pants can plausibly cut into sales; death through a glamorous vodka brand like the one parodied on the next page might similarly bring up second thoughts among liquor purchasers. Such guerrilla design work in effect grabs the semiotic handle of branding and gives it a disturbing yank.

THINGS ARE NOT INEVITABLE

What we now have could have been different, not just in the sense of one technology or product as opposed to another but in the way whole systems of production and consumption came together. Looking back, George Basalla says, the internal combustion engine was not the inevitable power source for the car. It was dirty, it needed a fuel not readily available to consumers, and required a large number of interacting parts. Steam power was more efficient and ran on cheap oil distillates that burned a primary (and endlessly available) fuel—water. Along came, at just the wrong moment from the standpoint of the dozen or so steam car makers of the time, discoveries of vast oil supplies in Texas and California. And a decisive liability of the steam engine, says Basalla, was its "identification with the technology of the previous century,"[53] including the imagery of black smoke from coal-burning steam locomotives and other dirty appliances. The steam engine producers were unable to launch an active marketing campaign that might have countered such imagery or an alternative physical

Adbuster twist on vodka ad campaign. ©2002 Courtesy www.adbusters.org

design to contradict the unpleasant connotations. Here is a case where more appealing form and marketing might have saved a cleaner and more efficient product. Who knows what kind of technical improvements might have then followed. The contest between oil and water was evidently a close one. "Under different conditions," Basalla says, "the steam engine might have won."[54]

One choice we may now be facing is how desktop personal-factory manufacturing will take place. Machines and the material "goop" they use will arise in a more or less coherent way. As desktop manufacturing declines in price—a target of $500 for the basic unit is the goal—there will be tremendous potential for vast amounts of new stuff, including waste in the process of making it. Radically decentralized production may make it harder still to control who makes what and with what effect. Personal factories, like the personal airplanes and some other "modern miracles" also once thought just around the corner, may of course not materialize. But there needs to be readiness given the massive consequences should the prognosticators this time be right. The early resistance to genetically engineered foods, based not just on individual health effects but also eco-system concerns, discouraged the lash-ups from setting in that would have made later interventions much more difficult. There must be a similar timeliness with personal factories—not in blocking them altogether, but in affecting their makeup. Otherwise, past calamities will repeat: a technological breakthrough will increase the environmental load by making it still cheaper to have still more. But if the new machines can work only with environmentally benign materials and safe procedures, they can be changed from a potential liability to a source of improvement as they replace old-style factories and their polluting processes. There might also be, as in the design visionary's imaginings, a spreading around of the fun and creativity of making things.

THE CREATIVE COMMONWEALTH

I have argued for the normality of creative expression through material goods—both for producers and consumers. Artifacts help people signal and achieve affiliation and solidarity while also marking them off from one another. When it comes to goods, as with so many other realms, the devil and the decencies are in the details rather than any generalizations about the nature of consumption per se. In the current U.S. context, inequality in personal wealth and income has increased to a degree unique in contexts otherwise characterized as democratic. Having severely differential access to goods not only alters life chances of individuals but warps effective citizenship and deforms social membership. It may even help signal to those that have that the "have-nots" are not fully human: why else would they live like that? For those on the bottom, it may yield either sycophantic deference or intense resistance. Such attitudes, from above and below, were common in prior eras when wealth differences yielded people who ate, dressed, and smelled so differently. Translated into contemporary contexts of goods' access—to computer technology as one crucial type of commodity—such inequality remains a hindrance to the trust and mutuality required by democracy or for creative economic productivity.

This pattern of inequality also unjustly compensates the sources of the wealth. Corporate boardrooms do not contain the genius of production, nor does it reside in the offices of engineers, marketers, or designers. Production success comes from the cultural currents that make up social life in general and from all over the world—"from the vapor of available meaningful images wafting among all the ranks, all the colors, all the genders."[55] What might look like a product that arose out of a professional design school in fact came from the travels of design students through Tibet or the slums of Toledo. Even the ragtag homeless and meandering crazies of the streets make a mark on couture and all the stuff that then spills from the runways. In Italy, there is a special chic from simulating the look of poverty (*falso povero*); as the designer Christian Lacrois remarked in *Vogue*, "It's terrible to say, very often the most exciting outfits are from the poorest people."[56] Maybe that means they should have a share of the proceeds. Where *is* their spare change?

In the city and across the globe, the cultures people produce together contain the solutions that make economies possible. Since such sensibility is a common project with mutual appropriation the rule rather than the exception, the economic goods that come out of this cornucopia are plausibly common wealth as well. Some creators are handsomely compensated, but others, perhaps gratuitously appreciated for their "spirit," are largely left out of the remuneration loop. A simple appreciation that any one's genius ipso facto reflects the common genius would be a start toward shared responsibility. This justification for sharing does not replace others, nor eliminate the arduous moral and political struggles to achieve it. Instead, I mean that super-profits not only excessively exploit labor, they also exploit the labor of love—perhaps an even uglier injustice.

To relax in the war on goods is not to surrender to the opposite extreme of honoring profligate luxury, waste, and indifference. While still giving the frivolous its due, no one has to buy into social or natural dandyism. In contrast to his more purist colleagues on the German left, Walter Benjamin, writing his "Arcades Project" in the midst of the rise of fascism, was able to see fashion "as the antithesis of uniforms, and concern with fashion as a realm of genuine freedom in the modern world."[59] He was striving for, as Marshall Berman calls it, "a Marxism with charm." There are different ways that material can function as meaning. If distinction requires usurping nature and community with a 20-room house and a staff of serfs, people will seek just that. But what we know about humans indicates how varied can be the structures under which their fights for love and glory can operate. Subtle distinction works wonders. We need to create an envelope that capitalizes on this penchant for nuance, not one that wastes it.

Notes

Chapter 1

1. I mimic Howard Becker's terms and analytic strategy. See Howard Becker, *Art Worlds* (Berkeley: University of California Press, 1982).

2. See Toaster Foundation Museum 2001 at www.toaster.org.

3. Bruno Latour attributes this term to John Law, who evidently used it in an early draft of a paper that was later published without it. See John Law, "On the Methods of Long-Distance Control: Vessels, Navigation, and the Portuguese Route to India," in *Power, Action, and Belief: A New Sociology of Knowledge?* ed. John Law (London: Routledge and Kegan Paul, 1986). See also: John Law, "Of Ships and Spices," (unpublished essay, CSI, 1984).

4. Bruno Latour, *Science in Action: How to Follow Scientists and Engineers through Society* (Cambridge, Mass.: Harvard University Press, 1987), 108.

5. Andrew Pickering, *The Mangle of Practice: Time, Agency, and Science* (Chicago: University of Chicago Press, 1995), 17.

6. Henry Petroski, *Design Paradigms: Case Histories of Error and Judgment in Engineering* (New York: Cambridge University Press, 1994).

7. Zigmunt Bauman, "Industrialism, Consumerism, and Power," *Theory, Culture, and Society* 1.3 (1983): 38–39. J. Alt, "Beyond Class: The Decline of Industrial Labor and Leisure," *Telos.* 28 (1976).

8. Thorstein Veblen, *The Theory of the Leisure Class: An Economic Study of Institutions* (New York: Modern Library, 1934).

9. See also Nikolaus Pevsner, *Pioneers of Modern Design: From William Morris to Walter Gropius*, 2nd ed. (Harmondsworth, Middlesex, England: Penguin, 1960), 46. Georg Simmel formulated the idea of hierarchical emulation. See Georg Simmel, "Fashion," *American Journal of Sociology* 62 (1957 [1904]).

10. Barry Commoner, *The Closing Circle; Nature, Man, and Technology* (New York: Knopf, 1971).

11. Ellen Lupton and J. Abbott Miller, *The Bathroom, the Kitchen, and the Aesthetics of Waste: A Process of Elimination* (New York: Kiosk, 1992), 5, 71.

12. See Ellen Lupton, *Mechanical Brides: Women and Machines from Home to Office* (Princeton: Princeton Architectural Press, 1993).

13. Quoted in Isabel Wilkerson, "The Man Who Put Steam in Your Iron," *New York Times,* July 11, 1991. Strasser attributes first use to a *Business Week* article in 1955. See Susan Strasser, *Waste and Want: A Social History of Trash* (New York: Henry Holt, 1999), 274.

14. Bryan Lawson, *How Designers Think* (Cambridge, England: Cambridge University Press, 1991).

15. Stuart Ewen, *Captains of Consciousness: Advertising and the Social Roots of the Consumer Culture* (New York: McGraw-Hill, 1976), 99.

16. Lupton and Miller, *The Bathroom, the Kitchen, and the Aesthetics of Waste: A Process of Elimination* 5, 71.

17. See, for example, Brenda Jo Bright, "Remappings: Los Angeles Low Riders," in *Looking High and Low,* ed. Brenda Jo Bright and Liza Bakewell (Tucson: University of Arizona Press, 1995), 93. Early on, Stuart Hall criticized the "highly dubious" romanticizing of such practices. See Stuart Hall, "Notes on Decontructing 'the Popular'" in *People's History and Socialist Theory*, ed. Raphael Samuel (London: Routledge, 1981).

18. Francesca Bray, *Technology and Gender* (Berkeley: University of California Press, 1997), 39.

19. Robert Redfield, *The Folk Culture of Yucatan* (Chicago: University of Chicago Press, 1941).

20. Miriam Starck, "Technical Choices and Social Boundaries in Material Culture Patterning: An Introduction," in *The Archaeology of Social Boundaries*, ed. Miriam Starck (Washington, DC: Smithsonian Institution Press, 1998), 5.

21. Mary Douglas and Baron Isherwood, *The World of Goods: Towards an Anthropology of Consumption*, 2nd ed. (New York: Basic Books, 1996 [1979]).

22. Ibid., 45.

23. Ibid., 37.

24. Bray, *Technology and Gender,* 109.

25. Maurice Freedman, "Ritual Aspects of Chinese Kinship and Marriage," in *Family and Kinship in Chinese Society*, ed. Maurice Freedman (Stanford, Calif.: Stanford University Press, 1970).

26. Daniel Miller, Peter Jackson, Nigel Thrift, Beverly Holbrook, and Michael Rowlands, *Shopping, Place, and Identity* (London: Routledge, 1998), 141.

27. Ibid.

28. Mort, *Cultures of Consumption*, 188.

29. Alfred Gell, *Art and Agency* (Oxford: Clarendon, 1998), 231.

30. Douglas and Isherwood, *The World of Goods: Towards an Anthropology of Consumption.*

31. Mort, *Cultures of Consumption,* 188. Ozick uses the term "synthetic sublime." See Ozick, "The Synthetic Sublime," *New Yorker,* Feb. 22 and March 1 (combined issue), 1999.

32. I am invoking, as do Douglas and Isherwood, the sociological school of ethnomethodology. See Harold Garfinkel, *Studies in Ethnomethodology* (Englewood Cliffs, N.J.: Prentice Hall, 1967). See also Melvin Pollner, *Mundane Reason: Reality in Everyday and Sociological Discourse* (New York: Cambridge University Press, 1987).

33. Gell, *Art and Agency.*

34. Michael Dietler and Ingrid Herbich, "*Habitus,* Techniques, Style: An Integrated Approach to the Social Understanding of Material Culture and Boundaries," in *The Archaeology of Social Boundaries,* ed. Miriam T. Stark (Washington, DC: Smithsonian Institution Press, 1998).

35. David Keightley, "Archaeology and Mentality: The Making of China," *Representations* 18 (spring 1987).

36. A. Leroi-Gourhan, *Gesture and Speech,* trans. Anna Berger (Cambridge: MIT Press, 1993), 305.

37. See Heather Lechtman, "Style in Technology: Some Early Thoughts," in *Material Culture: Style, Organization, and Dynamics of Technology,* eds. H. Lechtman and R. S. Merrill (New York: West, 1977).

38. Daniel Bell, *The Cultural Contradictions of Capitalism* (New York: Basic Books, 1976), 70.

39. See, for example, Shoshana Zuboff, *In the Age of the Smart Machine* (New York: Basic Books, 1989); Tom Peters, *The Pursuit of Wow* (New York: Vintage, 1994).

40. On the limits of advertising, see Michael Schudson, *Advertising, the Uneasy Persuasion* (New York: Basic Books, 1986).

41. Stanley Lieberson, *A Matter of Taste: How Names, Fashions, and Culture Change* (New Haven, Conn.: Yale University Press, 2000), 273.

42. Ibid., 91, 170.

43. Ibid., 163, 174.

44. Lieberson goes to some trouble to show that the popularity of "Marilyn" came before the stardom of Marilyn Monroe (the stage name of Norma Jean Baker)—she got on board a name already on the rise.

Chapter 2

1. Pierre Bourdieu, *The Logic of Practice,* trans. Richard Nice (Cambridge, England: Polity, 1990). A similar definition of design: "the conscious process to develop physical objects with functional, ergonomic, economical and aesthetic concern." See Rune Monö, *Design for Product Understanding* (Stolkholm: Liber, 1997), 151.

2. The bulk of my interviews ranged over the 1994–1998 period. I toured the offices and workshops of about 25 design offices and in several instances hung

around for several hours or a full day, watching work go on, including focus groups and other design research activities. I have had dozens of more casual conversations with people in related fields (e.g., model makers, computer support staff, showroom salesreps, and manufacturers). Most design informants were the principals, but I have interviewed designers at beginning levels and some senior designers working in independent consultancies as well as in such companies as Whirlpool, Chrysler, Black and Decker, and Apple. I visited almost all designers in Los Angeles, San Diego, and Ventura counties except those in auto studios, where my coverage was spottier. Names were taken from phone directory Yellow Pages, membership listings in the Industrial Designers Society of America, and snowball-style referrals. I have also interviewed designers working in the U.S. East, Midwest, Bay Area, and to a lesser degree in other parts of the world—Sydney and London in particular.

3. Industrial Designers Society of America (IDSA) *IDSA Compensation Study* (Great Falls, Va.: Industrial Designers Society of America, 1996).

4. Brian Dumaine, "Design That Sells and Sells And . . ." *Fortune,* March 11, 1991: 88.

5. Neil Fligstein, "The Intraorganizational Power Struggle: Rise of Finance Personnel to Top Leadership in Large Corporations 1919-1979," *American Sociological Review* 52.1 (1987).

6. Source of data and estimate from James Ryan, president, Industrial Designers Society of America, interview with author, 1997, and IDSA, "Conference Registration Data," *IDSA* (Washington, DC: 1997).

7. Jim Kaufman, "TNT: Industrial Design Curriculums." See the website, www.idsa.org/whatsnew/gged_proceed/paper015.htm.

8. Gary Lee Downey, *The Machine in Me* (New York: Routledge, 1998), 226.

9. Sheryle Bagwell, "Design: It's More Than Art, It's the Competitive Edge," *Australian Financial Review Magazine* 1992: 8.

10. Clement Greenberg, *Art and Culture: Critical Essays* (Boston: Beacon Press, 1978).

11. Gottfried Semper, *Der Stil in Den Technischen Und Tektonischen Kunsten, Oder Praktische Asthetik : Ein Handbuch Fur Techniker, Kunstler Und Kunstfreunde* (Mittenwald: Maander, 1977) as quoted in Eva Zeisel, "The Magic Language of Design" (unpublished paper, 2001).

12. No author, "Iomega: The Right Stuff," *Journal of Business and Design,* 1996. The CEO of Crown Forklift trucks gave a similar testimonial that it was design that built his company (see chapter 3).

13. No author, "Verse 504 and 514 Voice Access Microphones," *I.D. Magazine,* August 2001.

14. Edward De Bono, *Lateral Thinking: Creativity Step by Step* (New York: Perennial Library, 1990).

15. Anne Hollander, *Seeing through Clothes* (New York: Penguin, 1988).

16. Advertisement, *I.D. Magazine,* August 2001.

17. Josep Lluscà, "Redefining the Role of Design" *Innovation* magazine, 15(3)1996: 25.

18. Eva Zeisel, "Acceptance Speech," *Industrial Design Society of America Annual Meeting* (Washington, DC: 1997).

19. Mark Granovetter, "The Strength of Weak Ties," *American Journal of Sociology*, 78 (1975).

20. See, e.g., David Woodruff and Elizabeth Lesley, "Surge at Chrysler," *Business Week*, Nov. 9, 1992: 89. Alex Taylor III, "U.S. Cars Come Back," *Fortune*, Nov. 16, 1992: 64.

21. The designer called it a "Rodney Dangerfield attitude," referring to the U.S. comic's depiction of an ignorant businessman who late in life returns to college where he enjoys ridiculing the idea of book knowledge and expertise.

22. Ivan Hybs, "Beyond the Interface," *Leonardo* 29 (1996).

23. The *I.D. Magazine* awards do so consistently, as for example this attribution for a winning piece of upholstered furniture: "Client/company: Umbra, Toronto, Ontario; Consultant Design: Karim Rashid Inc. New York. Karim Rashid, principal; Materials/Fabrication: polyurethane foam covered in 100 percent polyester fabric; Hardware/Software: Apple Power Mac G3, Adobe Photoshop, Ashlar Vellum 3D, Form Z." No author, "Q Chaise," *I.D. Magazine,* August 2001.

24. Kathryn Henderson, *On Line and on Paper (inside Technology)* (Boston: MIT Press, 1998). See also Eugene S. Ferguson, *Engineering and the Mind's Eye* (Cambridge: MIT Press, 1992), 37; Bryan Laffitte, "Drawing as a Natural Resource in Design," in *Natural Resources* (Santa Fe, N.M.: Industrial Designers Society of America, 1995), *Design Education Conference Proceedings*, 43.

25. Tom Kelley and Jonathan Littman, *The Art of Innovation: Lessons in Creativity from IDEO, America's Leading Design Firm* (New York: Currency/Doubleday, 2001).

26. Michael Hiltzik, "High-Tech Pioneer William Hewlett Dies," Jan. 13 2001, A1.

27. For an extraordinary ergonomic study of human defecation, urination, and personal hygiene appropriate to the design of bathroom fixtures, see Alexander Kira, *The Bathroom*, 2nd ed. (New York: Viking, 1976).

28. Kelley and Littman, *The Art of Innovation: Lessons in Creativity from Ideo, America's Leading Design Firm,* 38.

29. This account from Henry Petroski, *The Evolution of Useful Things* (New York: Random House, 1992), 84. See also Robert M. McMath, "Throwing in the Towel," *American Demographics*, November 1996.

30. Paul duGay et al., *Doing Cultural Studies: The Story of the Sony Walkman* (London: Sage, 1997).

31. On "affordances," see Donald Norman, *The Design of Everyday Things* (New York: Doubleday, 1988).

32. Lupton, *Mechanical Brides: Women and Machines from Home to Office.*

33. Black and Decker lecture, annual meeting of the Industrial Designers Society of America, 1998.

34. Galen Cranz, *The Chair: Rethinking Culture, Body, and Design* (New York: Norton, 1999), 52.

35. Vitruvius Pollio, *Vitruvius: The Ten Books on Architecture.*, trans. Morris Hicky Morgan (New York: Dover, 1960), 103. Quoted in Sanders, 1996: 13.

36. Sanders, 1996, 15

37. Edson Armi, *The Art of American Car Design* (University Park: Pennsylvania State University, 1990), 155.

Chapter 3

1. Daniel Bell, *The Cultural Contradictions of Capitalism,* 70.

2. Petroski, *The Evolution of Useful Things*, 32.

3. Philip Nobel, "Can Design in America Avoid the Style Trap?" *New York Times,* Nov. 26, 2000, Sec. 2, p. 33.

4. Dennis Altman, *The Homosexualization of America* (New York: St. Martin's Press, 1982), 154; see also Elizabeth Wilson, "Fashion and the Postmodern Body," in *Chic Thrills: A Fashion Reader*, ed. Juliet Ash and Elizabeth Wilson (Berkeley: University of California Press, 1993).

5. Max Eastman, quoted in Michelle Helene Bogart, *Artists, Advertising, and the Borders of Art* (Chicago: University of Chicago Press, 1995), 54.

6. David Harvey, *The Condition of Postmodernity: An Enquiry into the Origins of Cultural Change* (Oxford, England: Blackwell, 1989), 328.

7. Charles Baudelaire, *The Painter of Modern Life*, trans. Jonathan Mayne (London: Phaidon, 1970) 2, 3.

8. Gell, *Art and Agency,* 71.

9. Becker, *Art Worlds*.

10. James Atlas, "An Interview with Richard Stern," *Chicago Review* 45.3, 45.4 (1999): 43.

11. Latour, *Science in Action: How to Follow Scientists and Engineers through Society*.

12. F. Klingender, *Art and the Industrial Revolution* (Frogmore, St. Albans, Hertsfordshire, England: Paladin, 1972 [1947]).

13. National Museum, "Beneath the Skin: Technical Artists" (London: National Museum of Science and Industry, 1999).

14. Cyril Stanley Smith, *A Search for Structure: Selected Essays on Science, Art, and History* (Cambridge: MIT Press, 1981), 194.

15. Victor Papanek, *The Green Imperative* (New York: Thames and Hudson, 1995), 51.

16. Cyril S. Smith, *A Search for Structure: Selected Essays on Science, Art, and History,* 328.

17. Petroski, *The Evolution of Useful Things,* 114.

18. Cyril Stanley Smith, "Art, Technology, and Science: Notes on Their Historical Interaction," in *Perspectives in the History of Science and Technology*, ed. Duane H. D. Roller (Norman: University of Oklahoma Press, 1971), as cited in Virginia Postrel, *The Future and Its Enemies: The Growing Conflict over Creativity, Enterprise, and Progress* (New York: Free Press, 1998), 134.

19. Cyril S. Smith, *A Search for Structure: Selected Essays on Science, Art, and History,* 329.

20. James Adovasio, quoted in Natalie Angier, "Furs for Evening, but Cloth Was the Stone Age Standby," *New York Times,* Dec. 14, 1999.

21. Johan Huizinga, *Homo Ludens: A Study of the Play Element in Culture* (Boston: Beacon, 1950), 28, cited in Postrel, *The Future and Its Enemies: The Growing Conflict over Creativity, Enterprise, and Progress,* 175.

22. Cyril S. Smith, *A Search for Structure: Selected Essays on Science, Art, and History* 210, 215, 230.

23. Cyril S. Smith 1971: 43

24. For mining and missiles, see Cyril S. Smith, *A Search for Structure: Selected Essays on Science, Art, and History*, 202. Textiles: The spinning jenny and waterframe stem from the desire for calico prints; the specific idea for the technology is said to have arisen from an eighteenth-century chess-playing machine. See Standage, Tom, *The Turk: The Life and Times of the Famous 18th Century Chess-Playing Machine,* New York: Walker & Co.; Chandra Mukerji, *From Graven Images: Patterns of Modern Materialism* (New York: Columbia University Press, 1983); and L. C. A. Knowles as cited in Mukerji, *From Graven Images: Patterns of Modern Materialism*, 221. For chemicals, see Simon Garfield, *Mauve: How One Man Invented a Color That Changed the World* (New York: W. W. Norton, 2001); George Basalla, *The Evolution of Technology* (New York: Cambridge University Press, 1988); and Keith Chapman, *The International Petrochemical Industry* (Cambridge: Blackwell, 1991). For plastics, see *Early American Ironware, Cast and Wrought*, 1963, Henry J. Kaufman, 1966, "Their Historical Interaction" as cited in Cyril Smith 1971 "Art, Technology and Science: Notes in *Perspectives in the History of Science and Technology*, ed. Duane H.D. Roller (Normal, Okla.: University of Oklahoma Press, 1971): 129–65.

25. Michael Snodin, *Ornament: A Social History since 1450* (New Haven, Conn.: Yale University Press, 1996).

26. Basalla, *The Evolution of Technology,* 8.

27. David Hounshell, *From the American System to Mass Production 1800–1932* (Baltimore: Johns Hopkins University Press, 1984).

28. National Museum of Science and Industry, display copy, London: 1999.

29. Roland Barthes, *Mythologies* (London: Vintage, 1993 [1957]) 90, 88.

30. Michael Schwartz and Frank Romo, *The Rise and Fall of Detroit* (Berkeley: University of California Press, forthcoming), citing Henry Ford and Samuel Crowther, *Today and Tomorrow* (Garden City, N.Y.: Doubleday, Page, 1926), 186–88.

31. Jeffrey Meikle, "From Celebrity to Anonymity: The Professionalization of American Industrial Design," *Raymond Loewy: Pioneer of American Industrial Design*, ed. Angela Schönberger (Berlin: Prestel, 1990), 52.

32. Hounshell, *From the American System to Mass Production 1800–1932*, 276.

33. Alfred Chandler, *The Visible Hand: The Managerial Revolution in American Business* (Cambridge, Mass.: Harvard University Press, 1977).

34. Stephen Bayley, *Harley Earl and the Dream Machine* (New York: Knopf, 1983), 116.

35. Arthur Pound, *The Turning Wheel; The Story of General Motors through Twenty-Five Years, 1908–1933* (Garden City, N.Y.: Doubleday, Doran, 1934), 293-94.

36. Raymond Loewy, quoted in Petroski, *The Evolution of Useful Things,* 168.

37. Armi, *The Art of American Car Design,* 53.

38. Kirk Varnedoe and Adam Gopnik, *High and Low* (New York: Museum of Modern Art, 1991), 407.

39. Brian Dumaine, "Five Products U.S. Companies Design Badly," *Fortune,* November 21, 1988: 130. The other badly designed product types cited were small appliances, home furniture, stoves, and air conditioners.

40. Braudel, 1981: 243

41. Richard Klein, *Cigarettes Are Sublime* (Durham, N.C.: Duke University Press, 1993).

42. Erving Goffman, *Interaction Ritual; Essays in Face-to-Face Behavior* (Chicago: Aldine, 1967).

43. Jack Goody, *Cooking, Cuisine, and Class* (Cambridge, England: Cambridge University Press, 1982).

44. Sydney Mintz, "Time, Sugar, and Sweetness," *Marxist Perspectives* 2 (1979).

45. Mark Pendergrast, *Uncommon Grounds: The History of Coffee and How It Transformed Our World* (New York: Basic Books, 1999).

46. Cranz, *The Chair: Rethinking Culture, Body, and Design,* 32–33.

47. Edward Lucie-Smith, *A History of Industrial Design* (New York: Van Nostrand, 1983).

48. Witold Rybczynski, *Home: A Short History of an Idea* (New York: Penguin, 1986), 97. See also Cranz, *The Chair: Rethinking Culture, Body, and Design.*

49. Cranz, *The Chair: Rethinking Culture, Body, and Design,* 287.

50. Ruth Rubinstein, *Dress Codes* (Boulder, Colo.: Westview, 1995), cites L. H. Newburgh, ed., *The Physiology of Heat Regulation and the Science of Clothing* (New York: Stretchet Haffner, 1968), and an essay from that book by H. C. Bazett, "The Regulation of Body Temperature."

51. Quentin Bell, *On Human Finery* (London: Hogarth, 1947).

52. Lucie-Smith, *A History of Industrial Design.*

53. Cyril S. Smith, *A Search for Structure: Selected Essays on Science, Art, and History,* 325.

54. Baudelaire, *The Painter of Modern Life,* 8.

55. The term is from Schumpeter, who used it in a different context. Schumpeter, quoted in Herman Daly, *Beyond Growth: The Economics of Sustainable Development* (Boston: Beacon, 1996), 6.

56. Terry Smith, *Making the Modern: Industry, Art, and Design in America* (Chicago: University of Chicago Press, 1993).

57. Dirac, quoted in Edward Rothstein, "Recurring Patterns, the Sinews of Nature," *New York Times,* October 9, 1999.

58. K. C. Cole, "A Career Boldly Tied by Strings,"*New York Times* Feb. 4, 1997: A1, A16. Similar reports come from Benoit Mandelbrot, Richard Feyman, Leon Szilard, Jonas Salk, C. Radharisna Rao, and Arthur C. Clarke. For still another collection see Graham Farmelo, ed., *It Must Be Beautiful: Great Equations of Modern Science* (New York: Granta, 2002).

59. See Antonio Damasio, *Descartes' Error: Emotion, Reason, and the Human Brain* (New York: Plenum, 1994). For still other testimonials, see John D. Barrow, *The Artful Universe* (Oxford, England: Oxford University Press, 1995); Enrico Coen, *The Art of Genes* (Oxford, England: Oxford University Press, 1999); Philip Ball, *The Self-Made Tapestry* (Oxford, England: Oxford University Press, 1998); Brian Greene, *The Elegant Universe* (New York: Norton, 1999); and Edward Rothstein, *Emblems of Mind* (New York: Avon, 1996).

60. R. D'Andrede, "Culturally Based Reasoning," in *Cognition in Social Worlds*, ed. A. Gellatly, D. Rogers, and J. Sloboda (New York: McGraw-Hill, 1989).

61. Edwin Hutchins, "Mental Models as an Instrument for Bounded Rationality, Distributed Cognition and HCI Laboratory, Department of Cognitive Science, University of California-San Diego, 1999).

62. Yi-Fu Tuan, "The Significance of the Artifact," *Geographical Review* 70 (1980). See also Robert Sack, *Place, Modernity, and the Consumer's World* (Baltimore: Johns Hopkins University Press, 1992), 4.

63. Damasio, *Descartes Error: Emotion, Reason, and the Human Brain,* 54, 205, 219.

64. Gilles Fauconnier and Mark Turner, "Conceptual Integration Networks," *Cognitive Science* 22.2 (1998).

65. William Leach, *Land of Desire: Merchants, Power, and the Rise of a New American Culture* (New York: Pantheon, 1993).

66. Ibid.

67. Coco Chanel, quoted in Peter Wollen, ed., *Addressing the Century* (London: Hayward Gallery, 1998), 13.

68. Wollen, *Addressing the Century*; and Judith Clark, "Kenetic Beauty: The Theatre of the 1920s," in the same book.

69. Stephen Kern, *The Culture of Time and Space, 1880–1918* (Cambridge, Mass.: Harvard University Press, 1983), 155.

70. Reynal Guillen, "The Air-Force, Missiles and the Rise of the Los Angeles Aerospace Technopole," *Journal of the West* 36(3) 1997: 60–66.

71. William Owen, "Design for Killing: The Aesthetic of Menace Sells Guns to the Masses," *I.D. Magazine,* September/October 1996: 57.

72. Thanks to Tom Armbruster for this comparison.

73. See Penny Sparke et al., *Design Source Book* (Secaucus, N.J.: Chartwell, QED, 1986), 103.

74. London Design Museum, *Interactive Computer Program*, 1993, London Design Museum, April 4, 1993.

75. Georges Pompidou Centre, "Manifeste," Paris: Centre Pompidou, 1992, wall copy.

76. Paul Hawken, Amory Lovins, and L. Hunter Lovins, *Natural Capitalism* (Boston: Little, Brown, 1999), 118.

77. Gell, *Art and Agency*.

78. Alfred Gell, "The Technology of Enchantment and the Enchantment of Technology," *Anthropology, Art, and Aesthetics*, ed. J. Coote and A. Shelton (Oxford, UK: Clarendon Press, 1992).

79. Henry Petroski, *Invention by Design: How Engineers Get from Thought to Thing* (Cambridge, Mass.: Harvard University Press, 1996), 137.

80. No author, "Genesis Protective Eyewear," *I.D. Magazine*, March 2001.

81. Comments by Thomas Bidwell, "Natural Resources," paper presented at the annual meeting of the Industrial Designers Society of America (IDSA), 1995, Santa Fe, N.M.

82. James R. Sackett, "Style and Ethnicity in Archaeology," *The Uses of Style in Archaeology*, ed. Margaret W. Conkey and Christine Hastorf (Cambridge, England: Cambridge University Press, 1990).

83. Ibid., 32.

84. Patricia Brown, "Maya Lin: Making History on a Human Scale," *New York Times*, May 21, 1998, F–1.

85. Garfinkel, *Studies in Ethnomethodology*; Don Zimmerman, "The Practicalities of Rule Use," in *Understanding Everyday Life; Toward the Reconstruction of Sociological Knowledge*, ed. Jack D. Douglas (Chicago: Aldine, 1970).

86. Charles Bazerman, *The Language of Edison's Light* (Cambridge: MIT Press, 1999); Thomas Hughes, *American Genesis: A Century of Invention and Technological Enthusiasm, 1870–1970* (New York: Viking, 1989).

87. Rosalind H. Williams, *Dream Worlds: Mass Consumption in Late Nineteenth-Century France* (Berkeley: University of California Press, 1982), 228.

88. See J. Maxwell Atkinson, *Our Masters' Voices : The Language and Body Language of Politics* (New York: Methuen, 1984).

89. Bruno Latour, *Aramis or the Love of Technology* (Cambridge, Mass.: Harvard University Press, 1996).

90. Cyril S. Smith, *A Search for Structure: Selected Essays on Science, Art, and History*.

91. See C. Wright Mills, "Situated Actions and Vocabularies of Motive," *American Sociological Review* 5.6 (1940).

92. Bourdieu, *The Logic of Practice*. See also Garfinkel, *Studies in Ethnomethodology*.

Chapter 4

1. Diana Crane, "Diffusion Models and Fashion: A Reassessment," *Annals of the American Academy of Political and Social Science* 56 (November), 1999.

2. D. Langley Moore, *Fashion through Fashion Plates 1771–1970* (New York: C. N. Potter, 1971), cited in Neil McKendrick, "Commercialization and the Economy," *The Birth of a Consumer Society*, ed. Neil McKendrick, John Brewer, and J. H. Plumb (Bloomington: Indiana University Press, 1982).

3. Leora Auslander, *Taste and Power: Furnishing Modern France* (Berkeley: University of California Press, 1996).

4. Fernand Braudel, *Civilization and Capitalism, 15th–18th Century*, trans. Sian Reynolds (London: Collins, 1981), 317. For a history that covers the fourteenth century as well, see Christopher Breward, *The Culture of Fashion* (Manchester, England: Manchester University Press, 1995).

5. Bray, *Technology and Gender*, 138.

6. Craig Clunas, *Superfluous Things: Material Culture and Social Status in Early Modern China* (Cambridge, England: Polity, 1992), 165. See also, for fourteenth-century European fashion, Gilles Lipovetsky, *The Empire of Fashion: Dressing Modern Democracy*, trans. Catherine Porter (Princeton, N.J.: Princeton University Press, 1994).

7. Neil McKendrick, introduction to *The Birth of a Consumer Society*, ed. Neil McKendrick, John Brewer, and J. H. Plumb (Bloomington: Indiana University Press, 1982), 2.

8. Braudel, *Civilization and Capitalism, 15th–18th Century*, 316, quoted in Lieberson, *A Matter of Taste: How Names, Fashions, and Culture Change*, 9.

9. Alois Riegl, *Problems of Style: Foundations for a History of Ornament*, trans. Evelyn Kain (Princeton, N.J.: Princeton University Press, 1992 [1893]).

10. Dietler and Herbich, "*Habitus*, Techniques, Style: An Integrated Approach to the Social Understanding of Material Culture and Boundaries," 254.

11. Ascherson, Neil, "Any Colour You Like, So Long as It's Black . . ." (Sic) *Observer*, Jan. 24, 1999, 29.

12. Quote in Douglas and Isherwood, *The World of Goods: Towards an Anthropology of Consumption*, 110.

13. Gell, *Art and Agency* 256.

14. Ibid., 84.

15. Stephan Huyler, *From the Ocean of Painting: India's Popular Painting Traditions, 1589 to the Present* (New York: Rizzoli, 1994).

16. Miguel Covarrubias, *Island of Bali* (New York: Knopf, 1937).

17. Lila M. O'Neale, *Yurok-Karok Basket Weavers* (Berkeley: University of California Press, 1932).

18. E. Perkins, "The Consumer Frontier: Household Consumption in Early Kentucky," *Journal of American History* 78 (1991), as cited in Paul Glennie, "Consumption within Historical Studies," *Acknowledging Consumption*, ed. Daniel Miller (London: Routledge, 1995), 176.

19. Philip D. Morgan, *Slave Counterpoint: Black Culture in the Eighteenth Century Chesapeake and Lowcountry* (Chapel Hill: University of North Carolina Press, 1998), quoted in Edmund S. Morgan, "The Big American Crime," *New York Review*, Dec. 3, 1998.

20. Veblen, *The Theory of the Leisure Class: An Economic Study of Institutions*, 85.

21. Herbert Blumer, "Fashion: From Class Differentiation to Collective Selection," *Sociological Quarterly* 10, as quoted in Fred Davis, *Fashion, Culture, and Identity* (Chicago: University of Chicago Press, 1992), 118.

22. Pierre Bourdieu, *The Field of Cultural Production*, trans. Randal Johnson (New York: Columbia University Press, 1993), 106.

23. Howard S. Becker, "The Power of Inertia," *Qualitative Sociology* 18 (1995).

24. Cranz defines style as the "way all the parts of a composition are assembled around its main idea or attitude" Cranz, *The Chair: Rethinking Culture, Body, and Design*, 69.

25. See Ian Hodder, "Style as Historical Quality," in *The Uses of Style in Archaeology*, ed. Margaret Conkey and Christine Hastorf (Cambridge, England: Cambridge University Press, 1990).

26. Oliver Sacks, quoted in Calvin Tomkins, "The Maverick," *New Yorker*, July 7, 1997.

27. Gell, *Art and Agency*, 167.

28. Ibid., 218.

29. Agnes Brooks Young, *Recurring Cycles of Fashion, 1760–1937* (New York: Harper and Brothers, 1937) 205–6, cited in Lieberson, *A Matter of Taste: How Names, Fashions, and Culture Change*, 96.

30. Henry Dreyfuss, quoted in Bayley, *Harley Earl and the Dream Machine*.

31. Crane, "Diffusion Models and Fashion: A Reassessment."

32. Candace Shewach, "Interview with Author, Commenting on Barbara Barry's Design for Hbf, Inc." (1994). Interview at Pacific Design Center Exhibit Los Angeles, Calif.

33. Balzac, quoted in Williams, *Dream Worlds: Mass Consumption in Late Nineteenth-Century France*.

34. Basalla, *The Evolution of Technology*, 107.

35. W. Brian Arthur, "Self-Reinforcing Mechanisms in Economics," in *The Economy as an Evolving Complex System*, ed. Philip W. Anderson, Kenneth J. Arrow, and David Pines (Redwood City, Calif.: Addison-Wesley, 1988).

36. Philip Jackman, "A Calculated Distribution of Phone Keys," *Globe and Mail*, July 10, 1997.

37. Jacob Rabinow, *Inventing for Fun and Profit* (San Francisco: San Francisco Press, 1990).

38. Tom Kelley and Jonathan Littman, *The Art of Innovation: Lessons in Creativity from IDEO, America's Leading Design Firm* (New York: Currency/Doubleday, 2001), 187.

39. Paul Willis, "The Motorcycle within the Subcultural Group," *Working Papers in Cultural Studies, University of Birmingham* 2 (no date), as cited in Dick Hebdige, *Hiding in the Light* (London: Routledge, 1988), 86.

40. Hebdige, *Hiding in the Light*, 86.

41. Ibid., 96.

42. Adrian Forty, *Objects of Desire: Design and Society since 1750* (London: Thames and Hudson, 1992).

43. Surya Vanka, "The Cross-Cultural Meanings of Color," in *Proceedings of the Annual Meetings of the Industrial Designers Society of America*, ed. Paul Nini (San Diego, Calif.: Industrial Designers Society of America, 1998).

44. At least these are the impressions of Mike Nuttal, principal at Palo Alto's IDEO Design.

45. Peter Kilborn, "Dad, What's a Clutch?" *New York Times*, May 28, 2001: A8.

46. For general access to plumbing companies' promotional materials, as well as anthropological interpretations of bathroom modernity, see the website www.thethirdfloor.com/toilet/.

47. Terence Conran, *The Bed and Bath Book* (London: Mitchell Beazley, 1978) 226; see also Kira, *The Bathroom*.

48. Conran, *The Bed and Bath Book*, 226.

49. Toilets vary, by country, in terms of tendency for all material to disappear without leaving a trace; ease of flushing away fecal material while still sitting; odors emitted from standing waste; tendency for droppings to "splash back"; capacity to visually observe waste (sometimes medically important); likelihood of overflow and mechanism for dealing with it should it occur.

50. Conran, *The Bed and Bath Book*, 221.

51. Hawken, Lovins, and Lovins, *Natural Capitalism*, 118.

52. So, in the words of NASA Flight Center engineer Howard Winsett, "A major design feature of what is arguably the world's most advanced transportation system was determined over two thousand years ago by the width of a horse's ass." Forwarded e-mail message from Howard Winsett, NASA Dryden Flight Research Center.

53. Arthur, "Self-Reinforcing Mechanisms in Economics." For a catalog of instances, see Malcolm Gladwell, *The Tipping Point*.

54. McMath, "Throwing in the Towel."

55. Jamie Kitman, "All Hail the Crown Victoria," *Metropolis*, May 2000.

56. Raymond Williams, *The Country and the City* (New York: Oxford University Press, 1973).

57. Stewart Brand, *How Buildings Learn* (New York: Viking, 1994).

58. Phone interview with author, Nov. 16, 2001.

59. Sackett, "Style and Ethnicity in Archaeology," 36.

60. No author, "African Beauty," *Home Furnishings News (HFN)*, March 26, 2000.

61. Ellery J. Chun, "Obituary," *West Hawaii Today*, June 7, 2000. See also Thomas Steele, *The Hawaiian Shirt: Its Art and History* (New York: Abbeville, 1984).

62. See Orlando Patterson, "Ecumenical America: Global Culture and the American Cosmos," *World Policy Journal*, summer 1994.

63. Edward Said, *Culture and Imperialism* (London: Chatto & Windus, 1993). quoted in Miller, Jackson, Thrift, Holbrook and Rowlands, *Shopping, Place, and Identity*, 21.

64. Richard Caves, *Creative Industries: Contracts between Art and Commerce* (Cambridge, Mass.: Harvard University Press, 2000), 211.

65. Papanek, *The Green Imperative*, 62.

66. Jane Jacobs, *The Nature of Economies* (New York: Random House, 2000).

67. Claude S. Fischer, *America Calling: A Social History of the Telephone to 1940* (Berkeley: University of California Press, 1992).

68. Basalla, *The Evolution of Technology*, 139–41.

69. Ibid., 185.

70. AnnaLee Saxenian, *Regional Advantage: Culture and Competition in Silicon Valley and Route 128* (Cambridge, Mass.: Harvard University Press, 1994), 100.

71. Dan Lynch, cited in Postrel, *The Future and Its Enemies: The Growing Conflict over Creativity, Enterprise, and Progress,* 181.

72. Jerry Yang, "Turn on, Type in, and Drop Out," *Forbes ASAP,* Dec. 1, 1997, cited in Postrel, *The Future and Its Enemies : The Growing Conflict over Creativity, Enterprise, and Progress,* 181.

73. No author, "Hackers Rule," *The Economist*, Feb. 20, 1999.

74. Innovation Sports, available at http://www.isports.com/by_cust.htm, April 25, 2001.

75. Neil McKendrick, "Commercialization and the Economy," in McKendrick, et al., *The Birth of a Consumer Society*, 113.

76. David Brooks, *Bobos in Paradise* (New York: Simon and Schuster, 2000).

77. Colleen McDannell, *The Christian Home in Victorian America, 1840–1890* (Bloomington: Indiana University Press, 1986), 49, as quoted in Karen Halttunen, "From Parlor to Living Room: Domestic Space, Interior Decoration, and the Culture of Personality," in *Consuming Visions*, ed. Simon J. Bronner (New York: Norton, 1989), 164.

78. Adolf Loos, "Ornament and Crime," *Programs and Manifestoes on 20th Century Architecture*, ed. Ulrich Conrads (Cambridge: MIT Press, 1971 [1908]), 20–21.

79. Often attributed to modernist precursor Louis Sullivan, but was first used by Horatio Greenough. See John Pile, *Dictionary of 20th-Century Design* (New York: Roundtable Press, 1990), 84.

80. Cranz, *The Chair: Rethinking Culture, Body, and Design*, 143.

81. Reyner Banham, *Theory and Design in the First Machine Age* (New York: Praiger) 1970: 21

82. Tom Wolfe, *From Bauhaus to Our House* (London: Johnathan Cape, 1982), 77. See also Reyner Banham, *The Architecture of the Well-Tempered Environment*.

83. Cranz, *The Chair: Rethinking Culture, Body, and Design,* 87.

84. Philip Johnson, quoted in Rybczynski, *Home: A Short History of an Idea*, 211.

85. George Kubler, *The Shape of Time: Remarks on the History of Things* (New Haven, Conn.: Yale University Press, 1962).

86. Eric Norcross, "Evolution of the Sunbeam T-20," *Hotwire: The Newsletter of the Toaster Museum Foundation, Charlottesville, Va.*

87. Papanek, *The Green Imperative*.

88. DuGay et al., *Doing Cultural Studies: The Story of the Sony Walkman*, 59.

Chapter 5

1. Charlie Porter, "Dior Postpones Retrospective of Galliano's Work," *Guardian*, Oct. 16, 2001.

2. Hebdige, *Hiding in the Light*.

3. Bray, *Technology and Gender*, 144.

4. Fred Davis, *Fashion, Culture, and Identity*, 118.

5. Ray Oldenburg, *The Great Good Place* (New York: Marlowe, 1989). Regarding shopping on the U.S. western frontier, see E. Perkins, "The Consumer Frontier: Household Consumption in Early Kentucky," *Journal of American History* 78 (1991).

6. Jane Jacobs, *The Death and Life of Great American Cities* (New York: Random House, 1961).

7. McKendrick, "Introduction," 6.

8. Basalla, *The Evolution of Technology*.

9. Emmanuel Cooper, *Ten Thousand Years of Pottery* (London: British Museum Press, 2000), 234–35.

10. Jules Lubbock, *The Tyranny of Taste* (New Haven, Conn.: Yale University Press, 1995), 221.

11. McKendrick, "Commercialization and the Economy," 140–43.

12. Deidre Lynch, "Counter Publics: Shopping and Women's Sociability," in *Romantic Sociability: Essays in British Cultural History, 1776–1832*, ed. Gillian Russell and Clara Tuite (Cambridge, England: Cambridge University Press, forthcoming), as quoted in Sarah Boxer, "I Shop, Ergo I Am: The Mall as Society's Mirror," *New York Times*, March 28, 1998.

13. Judith Walkowitz, "Going Public: Shopping, Street Harassment, and Streetwalking in Late Victorian London," *Representations* 62 (spring (1998): 51.

14. Leach, *Land of Desire: Merchants, Power, and the Rise of a New American Culture*, 132.

15. Ibid., 89. Artists of all sorts spend career time doing store windows, as have some industrial designers.

16. Viviana A. Rotman Zelizer, *The Social Meaning of Money* (New York: Basic Books, 1994). James G. Carrier, *Gifts and Commodities: Exchange and Western Capitalism since 1700* (New York: Routledge, 1995), 16, 177.

17. Marjorie L. DeVault, *Feeding the Family* (Chicago: University of Chicago Press, 1991).

18. Malcolm Gladwell, "The Pitchman: Ron Popeil and the Conquest of the American Kitchen," *New Yorker*, Oct. 30, 2000: 70.

19. IDSA, *Annual Meeting, Industrial Designers Society of America (IDSA)* (Santa Fe, N.M.: 1995).

20. DuGay et al., *Doing Cultural Studies: The Story of the Sony Walkman*.

21. Philip Kasinitz, *Caribbean New York: Black Immigrants and the Politics of Race* (Ithaca, N.Y.: Cornell University Press, 1992).

22. Miller et al., *Shopping, Place, and Identity*, 164.

23. Richard Appelbaum, David Smith, and Brad Christerson, "Commodity Chains and Industrial Restructuring in the Pacific Rim: Garment Trade and Manufacturing," *Commodity Chains and Global Capitalism*, ed. Gary Gereffi and Miguel Korzeniewicz (Westport, Conn.: Greenwood, 1994); Susan Strasser,

Satisfaction Guaranteed: The Making of the American Mass Market (New York: Pantheon, 1989), 284.

24. Strasser, *Satisfaction Guaranteed: The Making of the American Mass Market.*

25. Kim Hastreiter, "Design for All," *Paper* Magazine, May 2001: 105.

26. Paco Underhill, *Why We Buy: The Science of Shopping* (New York: Simon and Schuster, 1999), 162.

27. Strasser, *Satisfaction Guaranteed: The Making of the American Mass Market.*

28. Underhill, *Why We Buy: The Science of Shopping*, 174. See also Nicole Biggart, *Charismatic Capitalism* (Chicago: University of Chicago Press), 1990.

29. Ibid., 111.

30. Ibid., 174.

31. See A. F. Robertson, *Life Like Dolls: The Natural History of a Commodity*, (New York: Routledge, 2003).

32. Petroski, *The Evolution of Useful Things*, 167.

33. Gladwell, "The Pitchman: Ron Popeil and the Conquest of the American Kitchen," 71.

34. Ibid., 68.

35. Mary Morris, vice president of Ross-Simons. See Beth Viveiros, "A New Setting," *Direct Marketing Intelligence*, May 1, 2002.

36. Hawken, Lovins, and Lovins, *Natural Capitalism.*

37. For one useful commentary, see R. Shields, "Social Spatialisation and the Built Environment: The West Edmonton Mall," *Environment and Planning D: Society and Space* 7 (1989).

38. Fredric Jameson, *Postmodernism* (Durham, N.C.: Duke University Press, 1991).

39. Susan S. Fainstein, *The City Builders* (Cambridge, Mass.: Blackwell, 1994), 230.

40. Michael Fried, "Art and Objecthood," *Minimal Art: A Critical Anthology*, ed. Gregory Battcock (New York: Dutton, 1968), cited in Richard Sennett, *The Conscience of the Eye* (New York: Alfred Knopf, 1990).

Chapter 6

1. Michael Storper, *The Regional World* (New York: Guilford, 1997).

2. J. Nicholas Entrikin, *The Betweenness of Place: Towards a Geography of Modernity* (Baltimore: The Johns Hopkins University Press, 1991), 13.

3. Raymond Williams, *The Country and the City* (New York: Oxford University Press, 1973), 22.

4. The concept appears in L. J. Hanifan, *The Community Center* (Boston: Silver, Burdette, 1920), 78-79, and later in Jane T. Jacobs, *The Death and Life of Great American Cities* (New York: Random House, 1961).

5. Jacobs, *The Nature of Economies*, 26.

6. See Harvey Molotch, William Freudenburg, and Krista Paulsen, "History

Repeats Itself, but How? City Character, Urban Tradition, and the Accomplishment of Place," *American Sociological Review* 65 (2000).

7. Blaise Cendrars, *Hollywood: Mecca of the Movies*, trans. Garrett White (Berkeley: University of California Press, forthcoming [1936]), 2 of the translated typed text.

8. Daniel Bell, *The Cultural Contradictions of Capitalism.*

9. Jean Baudrillard, *America* (New York: Verso, 1989), 104.

10. No author, "California Design: Funk Is In: Brash, Passionate Newcomers Are Taking on Austere Eurostyle," *Business Week Special Bonus Issue*, August 1990: 172.

11. Lewis MacAdams, "The Blendo Manifesto," *California Magazine,* March 1984.

12. Barbara Thornburg, "Sitting on Top of the World," *Los Angeles Times Magazine,* Oct. 11, 1992.

13. Harold Brodkey, "Hollywood Closeup," *New Yorker,* May 3, 1992: 69.

14. Kevin Robins, "Tradition and Translation: National Culture in Its Global Context," *Enterprise and Heritage*, ed. John Corner and Sylvia Harvey (London: Routledge, 1990).

15. Justin Stagl, *A History of Curiosity: The Theory of Travel, 1550–1800* (Chur, Switzerland: Harwood, 1995).

16. William E. Myer, "Indian Trails of the Southeast," Forty-second Annual Report of the Bureau of American Ethnology (Washinton, DC: Smithsonian Institution), 1924, as cited in John Brinkerhoff Jackson, *A Sense of Place, a Sense of Time* (New Haven, Conn.: Yale University Press, 1994).

17. Donald Lundberg, E. M. Krishnamoorthy, and Mink H. Stavenga, *Tourism Economics* (New York: Wiley and Sons, 1995).

18. Strasser, *Satisfaction Guaranteed: The Making of the American Mass Market*, 109.

19. John Findlay, *Magic Lands: Western Cityscapes and American Culture after 1940* (Berkeley: University of California Press, 1992).

20. Sack, *Place, Modernity, and the Consumer's World,* 164.

21. Lundberg, Krishnamoorthy and Stavenga, *Tourism Economics.*

22. William Kreysler, telephone interview with author, 1997.

23. Ash Amin and Nigel Thrift, "Neo-Marshallian Nodes in Global Networks," *International Journal of Urban and Regional Research* 16.4 (1992): 579.

24. Rubinstein, *Dress Codes,* 225. Rubinstein cites Valerie Steele, *Paris Fashion* (New York: Oxford University Press, 1988), 23.

25. Rosalind Williams, *Dream Worlds: Mass Consumption in Late Nineteenth-Century France.*

26. No author, "LAX Gateway," *I.D. Annual Design Review*, 114.

27. Storper, *The Regional World.*

28. Goody, *Cooking, Cuisine, and Class.*

29. Gerald Hirshberg, "Comments," *Why Design* (San Diego, Calif.: Industrial Designers Society of America, 1998).

30. Carey McWilliams, *Southern California: An Island on the Land* (Salt Lake City: Peregrine Smith, 1973 [1946]).

31. "L'isola Advertisement," *New York Times*, May 4, 1986.

32. But see Saskia Sassen, *The Mobility of Capital and Labor* (New York: Cambridge University Press, 1988).

33. Mort, *Cultures of Consumption*.

34. Suzanne Reimer, Paul Stallard, and Deborah Leslie, "Commodity Spaces: Speculations on Gender, Identity and the Distinctive Spatialities of Home Consumption," unpublished paper, 1998.

35. Allen Scott, *Technopolis: The Geography of High Technology in Southern California* (Berkeley: University of California Press, 1993). Also see Barney Brantingham, "Those High-Flyin Loughead Brothers," *Santa Barbara News-Press,* Dec. 27, 1992.

36. Thomas S. Hines, *Richard Neutra and the Search for Modern Architecture* (Berkeley: University of California Press, 1994), 28.

37. Ibid., 78.

38. Preston Lerner, "One for the Road," *Los Angeles Times Magazine,* Feb. 9, 1992: 33.

39. United Nations Conference on Trade and Development, *Handbook of International Trade and Devlopment Statistics* (New York: United Nations, 1994).

40. Michael Porter, *The Competitive Advantage of Nations* (New York: Free Press, 1990); see also Alan Pred, *The Spatial Dynamics of U.S. Urban-Industrial Growth* (Cambridge: MIT Press, 1966).

41. Storper, *The Regional World*, 116.

42. Guido Martinotti, "A City for Whom?" *The Urban Moment,* ed. Sophie Body-Gendrot and Robert Beauregard (Thousand Oaks, Calif.: Sage, 2002).

43. Alfred Hitchcock, "Alfred Hitchcock on His Films," *The Listener,* Aug. 6, 1964.

44. Interview by Richard Appelbaum and Edna Bonacich at Bugle Boy, 1991. See Richard Appelbaum and Edna Bonacich, *Behind the Label* (Berkeley: University of California Press, 2000). I am grateful for access to the original interview transcripts.

45. Corky Newman, president of the California Mart. See Vicki Torres, "Bold Fashion Statement: Amid Aerospace Decline, L.A. Garment Industry Emerges as a Regional Economic Force," *Los Angeles Times*, March 12, 1995, D–1.

46. See Edward Soja, *Postmodern Geographies* (New York: Verso, 1989).

47. Riley Doty, "Comment on 'the Arts and Crafts Movement in California' Oakland Museum Show," *Arts and Crafts,* Aug., 27–28, 1993: 28.

48. No author, "Big Personality Pieces," *House Beautiful,* February 1987. See also Tim Street-Porter, *Freestyle: The New Architecture and Interior Design from Los Angeles* (New York: Stewart, Tabori, and Chang, 1986).

49. Doty endorsed this view of Henry-Russell Hitchcock in "Comment on 'the Arts and Crafts Movement in California' Oakland Museum Show," 93.

50. Reyner Banham, *The Architecture of the Well-Tempered Environment* (London: The Architectural Press, 1963), 208. See also Wolfe, *From Bauhaus to Our House,* 86.

51. Lee Fleming, "Remaking History," *Garden Design,* September/October 1992.

52. David DeMarse, director of marketing and business planning, American Seating Co., interview with author, 1992.

53. Ibid.

54. Martin Filler, "Frank Gehry and the Modern Tradition of Bentwood Furniture," *Frank Gehry: New Bentwood Furniture Designs* (Montreal: Montreal Museum of Decorative Arts, 1992), 102.

55. Bright, "Remappings: Los Angeles Low Riders."

56. This and the following quote from the Ford executive come from Paul Lienert, "Detroit's Western Front," *California Business*, December 1989: 38.

57. David Gebhard, introduction to *California Crazy: Roadside Vernacular Architecture*, eds. Jim Heimann and Rip Georges (San Francisco: Chronicle Books, 1980), 11.

58. Leonard Pitt and Dale Pitt, *Los Angeles, A to Z* (Berkeley: University of California Press, 1997), 376.

59. Nancy Moure, *California Art: 450 Years of Painting and Other Media* (Los Angeles: Dustin, 1998).

60. Varnedoe and Gopnik, *High and Low*, 154.

61. Christopher Knight, "Mike Kelley, at Large in Europe," *Los Angeles Times*, July 5, 1992.

62. Adam Gopnik, "Diebenkorn Redux," *New Yorker*, May 24 1993: 97.

63. Paola Antonelli, "Economy of Thought, Economy of Design," *Arbitare* 1994.

64. Angela McRobbie, "Second-Hand Dresses and the Role of the Ragmarket," in *Zoot Suits and Second-Hand Dresses*, ed. Angela McRobbie (Boston: Unwin and Hyman, 1988); Angela McRobbie, *British Fashion Design* (London: Routledge, 1998).

65. Calvin Tomkins, "The Maverick," *New Yorker*, July 7, 1997: 43.

66. Frank Gehry, interview by Charlie Rose, *Charlie Rose Show* (Public Broadcasting System, 1993) See also: Martin Filler, "Ghosts in the House," *New York Review of Books*, Oct. 21, 1999: 10.

67. Robert Andrews and Ron Hill, "Art and Auto Design in California," in *The Arts: A Competitive Advantage for California*, KPMG Marwick LLP (Sacramento: California Arts Council, 1994), 28, 29.

68. Ibid., 4.

69. Sharon Zukin, *The Cultures of Cities* (Cambridge, Mass.: Blackwell, 1995), 155.

70. Bernard Beck, "Reflections on Art and Inactivity" (Evanston, Ill.: CIRA Seminar Series Monograph, Culture and the Arts Workgroup. Center for Interdisciplinary Research in the Arts, Northwestern University, 1988), Vol. 1.

71. Fred Block, *The Vampire State: And Other Myths and Fallacies about the U.S. Economy* (New York: New Press, 1996), 233.

72. Ernest Raia, "Quality in Design," *Purchasing*, April 6, 1989.

73. Scott Lash and John Urry, *Economies of Signs and Space* (London: Sage, 1994), 123.

74. Rybczynski, *Home: A Short History of an Idea*, 3.

75. No author, "Collar Wide Open," *Details*, June 2001.

76. Hollander, *Seeing through Clothes*.

77. Ibid., 154.

78. Rosemary Brantley, interview with author, (July 6, 1992).

79. Chris Woodyard, "Surf Wear in Danger of Being Swept Aside by Slouchy, Streetwise Look," *Los Angeles Times*, June 21, 1992.

80. Martin Battersby, *The Decorative Thirties* (New York: Whitney Library of Design, 1988).

81. W. Robert Finegan, *California Furniture: The Craft and the Artistry* (Chatsworth, Calif.: Windsor, 1990).

82. Charles McGrath, "Rocking the Pond," *New Yorker*, Jan. 24, 1994: 50.

83. Allen Scott, "French Cinema," *Theory, Culture, & Society* 17.1 (2000).

84. Allen Scott, "The US Recorded Music Industry," *Environment and Planning A* 31 (1999).

85. Claudia Eller, "All the Rage; Fashion's Top Names Take on Hollywood with Agents, Deals," *Los Angeles Times,* May 29, 1998.

86. Hiltzik, "High-Tech Pioneer William Hewlett Dies," A1.

87. Ashley Dunn, "It's Alive; Well, Sort Of," *Los Angeles Times,* July 6, 1998.

88. Charles Gandy and Susan Zimmermann-Stidham, *Contemporary Classics: Furniture of the Masters* (New York: McGraw-Hill, 1981), 136.

89. Doug Stewart, "Eames: The Best Seat in the House," *Smithsonian,* May 1999: 84.

90. Michael Hiltzik, *Dealers of Lightning* (New York: Harper Collins, 1999).

91. AnnaLee Saxenian, *Regional Advantage: Culture and Competition in Silicon Valley and Route 128* (Cambridge, Mass.: Harvard University Press, 1994). For the California case especially, see Andy C. Pratt, "The New Media, The New Economy, and New Spaces" *Geoforum* 31 (2000).

92. Arnaldo Bagnasco, *Tre Italie: La Problematica Territoriale Dello Sviluppo Italiano* (Bologna: Il mulino, 1977). See also Michael Piore and Charles Sabel, *The Second Industrial Divide: Possibilities for Prosperity* (New York: Basic Books, 1990).

93. Brooks, *Bobos in Paradise*.

94. Martin Gannon, *Understanding Global Cultures* (Thousand Oaks, Calif.: Sage, 2001), 231.

95. R. F. Imrie, "Industrial Restructuring, Labor, and Locality: The Case of the British Pottery Industry," *Environment and Planning A* 21 (1989).

96. Wall copy, Permanent Product Exhibition, London Design Museum, 1998.

97. *CM Magazine* Sept. 6, 1996, p. 6, quoted in Reimer and Leslie, ms. 9.

98. Diana Crane, *Fashion and Its Social Agendas* (Chicago: University of Chicago Press, 2000), 138.

99. Conran, *The Bed and Bath Book*.

100. Petroski, *The Evolution of Useful Things,* 165.

101. See also Hugh Aldersey-Williams, 1992.

102. Bruce Nussbaum, "Smart Design: Quality Is the New Style," *Business Week*, April 11, 1988: 106.

103. Sibylle Kicherer, *Olivetti: A Study of the Corporate Management of Design* (New York: Rizzoli, 1990).

104. Bagnasco, *Tre Italie : La Problematica Territoriale Dello Sviluppo Italiano*. See also Michael J. Piore and Charles F. Sabel, *The Second Industrial Divide : Possibilities for Prosperity* (New York: Basic Books, 1990).

105. Appelbaum, Smith, and Christerson, "Commodity Chains and Industrial Restructuring in the Pacific Rim: Garment Trade and Manufacturing."

106. Amin and Thrift, "Neo-Marshallian Nodes in Global Networks," 578, 579.

107. Saskia Sassen, *The Global City* (New York: Princeton University Press, 1991), 213.

108. Mike Davis, *Ecology of Fear* (New York: Random House, 1998).

109. The phrase is inspired by the title of Howard Becker's collection of essays: *Doing Things Together*.

110. For the founding statement, see Garfinkel, *Studies in Ethnomethodology*; see also John Heritage, *Garfinkel and Ethnomethodology* (New York: Polity, 1984).

Chapter 7

1. Gary Gereffi and Miguel Korzeniewicz, eds., *Commodity Chains and Global Capitalism* (Westport, Conn.: Greenwood, 1994).

2. Gray Brechin, *Imperial San Francisco* (Berkeley: University of California Press, 1999).

3. Adam Hochschild, *King Leopold's Ghost* (New York: Houghton Mifflin, 1999).

4. Jon Lee Anderson, "Oil and Blood," *New Yorker*, Aug. 14, 2000: 49.

5. Adrienne Vitjoen, "South Africa/Conscience Raising." *Innovation* magazine, Fall 1996: 20.

6. Regarding the nineteenth-century United States, see Dolores Hayden, *Redesigning the American Dream: The Future of Housing, Work, and Family Life* (New York: Norton, 1986).

7. No author, "Six Hundred Miles Away," *Observer Magazine*, Nov. 19, 2000.

8. United Nations Conference on Trade and Development, *Handbook of International Trade and Development Statistics* (New York: United Nations, 1994). The countries with the richest fifth of the world's peoples were responsible, in 1990, for almost 85 percent of all world trade. See also Neil Fligstein, *The Architecture of Markets* (Princeton, N.J.: Princeton University Press, 2001), 197.

9. George Codding, *The International Telecommunication Union* (New York: Arno, 1972), 14, as cited in John Braithwaite and Peter Drahos, *Global Business Regulation* (Cambridge, England: Cambridge University Press, 2000), 332.

10. Mark Zacher and Brent A. Sutton, *Governing Global Networks: International Regimes for Transportation and Communications* (Cambridge, England: Cambridge University Press, 1996).

11. Braithwaite and Drahos, *Global Business Regulation*, 333.

12. Codding, *The International Telecommunication Union*, as cited in Braithwaite and Drahos, *Global Business Regulation*, 328.

13. Braithwaite and Drahos, *Global Business Regulation*.

14. Ibid., 505.

15. For an acute depiction of the liabilities of gradual, as opposed to sudden, environmental crises, see Thomas D. Beamish, "Accumulating Trouble: Complex Organization, a Culture of Silence, and a Secret Spill," *Social Problems* (2000).

16. Richard Sennett, "The Art of Making Cities," comments presented at the Annual Meeting of the Research Committee on the Sociology of Urban and Regional Development, International Sociological Association, 2000, Amsterdam, The Netherlands.

17. Maureen Jung, "The Comstocks and the California Mining Economy, 1848–1900: The Stock Market and the Modern Corporation," PhD Dissertation, Dept. of Sociology, University of California, Santa Barbara, 1988.

18. Corporate licensing generates $15 billion in annual U.S. retail sales. See Rachel Beck, "Logo Licensing on the Rise," Associated Press story, *Santa Barbara News-Press*, May 24, 1997.

19. See *www.fortunebrands.com*.

20. Barry Saferstein, "Collective Cognition and Collaborative Work: The Effects of Cognitive and Communicative Processes on the Organization of Television Production," *Discourse & Society* 3.1 (1992).

21. David Redhead, *Products of Our Time* (Boston: Birkhauser, 2000), 108.

22. Hugh Aldersey-Williams, *Nationalism and Globalism in Design* (New York: Rizzoli, 1992), 155.

23. Jay Wilson, "U.S. Companies May Be Resting on Dead Laurels," *Marketing News*, Nov. 6 (1989), 21.

24. Raia, "Quality in Design."

25. Bruce Nussbaum, "Product Development: Designed in America," *Business Week*, n.d. 1989.

26. Robert Croston, "Industrial Design Employment and Education Survey," *Industrial Designers Society of America*, ed. Paul Nini, CD-ROM ed. (San Diego, Calif.: Industrial Designers Society of America, 1998).

27. For Australia, see Bagwell, "Design: It's More Than Art, It's the Competitive Edge."

28. Bruce Nussbaum, "A New Golden Era of Design," comments at the Annual Meetings of the Industrial Designers Society of America, in Washington, DC, 1997.

29. See, e.g., Apple Advertisement, the *Guardian* (UK), May 8, 1999: 30.

30. Sack, *Place, Modernity and the Consumer's World*.

31. Full-page advertisement, the *Independent*, Feb. 12, 1999: 6.

32. Magali Sarfatti Larson, *Behind the Post-Modern Facade* (Berkeley: University of California Press, 1995).

33. Personal communication, Byron Glaser, Glaser-Higashi, 1998.

34. Diana Crane, "Globalization, Organizational Size, and Innovation in the French Luxury Fashion Industry," *Poetics* 24 (1997).

35. Marnell Jameson, "Fine Design at a Discount," *Los Angeles Times*, Feb. 4, 1999, E1.

36. See, for example, Target Corporation advertising insert, *New York Times*, Sept. 10, 2000, and *www.target.com*, 2001.

37. Naomi Klein, *No Logo: Taking Aim at the Brand Bullies* (New York: Picador, 2000), 421.

38. Ibid., 189.

39. Barnaby Feder, "Orthodontics Via Silicon Valley," *New York Times*, Aug. 18, 2000.

40. See Bruce Goldman, "Experts Foresee Desktop 'Factories' within 10 Years," *Stanford Report* 31.39, Aug. 25, 1999.

41. Quoted in Sibylle Kicherer, *Olivetti: A Study of the Corporate Management of Design* (New York: Rizzoli, 1990), 42.

42. *Business Week*, March 14, 1994: 60, as cited in Zukin, *The Cultures of Cities*, ms. 5.

43. Nick Graham, comments at annual meetings of Industrial Designers of America 1995 in Santa Fe, N.M.

44. See Charles MacKay, *Extraordinary Popular Delusions and the Madness of Crowds* (New York: Harmony, 1980 [1841, 1852]). Kee Warner and Harvey Molotch, "Information in the Marketplace: Media Explanations of the '87 Crash," *Social Problems* 40.2 (May 1993). Donald McCloskey, *The Rhetoric of Economics* (Madison: University of Wisconsin Press, 1985).

45. Bob Gerson, "Companies Come and Go but Brands Live on Forever," *TWICE (This Week in Consumer Electronics) Retailing/E-Tailing*, May 7, 2001. In regard to diversification stories, see Neil Fligstein, *The Transformation of Corporate Control* (Cambridge, Mass.: Harvard University Press, 1990).

Chapter 8

1. John Alroy, "A Multispecies Overkill Simulation of the End-Pleistocene Megafaunal Mass Extinction," *Science* 292 (2001). See also Tim Flannery, *The Eternal Frontier* (New York: Atlantic Monthly Press, 2001).

2. James Surowiecki, "Farewell to Mr. Fix-It," *New Yorker*, March 5, 2001.

3. Braithwaite and Drahos, *Global Business Regulation*, esp. 274, 275, 446, 447.

4. Rubinstein, *Dress Codes*.

5. Quoted in Jules Lubbock, *The Tyranny of Taste*, 95.

6. Maquelonne Toussaint-Samat 1990, as cited in Crane, *Fashion and Its Social Agendas*, 113.

7. Lubbock, *The Tyranny of Taste*.

8. Strasser, *Waste and Want: A Social History of Trash*, 154.

9. Lubbock, *The Tyranny of Taste*, 325.

10. Philippe Bourgois, *In Search of Respect: Selling Crack in the Barrio* (New York: Cambridge University Press, 1995).

11. Jonathan Glancey, "Modern Values," *Guardian*, Jan. 25, 1999.

12. See John Heskett, "Archaism and Modernism in Design in the Third Reich," *Block* 3, as cited in Dick Hebdige, *Hiding in the Light: On Images and Things* (New York: Routledge, 1988), 61.

13. For jokes about Soviet-era products; see e.g. http://homepage.ntlworld.com/LadaJokes.htm.

14. Manuel Castells, *End of Millennium*, Vol. 3 of *The Information Age*, 3 vols. (Malden, Mass.: Blackwell, 1998).

15. There was an apparently rueful saying among Soviet women: "After I'm dead, no one will know that I had taste." Michael Wines, "The Worker's State Is History, and Fashion Reigns," *New York Times*, 2001.

16. Tim McDaniel, *The Agony of the Russian Idea* (Princeton, N.J.: Princeton University Press, 1996), 131.

17. Martin McCauley, *Gorbachev* (London: Longman, 1998), 30.

18. See Mervyn Matthews, *Privilege in the Soviet Union* (London: Allen and Unwin, 1978), 177.

19. Celestine Bohlen, "Raisa Gorbachev, the Chic Soviet First Lady of the Glasnost Era, Is Dead at 67," *New York Times,* Sept. 21, 1999. See also Ilya Zemtsov, *The Private Life of the Soviet Elite* (New York: Crane Russak, 1985), 98.

20. Craig Calhoun, "The Radicalism of Tradition," *American Journal of Sociology* 88 (5): 1983: 886–914.

21. Pamela Sellers, "Fabric Trends Take Their Cue from the Environment," *California Apparel News,* June 26, July 1992: 206.

22. Strasser, *Satisfaction Guaranteed.*

23. Westat Inc., *Draft Final Report: Screening Survey of Industrial Subtitle D Establishments* (Rockville, Md.: Environmental Protection Agency Office of Solid Waste, 1987). I thank Samantha MacBride for referring this source to me.

24. Samantha MacBride, "Recycling Reconsidered: Producer vs. Consumer Wastes in the United States," unpublished research paper, Department of Sociology, New York University.

25. Pierre Desrochers, "Market Processes and the Closing of Industrial Loops: A Historical Reappraisal," *Journal of Industrial Ecology* 4.1 (2000).

26. Ibid.

27. Reid Lifset, "Moving from Products to Services," *Journal of Industrial Ecology* 4.1 (2000).

28. Quote from Keith Bradsher, "Is It Bold and New, or Just Tried and True?" *New York Times,* July 16, 2000, 11.

29. Chris Ryan, "Dematerializing Consumption through Service Substitution Is a Design Challenge," *Journal of Industrial Ecology* 4.1 (2000).

30. A. Bressand, C. Distler, and K. Nicolaidis, "Networks at the Heart of the Service Economy," *Strategic Trends in Services*, ed. A. Bressand and K. Nicolaidis (Grand Rapids, Mich.: Ballinger, 1989).

31. Wolfgang Sachs et al., *Greening the North: A Post-Industrial Blueprint for Ecology and Equity*, trans. Timothy Nevill (London: Zed, 1998).

32. Lance Compa and Tashia Hinchcliffe-Darricarrere, "Enforcing International Labour Rights through Corporate Codes of Conduct," *Columbia Journal of Transnational Law* 33 (1995).

33. Christopher D. Cook and A. Clay Thompson, "Silicon Hell," *Bay Guardian*, April 26, 2000.

34. Daly, *Beyond Growth: The Economics of Sustainable Development*, 42.

35. Hawken, Lovins, and Lovins, *Natural Capitalism*; William McDonough and Michael Braungart, *Cradle to Cradle: Remaking the Way We Make Things* (New York: North Point Press, 2002).

36. Sachs et al., *Greening the North: A Post-Industrial Blueprint for Ecology and Equity*.

37. Hawken, Lovins, and Lovins, *Natural Capitalism*, 113.

38. Hartmut Esslinger and Steven Skov Holt, "Integrated Strategic Design" *rana integrated strategic design magazine* 1 (1994): 52–54.

39. Daniel Becker of the Sierra Club, quoted in Danny Hakim, "The Station Wagon is Back, but Not as a Car," *New York Times*, March 19, 2002: A1, C2.

40. Hawken, Lovins, and Lovins, *Natural Capitalism*.

41. Gunnar Myrdal, *Beyond the Welfare State; Economic Planning and Its International Implications* (New Haven: Yale University Press, 1960).

42. Robert Baldwin and Martin Cave, *Understanding Regulation* (New York: Oxford University Press, 1999), 37.

43. Sachs et al., *Greening the North: A Post-Industrial Blueprint for Ecology and Equity*, 198.

44. McDonough and Braungart, 178.

45. Peter Grabosky and John Braithwaite, *Of Manners Gentle: Enforcement Strategies of Australian Business Regulatory Agencies* (Melbourne: Oxford University Press, 1986).

46. U. Hansen and I. Schoenheit, "Was Belohnen Die Konsumenten," *Absatzwirtschaft* 12 (1993), as cited in Sachs et al., *Greening the North: A Post-Industrial Blueprint for Ecology and Equity*.

47. See, for example, Papanek, *The Green Imperative*. Other related terms for variations on the idea include "materials flow accounting" (MFA), "substance flow analysis" (SFA), "life-cycle assessment (LCA), "energy analysis" and "environmentally extended input-output analysis" (IOA). For one summary, see Helias Udo de Haes et al., "Full Mode and Attribution Mode in Environmental Analysis," *Journal of Industrial Ecology* 4.1 (2000).

48. McDonough and Braungart, 174–76.

49. Percival Goodman and Paul Goodman, *Communitas: Means of Livelihood and Ways of Life* (Chicago: University of Chicago Press, 1947).

50. See John R. Logan and Harvey Luskin Molotch, *Urban Fortunes: The Political Economy of Place* (Berkeley: University of California Press, 1987). See also Peter K. Eisinger, *The Rise of the Entrepreneurial State: State and Local Economic Development Policy in the United States* (Madison: University of Wisconsin Press, 1988).

51. As a matter of law, the states of New York, Maine, Massachusetts, and Vermont follow California pollution rules.

52. United Nations Conference on Trade and Development, *Handbook of International Trade and Development Statistics*, 1994. The countries with the richest fifth of the world's peoples were responsible, in 1990, for almost 85 percent of all world trade.

53. Basalla, *The Evolution of Technology*, 202.

54. Ibid., 202.

55. Hollander, *Seeing through Clothes*.

56. Naomi Klein, *No Logo: Taking Aim at the Brand Bullies*.

57. Marshall Berman, "Walter Benjamin's Arcades Project," *Metropolis* 2000: 120.

BIBLIOGRAPHY

Aldersey-Williams, Hugh. *Nationalism and Globalism in Design*. New York: Rizzoli, 1992.

Alroy, John. "A Multispecies Overkill Simulation of the End-Pleistocene Megafaunal Mass Extinction." *Science* 292 (2001): 1893–96.

Alt, J. "Beyond Class: The Decline of Industrial Labor and Leisure." *Telos* 28 (1976): 55–80.

Altman, Dennis. *The Homosexualization of America*. New York: St. Martin's Press, 1982.

Amin, Ash, and Nigel Thrift. "Neo-Marshallian Nodes in Global Networks." *International Journal of Urban and Regional Research* 16, no. 4 (1992): 571–87.

Anderson, Jon Lee. "Oil and Blood." *New Yorker*, Aug. 14, 2000, 46–59.

Andrews, Robert, and Ron Hill. "Art and Auto Design in California." In *The Arts: A Competitive Advantage for California*, ed. Inc KPMG Marwick LLP, 67–72. Sacramento: California Arts Council, 1994.

Angier, Natalie. "Furs for Evening, but Cloth Was the Stone Age Standby." *New York Times*, Dec. 14, 1999, D1–2.

Antonelli, Paola. "Economy of Thought, Economy of Design." *Arbitare* (1994): 243–49.

Appelbaum, Richard, and Edna Bonacich. *Behind the Label*. Berkeley: University of California Press, 2000.

Appelbaum, Richard, David Smith, and Brad Christerson. "Commodity Chains and Industrial Restructuring in the Pacific Rim: Garment Trade and Manufacturing." In *Commodity Chains and Global Capitalism*, ed. Gary Gereffi and Miguel Korzeniewicz. Westport, Conn.: Greenwood, 1994.

Armi, Edson. *The Art of American Car Design*. University Park: Pennsylvania State University, 1990.

Arthur, Linda Boynton. "Clothing, Control, and Women's Agency: The Mitigation of Patriarchal Power" In *Negotiating at the Margins*, ed. Sue Fisher and Kathy Davis. New Brunswick: Rutgers University Press, 1993.

Arthur, W. Brian. "Self-Reinforcing Mechanisms in Economics." In *The Economy as an Evolving Complex System*, ed. Philip W. Anderson, Kenneth J. Arrow, and David Pines, 9–32. Redwood City, Calif.: Addison-Wesley, 1988.

Ascherson, Neal. "Any Colour You Like, So Long as It's Black . . . (Sic)." *Observer*, Jan. 24, 1999: 29.

Atkinson, J. Maxwell. *Our Masters' Voices: The Language and Body Language of Politics.* New York: Methuen, 1984.

Atlas, James. "An Interview with Richard Stern." *Chicago Review* 45, nos. 3 and 4 (1999): 23–43.

Auslander, Leora. *Taste and Power: Furnishing Modern France.* Berkeley: University of California Press, 1996.

Bagnasco, Arnaldo. *Tre Italie: La Problematica Territoriale Dello Sviluppo Italiano.* Bologna: Il mulino, 1977.

Bagwell, Sheryle. "Design: It's More Than Art, It's the Competitive Edge." *Australian Financial Review Magazine,* 1992, 8–36.

Baldwin, Robert and Martin Cave, *Understanding Regulation.* New York: Oxford University Press, 1999.

Ball, Philip. *The Self-Made Tapestry.* Oxford, England: Oxford University Press, 1998.

Banham, Reyner. *The Architecture of the Well-Tempered Environment.* London: Architectural Press, 1963.

——. *Theory and Design in the First Machine Age.* New York: Praeger, 1970.

Barrow, John D. *The Artful Universe.* Oxford, England: Oxford University Press, 1995.

Barthes, Roland. *Mythologies.* London: Vintage, 1993 (1957).

Basalla, George. *The Evolution of Technology.* New York: Cambridge University Press, 1988.

Battersby, Martin. *The Decorative Thirties.* New York: Whitney Library of Design, 1988.

Baudelaire, Charles. *The Painter of Modern Life.* Translated by Jonathan Mayne. London: Phaidon, 1970.

Baudrillard, Jean. *America.* New York: Verso, 1989.

Bauman, Zigmund. "Industrialism, Consumerism, and Power." *Theory, Culture, and Society* 1, no. 3 (1983): 32–43.

Bayley, Stephen. *Harley Earl and the Dream Machine.* New York: Knopf, 1983.

Bazerman, Charles. *The Language of Edison's Light.* Cambridge, Mass: MIT Press, 1999.

Bazett, H. C. "The Regulation of Body Temperature." In *The Physiology of Heat Regulation and the Science of Clothing*, ed. L. H. Newburgh, 109–17. New York: Stretchet Haffner, 1968.

Beamish, Thomas D. "Accumulating Trouble: Complex Organization, a Culture-of-Silence, and a Secret Spill." *Social Problems* (2000): 473–98.

Beck, Bernard. "Reflections on Art and Inactivity." CIRA Seminar Series Monograph, Culture and the Arts Workgroup. Vol. 1, 43–66. Center for Interdisciplinary Research in the Arts. Northwestern University, Evanston, Ill., 1988.

Beck, Rachel. "Logo Licensing on the Rise." *Santa Barbara News-Press* (Associated Press), May 24, 1997, D-1.

Becker, Howard S. *Art Worlds*. Berkeley: University of California Press, 1982.

Becker, Howard S. "The Power of Inertia." *Qualitative Sociology* 18 (1995): 301–10.

Bell, Daniel. *The Cultural Contradictions of Capitalism*. New York: Basic Books, 1976.

Bell, Quentin. *On Human Finery*. London: Hogarth, 1947.

Berman, Marshall. "Walter Benjamin's Arcades Project." *Metropolis,* 2000, 116–21.

Bidwell, Thomas. "Natural Resources." Paper presented at the annual meeting of the Industrial Designers Society of America (IDSA), 1995, in Santa Fe, New Mexico.

Biggart, Nicole. *Charismatic Capitalism: Direct Selling Organizations in America.* Chicago: University of Chicago Press, 1990.

Block, Fred. *The Vampire State: And Other Myths and Fallacies About the U.S. Economy.* New York: New Press, 1996.

Blumer, Herbert. "Fashion: From Class Differentiation to Collective Selection." *Sociological Quarterly* 10: 275–91.

Bogart, Michelle Helene. *Artists, Advertising, and the Borders of Art*. Chicago: University of Chicago Press, 1995.

Bohlen, Celestine. "Raisa Gorbachev, the Chic Soviet First Lady of the Glasnost Era, Is Dead at 67." *New York Times*, Sept. 21, 1999, C25.

Bono, Edward De. *Lateral Thinking: Creativity Step by Step*. New York: Perennial Library, 1990.

Bourdieu, Pierre. *The Logic of Practice*. Translated by Richard Nice. Cambridge, England: Polity, 1990.

——. *The Field of Cultural Production*. Translated by Randal Johnson. New York: Columbia University Press, 1993.

Bourgois, Philippe. *In Search of Respect: Selling Crack in the Barrio*. New York: Cambridge University Press, 1995.

Boxer, Sarah. "I Shop, Ergo I Am: The Mall as Society's Mirror." *New York Times*, March 28, 1998, 7.

Bradsher, Keith. "Is It Bold and New, or Just Tried and True?" *New York Times*, July 16, 2000, 1, 11.

Braithwaite, John, and Peter Drahos. *Global Business Regulation*. Cambridge, England: Cambridge University Press, 2000.

Brand, Stewart. *How Buildings Learn*. New York: Viking, 1994.

Brantingham, Barney. "Those High-Flyin Loughead Brothers." *Santa Barbara News Press*, Dec. 27, 1992, 2.

Braudel, Fernand. *Civilization and Capitalism, 15th–18th Century*. Translated by Sian Reynolds. London: Collins, 1981.

Bray, Francesca. *Technology and Gender.* Berkeley: University of California Press, 1997.

Brechin, Gray. *Imperial San Francisco.* Berkeley: University of California Press, 1999.

Bressand, A., C. Distler, and K. Nicolaidis. "Networks at the Heart of the Service Economy." In *Strategic Trends in Services*, ed. A. Bressand and K. Nicolaidis, 17–32. Grand Rapids, Mich.: Ballinger, 1989.

Bright, Brenda Jo. "Remappings: Los Angeles Low Riders." In *Looking High and Low*, ed. Brenda Jo Bright and Liza Bakewell, 89–123. Tucson: University of Arizona Press, 1995.

Brodkey, Harold. "Hollywood Closeup." *New Yorker*, May 3, 1992, 64–69.

Brooks, David. *Bobos in Paradise.* New York: Simon and Schuster, 2000.

Brown, Patricia. "Maya Lin: Making History on a Human Scale" *New York Times* May 21, 1998, F1.

Calhoun, Craig. "The Radicalism of Tradition." *American Journal of Sociology* 88 (5) 1983: 886–914.

Carrier, James G. *Gifts and Commodities: Exchange and Western Capitalism since 1700.* New York: Routledge, 1995.

Carter, Dori. *Beautiful Wasps Having Sex.* New York: William Morrow, 2000.

Castells, Manuel. *End of Millennium.* Vol. 3 of *The Information Age.* 3 vols. Malden, Mass.: Blackwell, 1998.

Caves, Richard. *Creative Industries: Contracts between Art and Commerce.* Cambridge, Mass.: Harvard University Press, 2000.

Cendrars, Blaise. *Hollywood: Mecca of the Movies.* Translated by Garrett White. Berkeley: University of California Press, forthcoming (1936).

Centre, Georges Pompidou. "Manifeste." Paris: Centre Pompidou, 1992.

Chandler, Alfred. *The Visible Hand: The Managerial Revolution in American Business.* Cambridge, Mass.: Harvard University Press, 1977.

Chapman, Keith. *The International Petrochemical Industry.* Cambridge, Mass.: Blackwell, 1991.

Chun, Ellery J. "Obituary." *West Hawaii Today*, June 7, 2000.

Clark, Judith. "Kinetic Beauty: The Theatre of the 1920s." In *Addressing the Century: 100 Years of Art and Fashion*, ed. Peter Wollen, 79–87. London: Hayward Gallery, 1998.

Clunas, Craig. *Superfluous Things: Material Culture and Social Status in Early Modern China.* Cambridge, England: Polity, 1992.

Codding, George. *The International Telecommunication Union.* New York: Arno, 1972.

Coen, Enrico. *The Art of Genes.* Oxford, England: Oxford University Press, 1999.

Cole, K. C. "A Career Boldly Tied by Strings."*Los Angeles Times,* Feb. 4, 1997, 1.

Commoner, Barry. *The Closing Circle; Nature, Man, and Technology.* New York: Knopf, 1971.

Compa, Lance, and Tashia Hinchcliffe-Darricarrere. "Enforcing International Labour Rights through Corporate Codes of Conduct." *Columbia Journal of Transnational Law* 33 (1995): 663–89.

Conran, Terence. *The Bed and Bath Book.* London: Mitchell Beazley, 1978.

Cook, Christopher D., and A. Clay Thompson. "Silicon Hell." *Bay Guardian*, April 26, 2000, www.sfbg.com/News/34/30/siliconhell.html.

Cooper, Emmanuel. *Ten Thousand Years of Pottery*. London: British Museum Press, 2000.

Covarrubias, Miguel. *Island of Bali*. New York: Knopf, 1937.

Crane, Diana. "Globalization, Organizational Size, and Innovation in the French Luxury Fashion Industry." *Poetics* 24 (1997): 393–414.

———. "Diffusion Models and Fashion: A Reassessment." *Annals of the American Academy of Political and Social Science* 56 November 1999, 13–24.

———. *Fashion and Its Social Agendas*. Chicago: University of Chicago Press, 2000.

Cranz, Galen. *The Chair: Rethinking Culture, Body, and Design*. New York: Norton, 1999.

Creative Industries Task Force. *Creative Industries Mapping Document*. London: UK Department for Culture, Media and Sport, 1998.

Croston, Robert. "Industrial Design Employment and Education Survey." In *Industrial Designers Society of America*, ed. Paul Nini, CD-ROM. San Diego, Calif.: Industrial Designers Society of America, 1998.

Daly, Herman. *Beyond Growth: The Economics of Sustainable Development*. Boston: Beacon, 1996.

Damasio, Antonio. *Descartes Error: Emotion, Reason, and the Human Brain*. New York: Plenum, 1994.

D'Andrede, R. "Culturally Based Reasoning." In *Cognition in Social Worlds*, ed. A. Gellatly, D. Rogers, and J. Sloboda. New York: McGraw-Hill, 1989.

Davis, Fred. *Fashion, Culture, and Identity*. Chicago: University of Chicago Press, 1992.

Davis, Mike. *City of Quartz*. New York: Verso, 1990.

———. *Ecology of Fear*. New York: Random House, 1998.

Desrochers, Pierre. "Market Processes and the Closing of Industrial Loops: A Historical Reappraisal." *Journal of Industrial Ecology* 4, no. 1 (2000): 29–44.

DeVault, Marjorie L. *Feeding the Family*. Chicago: University of Chicago Press, 1991.

Dietler, Michael, and Ingrid Herbich. "*Habitus*, Techniques, Style: An Integrated Approach to the Social Understanding of Material Culture and Boundaries." In *The Archaeology of Social Boundaries*, ed. Mirian T. Stark. Washington, DC: Smithsonian Institution Press, 1998.

Doty, Riley. "Comment on 'the Arts and Crafts Movement in California' Oakland Museum Show." *Arts and Crafts*, Aug. 27–28, 1993.

Douglas, Mary, and Baron Isherwood. *The World of Goods: Towards an Anthropology of Consumption*. 2nd ed. New York: Basic Books, 1996 (1979).

Downey, Gary Lee. *The Machine in Me*. New York: Routledge, 1998.

DuGay, Paul, Stuart Hall, Linda Janes, Hugh Mackay, and Keith Negus. *Doing Cultural Studies: The Story of the Sony Walkman*. London: Sage, 1997.

Dumaine, Brian. "Five Products U.S. Companies Design Badly." *Fortune*, Nov. 21, 1988, 130.

———. "Design That Sells and Sells And . . ." *Fortune*, March 11, 1991, 86–94.

Dunn, Ashley. "It's Alive; Well, Sort Of." *Los Angeles Times*, July 6, 1998, D1.

Eisinger, Peter K. *The Rise of the Entrepreneurial State: State and Local Economic Development Policy in the United States*. Madison: University of Wisconsin Press, 1988.

Eller, Claudia. "All the Rage; Fashion's Top Names Take on Hollywood with Agents, Deals." *Los Angeles Times*, May 29, 1998, D1.

Eller, Claudia, and James Bates. "Attack of the Killer Franchise." *Los Angeles Times* May 11, 1997, D1, D4.

Entrikin, J. Nicholas. *The Betweenness of Place: Towards a Geography of Modernity*. Baltimore: Johns Hopkins University Press, 1991.

Esslinger, Hartmut and Steven Skov Holt, "Integral Strategic Design" *rana integrated strategic design magazine* 1 (1994): 52–54.

Ewen, Stuart. *Captains of Consciousness: Advertising and the Social Roots of the Consumer Culture*. New York: McGraw-Hill, 1976.

Fainstein, Susan S. *The City Builders*. Cambridge, Mass.: Blackwell, 1994.

Farmelo, Graham, ed. *It Must Be Beautiful: Great Equations of Modern Science*. New York: Granta Books, 2002.

Fauconnier, Gilles, and Mark Turner. "Conceptual Integration Networks." *Cognitive Science* 22, no. 2 (1998): 133–87.

Feder, Barnaby. "Orthodontics Via Silicon Valley." *New York Times*, Aug. 18, 2000, C1, 6.

Ferguson, Eugene S. *Engineering and the Mind's Eye*. Cambridge: MIT Press, 1992.

Filler, Martin. "Frank Gehry and the Modern Tradition of Bentwood Furniture." In *Frank Gehry: New Bentwood Furniture Designs*, 89–108. Montreal: Montreal Museum of Decorative Arts, 1992.

——. "Ghosts in the House." *New York Review of Books*, Oct. 21, 1999, 10–13.

Findlay, John. *Magic Lands: Western Cityscapes and American Culture after 1940*. Berkeley: University of California Press, 1992.

Finegan, W. Robert. *California Furniture: The Craft and the Artistry*. Chatsworth, Calif.: Windsor, 1990.

Fischer, Claude S. *America Calling: A Social History of the Telephone to 1940*. Berkeley: University of California Press, 1992.

Flannery, Tim. *The Eternal Frontier*. New York: Atlantic Monthly Press, 2001.

Fleming, Lee. "Remaking History." *Garden Design*, September/October 1992, 34–36.

Fligstein, Neil. "The Intraorganizational Power Struggle: Rise of Finance Personnel to Top Leadership in Large Corporations 1919-1979." *American Sociological Review* 52, no. 1 (1987): 44–58.

——. *The Transformation of Corporate Control*. Cambridge, Mass.: Harvard University Press, 1990.

Ford, Henry, and Samuel Crowther. *Today and Tomorrow*. Garden City, N.Y.: Doubleday, Page, 1926.

Forty, Adrian. *Objects of Desire: Design and Society since 1750*. London: Thames and Hudson, 1992.

Freedman, Maurice. "Ritual Aspects of Chinese Kinship and Marriage." In *Family and Kinship in Chinese Society*, ed. Maurice Freedman. Stanford, Calif.: Stanford University Press, 1970.

Fried, Michael. "Art and Objecthood." In *Minimal Art: A Critical Anthology*, ed. Gregory Battcock. New York: Dutton, 1968.

Gandy, Charles, and Susan Zimmermann-Stidham. *Contemporary Classics: Furniture of the Masters*. New York: McGraw-Hill, 1981.

Gannon, Martin. *Understanding Global Cultures*. Thousand Oaks, Calif.: Sage, 2001.

Garfield, Simon. *Mauve: How One Man Invented a Color That Changed the World*. New York: W. W. Norton, 2001.

Garfinkel, Harold. *Studies in Ethnomethodology*. Englewood Cliffs, N.J.: Prentice Hall, 1967.

Gebhard, David. Introduction to *California Crazy: Roadside Vernacular Architecture*, ed. Jim Heimann and Rip Georges. San Francisco: Chronicle, 1980.

Gehry, Frank. Interview by Charlie Rose. *Charlie Rose Show*, Public Broadcasting System, 1993.

Gell, Alfred. "The Technology of Enchantment and the Enchantment of Technology." In *Anthropology, Art, and Aesthetics*, ed. J. Coote and A. Shelton, 40–67. Oxford, England: Clarendon, 1992.

——. *Art and Agency*. Oxford, England: Clarendon, 1998.

Gereffi, Gary, and Miguel Korzeniewicz, eds. *Commodity Chains and Global Capitalism*. Westport, Conn.: Greenwood, 1994.

Gerson, Bob. "Companies Come and Go but Brands Live on Forever." *TWICE (This Week in Consumer Electronics) Retailing/E-Tailing*, May 7, 2001, 18.

Giddens, Anthony. *The Constitution of Society: Outline of the Theory of Structuration*. Berkeley: University of California Press, 1984.

Gladwell, Malcolm. "The Pitchman: Ron Popeil and the Conquest of the American Kitchen." *New Yorker*, October 30, 2000, 64–73.

——. *The Tipping Point*. New York: Little Brown, 2000.

Glancey, Jonathan. "Modern Values." *Guardian*, Jan. 25, 1999, G2, 10–11.

Glennie, Paul. "Consumption within Historical Studies." In *Acknowledging Consumption*, ed. Daniel Miller, 164–203. London: Routledge, 1995.

Goffman, Erving. *Interaction Ritual; Essays in Face-to-Face Behavior*. Chicago: Aldine, 1967.

Goldman, Bruce. "Experts Foresee Desktop 'Factories' within 10 Years." *Stanford Report* 31, no. 39, (August 25, 1999): 2, 7.

Goodman, Percival, and Paul Goodman. *Communitas: Means of Livelihood and Ways of Life*. Chicago: The University of Chicago Press, 1947.

Goody, Jack. *Cooking, Cuisine, and Class*. Cambridge, England: Cambridge University Press, 1982.

Gopnik, Adam. "Diebenkorn Redux." *New Yorker*, May 24, 1993, 97–110.

Grabler, Neal. *An Empire of Their Own: How the Jews Invented Hollywood*. New York: Anchor, 1989.

Grabosky, Peter, and John Braithwaite. *Of Manners Gentle: Enforcement Strategies of Australian Business Regulatory Agencies*. Melbourne: Oxford University Press, 1986.

Graham, Nick. "Comments" presented at the annual meeting of the Industrial Designers of America (IDSA), Santa Fe, N.M., 1995.

Granovetter, Mark. "The Strength of Weak Ties." *American Journal of Sociology* 78 (1975): 1360–80.

Greene, Brian. *The Elegant Universe*. New York: Norton, 1999.

Guillen, Reynal, "The Air-Force, Missiles, and the Rise of the Los Angeles Aerospace Technopole" *Journal of the West* 36 (3): 60–66.

Greer, J., and K. Bruno. *Greenwash: The Reality behind Corporate Environmentalism*. Penang/New York: Third World Network/Apex Press, 1996.

Haes, Helias Udo de, Gjalt Huppes Reinout Heijungs, Ester van der Voet, and Jean-Paul Hettelingh. "Full Mode and Attribution Mode in Environmental Analysis." *Journal of Industrial Ecology* 4, no. 1 (2000): 45–56.

Hall, Stuart. "Notes on Deconstructing the 'Popular'" in *People's History and Socialist Theory*, ed. Raphael Samuel, 227–40. London: Routledge, 1981.

Halttunen, Karen. "From Parlor to Living Room: Domestic Space, Interior Decoration, and the Culture of Personality." In *Consuming Visions*, ed. Simon J. Bronner, 157–89. New York: Norton, 1989.

Hakim, Danny. "The Station Wagon is Back, but Not as a Car," *New York Times* March 19, 2002: A1, C2.

Hanifan, L. J. *The Community Center*. Boston: Silver, Burdette, 1920.

Hansen, U., and I. Schoenheit. "Was Belohnen Die Konsumenten." *Absatzwirtschaft* 12 (1993).

Harvey, David. *The Condition of Postmodernity: An Enquiry into the Origins of Cultural Change*. Oxford, England: Blackwell, 1989.

Hastreiter, Kim. "Design for All." *Paper*, May 2001, 102–6.

Hawken, Paul, Amory Lovins, and L. Hunter Lovins. *Natural Capitalism*. Boston: Little, Brown, 1999.

Hayden, Dolores. *Redesigning the American Dream: The Future of Housing, Work, and Family Life*. New York: Norton, 1986.

Hebdige, Dick. *Hiding in the Light*. London: Routledge, 1988.

——. *Hiding in the Light: On Images and Things*. London: Routledge, 1988.

Henderson, Kathryn. *On Line and on Paper (Inside Technology)*. Boston: MIT Press, 1998.

Heritage, John. *Garfinkel and Ethnomethodology*. New York: Polity, 1984.

Heskett, John. "Archaism and Modernism in Design in the Third Reich." *Block* (3) 1980.

Hiltzik, Michael. *Dealers of Lightning*. New York: Harper Collins, 1999.

——. "High-Tech Pioneer William Hewlett Dies." *Los Angeles Times,* Jan. 13, 2001, A1, A10.

Hines, Thomas S. *Richard Neutra and the Search for Modern Architecture*. Berkeley: University of California Press, 1994.

Hirshberg, Gerald. "Comments." In *Why Design*. San Diego, Calif.: Industrial
Designers Society of America, 1998.

Hitchcock, Alfred. "Alfred Hitchcock on His Films." *Listener*, Aug. 6, 1964, 189–90.

Hochschild, Adam. *King Leopold's Ghost*. New York: Houghton Mifflin, 1999.

Hodder, Ian. "Style as Historical Quality." In *The Uses of Style in Archaeology*, ed.
Margaret Conkey and Christine Hastorf, 44–51. Cambridge, England:
Cambridge University Press, 1990.

Hollander, Anne. *Seeing through Clothes*. New York: Penguin, 1988.

Hounshell, David. *From the American System to Mass Production 1800–1932*.
Baltimore: Johns Hopkins University Press, 1984.

Hughes, Thomas. *American Genesis: A Century of Invention and Technological
Enthusiasm, 1870–1970*. New York: Viking, 1989.

Huizinga, Johan. *Homo Ludens: A Study of the Play Element in Culture*. Boston:
Beacon, 1950.

Hutchins, Edwin. "Mental Models as an Instrument for Bounded Rationality."
Unpublished Paper, University of California, San Diego. Distributed Cognition
and HCI Laboratory, Department of Cognitive Science, 1999.

Huyler, Stephan. *From the Ocean of Painting: India's Popular Painting Traditions, 1589
to the Present*. New York: Rizzoli, 1994.

Hybs, Ivan. "Beyond the Interface" *Leonardo* 29, No. 3 (1996): 215–23.

IDSA, "Conference Registration Data." Annual Meeting, Industrial Designers
Society of America Washington, DC, 1997.

———. *IDSA Compensation Study*. Great Falls, Va.: Industrial Designers Society of
America, 1996.

Imrie, R. F. "Industrial Restructuring, Labor, and Locality: The Case of the British
Pottery Industry." *Environment and Planning A* 21 (1989): 3–26.

Jackman, Philip. "A Calculated Distribution of Phone Keys." *Globe and Mail*, July
10, 1997.

Jackson, John Brinkerhoff. *A Sense of Place, a Sense of Time*. New Haven, Conn.: Yale
University Press, 1994.

Jacobs, Jane. *The Death and Life of Great American Cities*. New York: Random House,
1961.

———. *The Nature of Economies*. New York: Random House, 2000.

Jameson, Fredric. *Postmodernism*. Durham, N.C.: Duke University Press, 1991.

Jameson, Marnell. "Fine Design at a Discount." *Los Angeles Times*, Feb. 4, 1999,
E-1.

Jung, Maureen. "The Comstocks and the California Mining Economy, 1848–1900:
The Stock Market and the Modern Corporation." PhD Dissertation, University
of California, Santa Barbara, 1988.

Kasinitz, Philip. *Caribbean New York: Black Immigrants and the Politics of Race*. Ithaca,
N.Y.: Cornell University Press, 1992.

Kaufman, Henry J. *Early American Ironware, Cast and Wrought*. Rutland, VT: C. E.
Tuttle Co. 1966.

Keightley, David. "Archaeology and Mentality: The Making of China." *Representations* 18 (spring 1987): 91–128.

Kelley, Tom, and Jonathan Littman. *The Art of Innovation: Lessons in Creativity from IDEO, America's Leading Design Firm.* New York: Currency/Doubleday, 2001.

Kern, Stephen. *The Culture of Time and Space, 1880–1918.* Cambridge, Mass.: Harvard University Press, 1983.

Kicherer, Sibylle. *Olivetti: A Study of the Corporate Management of Design.* New York: Rizzoli, 1990.

Kilborn, Peter. "Dad, What's a Clutch?" *New York Times,* May 28, 2001, A1, A8.

Kira, Alexander. *The Bathroom.* 2nd ed. New York: Viking, 1976.

Kitman, Jamie. "All Hail the Crown Victoria." *Metropolis,* May 2000, 58, 143.

Klein, Naomi. *No Logo: Taking Aim at the Brand Bullies.* New York: Picador, 2000.

Klein, Richard. *Cigarettes Are Sublime.* Durham, N.C.: Duke University Press, 1993.

Klingender, F. *Art and the Industrial Revolution.* Frogmore, St. Albans, Hertfordshire, England: Paladin, 1972 (1947).

Knight, Christopher. "Mike Kelley, at Large in Europe." *Los Angeles Times,* July 5, 1992, 70.

Kubler, George. *The Shape of Time; Remarks on the History of Things.* New Haven, Conn.: Yale University Press, 1962.

Laffitte, Bryan. "Drawing as a Natural Resource in Design." In *Natural Resources,* 41–45. Santa Fe, N.M.: Industrial Designers Society of America, 1995.

Larson, Magali Sarfatti. *Behind the Post-Modern Facade.* Berkeley: University of California Press, 1995.

Lash, Scott, and John Urry. *Economies of Signs and Space.* London: Sage, 1994.

Latour, Bruno. *Science in Action: How to Follow Scientists and Engineers through Society.* Cambridge, Mass.: Harvard University Press, 1987.

———. *Aramis or the Love of Technology.* Cambridge, Mass.: Harvard University Press, 1996.

Law, John. "Of Ships and Spices." Essay, Department of Sociology, Lancaster University, Lancaster, UK, 1984.

———. "On the Methods of Long-Distance Control: Vessels, Navigation, and the Portuguese Route to India." In *Power, Action, and Belief: A New Sociology of Knowledge?* ed. John Law, 234–63. Boston: Routledge and Kegan Paul, 1986.

Lawson, Bryan. *How Designers Think.* Cambridge, England: Cambridge University Press, 1991.

Leach, William. *Land of Desire: Merchants, Power, and the Rise of a New American Culture.* New York: Pantheon, 1993.

Lechtman, Heather. "Style in Technology: Some Early Thoughts." In *Material Culture: Style, Organization, and Dynamics of Technology,* ed. H. Lechtman and R. S. Merrill, 3–20. New York: West, 1977.

Lerner, Preston. "One for the Road." *Los Angeles Times Magazine,* Feb. 9, 1992.

Leroi-Gourhan, A. *Gesture and Speech.* Translated by Anna Berger. Cambridge: MIT Press, 1993.

Lieberson, Stanley. *A Matter of Taste: How Names, Fashions, and Culture Change.* New Haven, Conn.: Yale University Press, 2000.

Lienert, Paul. "Detroit's Western Front." *California Business,* December 1989, 37–55.

Lifset, Reid. "Moving from Products to Services." *Journal of Industrial Ecology* 4, no. 1 (2000): 1–3.

Lipovetsky, Gilles. *The Empire of Fashion: Dressing Modern Democracy.* Translated by Catherine Porter. Princeton, N.J.: Princeton University Press, 1994.

Lluscà, Josep. "Redefining the Role of Design" *Innovation* magazine. 15(3)1996: 23–27.

Logan, John R., and Harvey Luskin Molotch. *Urban Fortunes: The Political Economy of Place.* Berkeley: University of California Press, 1987.

Loos, Adolf. "Ornament and Crime." In *Programs and Manifestoes on 20th Century Architecture,* ed. Ulrich Conrads, 19–24. Cambridge: MIT Press, 1971 (1908).

Lubbock, Jules. *The Tyranny of Taste.* New Haven, Conn.: Yale University Press, 1995.

Lucie-Smith, Edward. *A History of Industrial Design.* New York: Van Nostrand, 1983.

Lundberg, Donald, E. M. Krishnamoorthy, and Mink H. Stavenga. *Tourism Economics.* New York: Wiley and Sons, 1995.

Lupton, Ellen. *Mechanical Brides: Women and Machines from Home to Office.* New York; Princeton, N.J.: Cooper-Hewitt, National Museum of Design, Smithsonian Institution; Princeton Architectural Press, 1993.

Lupton, Ellen, and J. Abbott Miller. *The Bathroom, the Kitchen, and the Aesthetics of Waste: A Process of Elimination.* New York: Kiosk, 1992.

Lynch, Deidre. "Counter Publics: Shopping and Women's Sociability." In *Romantic Sociability: Essays in British Cultural History, 1776–1832,* ed. Gillian Russell and Clara Tuite. Cambridge, England: Cambridge University Press, forthcoming.

MacAdams, Lewis. "The Blendo Manifesto." *California Magazine,* March 1984, 78–89.

MacBride, Samantha. "Recycling Reconsidered: Producer vs. Consumer Wastes in the United States, 2001." Research paper, Department of Sociology, New York University.

MacKay, Charles. *Extraordinary Popular Delusions and the Madness of Crowds.* New York: Harmony, 1980 (1841).

Martinotti, Guido. "A City for Whom?" In *The Urban Moment,* ed. Sophie Body-Gendrot and Robert Beauregard. Thousand Oaks, Calif.: Sage, 2002.

Matthews, Mervyn. *Privilege in the Soviet Union.* London: Allen and Unwin, 1978.

McCauley, Martin. *Gorbachev.* London: Longman, 1998.

McCloskey, Donald. *The Rhetoric of Economics.* Madison: University of Wisconsin Press, 1985.

McDaniel, Tim. *The Agony of the Russian Idea.* Princeton, N.J.: Princeton University Press, 1996.

McDannell, Colleen. *The Christian Home in Victorian America, 1840–1890.* Bloomington: Indiana University Press, 1986.

McDonough, William and Michael Braungart. *Cradle to Cradle: Remaking the Way We Make Things*. New York: Northpoint Press, 2002.

McGrath, Charles. "Rocking the Pond." *New Yorker*, Jan. 24, 1994.

McKendrick, Neil. "Commercialization and the Economy." In *The Birth of a Consumer Society*, ed. Neil McKendrick, John Brewer and J. H. Plumb. Bloomington: Indiana University Press, 1982.

——. Introduction to *The Birth of a Consumer Society*, ed. Neil McKendrick, John Brewer, and J. H. Plumb. Bloomington: Indiana University Press, 1982.

McMath, Robert M. "Throwing in the Towel." *American Demographics*, November 1996: 60.

McRobbie, Angela. "Second-Hand Dresses and the Role of the Ragmarket." In *Zoot Suits and Second-Hand Dresses*, ed. Angela McRobbie, 23–49. Boston: Unwin and Hyman, 1988.

——. *British Fashion Design*. London: Routledge, 1998.

McWilliams, Carey. *Southern California: An Island on the Land*. Salt Lake City: Peregrine Smith, 1973 (1946).

Meikle, Jeffrey. "From Celebrity to Anonymity: The Professionalization of American Industrial Design." In *Raymond Loewy: Pioneer of American Industrial Design*, ed. Angela Schönberger, 51–62. Berlin: Prestel, 1990.

Melikian, Souren. "Designs in Shining Armor." *International Herald Tribune*, Dec. 5–6, 1998, 9.

Miller, Daniel. *A Theory of Shopping*. Cambridge, England: Polity, 1998.

Miller, Daniel, Peter Jackson, Nigel Thrift, Beverly Holbrook, and Michael Rowlands. *Shopping, Place, and Identity*. London: Routledge, 1998.

Mills, C. Wright. "Situated Actions and Vocabularies of Motive." *American Sociological Review* 5, no. 6 (1940): 904–13.

Mintz, Sydney. "Time, Sugar, and Sweetness." *Marxist Perspectives* 2 (1979): 56–73.

Molotch, Harvey, William Freudenburg, and Krista Paulsen. "History Repeats Itself, but How? City Character, Urban Tradition, and the Accomplishment of Place." *American Sociological Review* 65 (2000): 791–823.

Monö, Rune. *Design for Product Understanding*. Stockholm: Liber, 1997.

Moore, D. Langley. *Fashion through Fashion Plates 1771–1970*. New York: C. N. Potter, 1971.

Morgan, Edmund S. "The Big American Crime." *New York Review*, Dec. 3, 1998, 14.

Morgan, Philip D. *Slave Counterpoint: Black Culture in the Eighteenth Century Chesapeake and Lowcountry*. Chapel Hill: University of North Carolina Press, 1998.

Mort, Frank. *Cultures of Consumption*. London: Routledge, 1996.

Moure, Nancy. *California Art: 450 Years of Painting and Other Media*. Los Angeles: Dustin, 1998.

Mukerji, Chandra. *From Graven Images: Patterns of Modern Materialism*. New York: Columbia University Press, 1983.

Myer, William E. "Indian Trails of the Southeast" *Forty-second Annual Report of the*

Bureau of American Ethnology. Washington, DC: Smithsonian Institution, 1924, 727–857.

Myrdal, Gunnar. *Beyond the Welfare State: Economic Planning and Its International Implications.* New Haven, Conn.: Yale University Press, 1960.

Newburgh, L. H., ed. *The Physiology of Heat Regulation and the Science of Clothing.* New York: Stretchet Haffner, 1968.

Nobel, Philip. "Can Design in America Avoid the Style Trap?" *New York Times,* Nov. 26, 2000, Sec. 2, p. 33.

Norcross, Eric. ""Evolution of the Sunbeam T-20." *Hotwire: The Newsletter of the Toaster Museum Foundation,* Charlottesville, Va.

Norman, Donald. *The Design of Everyday Things.* New York: Doubleday, 1988.

Nussbaum, Bruce. "Smart Design: Quality Is the New Style." *Business Week,* April 11, 1988, 102–8.

———. "Product Development: Designed in America." *Business Week,* n.d. 1989, 137–50.

———. "A New Golden Era of Design" Comments at the Annual Meetings of the Industrial Designers Society of America, Washington, DC, 1997.

O'Neale, Lila M. *Yurok-Karok Basket Weavers.* Berkeley: University of California Press, 1932.

Oldenburg, Ray. *The Great Good Place.* New York: Marlowe, 1989.

Owen, William. "Design for Killing: The Aesthetic of Menace Sells Guns to the Masses." *I.D. Magazine,* September/October 1996, 54–61.

Ozick, Cynthia. "The Synthetic Sublime." *New Yorker,* Feb. 22 and March 1 (combined issue), 1999, 152–59.

Papanek, Victor. *The Green Imperative.* New York: Thames and Hudson, 1995.

Patterson, Orlando. "Ecumenical America: Global Culture and the American Cosmos." *World Policy Journal* (summer 1994): 104–5.

Pendergrast, Mark. *Uncommon Grounds : The History of Coffee and How It Transformed Our World.* New York: Basic Books, 1999.

Pereira, Joseph. "Off and Running." *Wall Street Journal,* July 22, 1993, 1, 8.

Perkins, E. "The Consumer Frontier: Household Consumption in Early Kentucky." *Journal of American History* 78 (1991): 486–510.

Peters, Tom. *The Pursuit of Wow.* New York: Vintage, 1994.

Petroski, Henry. *The Evolution of Useful Things.* New York: Random House, 1992.

———. *Design Paradigms: Case Histories of Error and Judgment in Engineering.* New York: Cambridge University Press, 1994.

———. *Invention by Design: How Engineers Get from Thought to Thing.* Cambridge, Mass.: Harvard University Press, 1996.

Pevsner, Nikolaus. *Pioneers of Modern Design: From William Morris to Walter Gropius.* 2nd ed. Harmondsworth, Middlesex, England: Penguin, 1960.

Pickering, Andrew. *The Mangle of Practice: Time, Agency, and Science.* Chicago: University of Chicago Press, 1995.

Pile, John. *Dictionary of 20th-Century Design.* New York: Roundtable Press, 1990.

Piore, Michael J., and Charles F. Sabel. *The Second Industrial Divide: Possibilities for Prosperity*. New York: Basic Books, 1990.

Pitt, Leonard, and Dale P. H. *Los Angeles, A to Z*. Berkeley: University of California Press, 1997.

Pollio, Vitruvius. *Vitruvius: The Ten Books on Architecture*. Translated by Morris Hicky Morgan. New York: Dover, 1960.

Pollner, Melvin. *Mundane Reason: Reality in Everyday and Sociological Discourse*. New York: Cambridge University Press, 1987.

Porter, Charlie. "Dior Postpones Retrospective of Galliano's Work." *Guardian*, Oct. 16, 2001, 15.

Porter, Michael. *The Competitive Advantage of Nations*. New York: Free Press, 1990.

Postrel, Virginia. *The Future and Its Enemies: The Growing Conflict over Creativity, Enterprise, and Progress*. New York: Free Press, 1998.

Pound, Arthur. *The Turning Wheel; The Story of General Motors through Twenty-Five Years, 1908–1933*. Garden City, N.Y.: Doubleday, Doran, 1934.

Pratt, Andy. "New Media, the New Economy, and New Spaces" *Geoforum* 31 (2000): 425–36.

Pred, Alan. *The Spatial Dynamics of U.S. Urban-Industrial Growth*. Cambridge: MIT Press, 1966.

Rabinow, Jacob. *Inventing for Fun and Profit*. San Francisco: San Francisco Press, 1990.

Raia, Ernest. "Quality in Design." *Purchasing*, April 6, 1989, 58–65.

Redfield, Robert. *The Folk Culture of Yucatan*. Chicago: University of Chicago Press, 1941.

Redhead, David. *Products of Our Time*. London: Birkhauser, August 2000.

Reimer, Suzanne, Paul Stallard, and Deborah Leslie. "Commodity Spaces: Speculations on Gender, Identity and the Distinctive Spatialities of Home Consumption." manuscript, Dept. of Geography, University of Hull, UK, 1998.

Riegl, Alois. *Problems of Style: Foundations for a History of Ornament*. Translated by Evelyn Kain. Princeton, N.J.: Princeton University Press, 1992 (1893).

Robertson, A. F. *Life Like Dolls: The Natural History of a Commodity*, New York: Routledge, 2003.

Robins, Kevin. "Tradition and Translation: National Culture in Its Global Context." In *Enterprise and Heritage*, ed. John Corner and Sylvia Harvey. London: Routledge, 1990.

Rothstein, Edward. *Emblems of Mind*. New York: Avon, 1996.

——. "Recurring Patterns, the Sinews of Nature." *New York Times*, Oct. 9, 1999, A15.

Rubinstein, Ruth. *Dress Codes*. Boulder, Colo.: Westview, 1995.

Ryan, Chris. "Dematerializing Consumption through Service Substitution Is a Design Challenge." *Journal of Industrial Ecology* 4, no. 1 (2000): 3–6.

Rybczynski, Witold. *Home: A Short History of an Idea*. New York: Penguin, 1986.

Sachs, Wolfgang, Reinhard Loske, Manfred Linz, with Ralf Behrensmeier et al. *Greening the North: A Post-Industrial Blueprint for Ecology and Equity*. Translated by Timothy Nevill. London: Zed, 1998.

Sack, Robert. *Place, Modernity, and the Consumer's World.* Baltimore: Johns Hopkins University Press, 1992.

Sackett, James R. "Style and Ethnicity in Archaeology." in *The Uses of Style in Archaeology,* ed. Margaret W. Conkey and Christine Hastorf, 32–43. Cambridge, England: Cambridge University Press, 1990.

Saferstein, Barry. "Collective Cognition and Collaborative Work: The Effects of Cognitive and Communicative Processes on the Organization of Television Production." *Discourse and Society* 3, no. 1 (1992): 61–86.

Said, Edward. *Culture and Imperialism.* London: Chatto and Windus, 1993.

Sassen, Saskia. *The Mobility of Capital and Labor.* New York: Cambridge University Press, 1988.

——. *The Global City.* New York: Princeton University Press, 1991.

Saxenian, AnnaLee. *Regional Advantage: Culture and Competition in Silicon Valley and Route 128.* Cambridge, Mass.: Harvard University Press, 1994.

Schudson, Michael. *Advertising, the Uneasy Persuasion.* New York: Basic Books, 1986.

Schwartz, Michael, and Frank Romo. *The Rise and Fall of Detroit.* Berkeley: University of California Press, forthcoming.

Scott, Allen. "The US Recorded Music Industry." *Environment and Planning A* 31 (1999): 1965–84.

——. "French Cinema." *Theory, Culture and Society* 17, no. 1 (2000): 1–37.

——. *Technopolis: The Geography of High Technology in Southern California.* Berkeley: University of California Press, 1993.

Sellers, Pamela. "Fabric Trends Take Their Cue from the Environment." *California Apparel News,* June 26, July 1992, 1, 5.

Semper, Gottfried. *Der Stil in Den Technischen Und Tektonischen Kunsten, Oder Praktische Asthetik: Ein Handbuch Fur Techniker, Kunstler Und Kunstfreunde.* Mittenwald: Maander, 1977.

Sennett, Richard. *The Conscience of the Eye.* New York: Alfred Knopf, 1990.

——. "The Art of Making Cities." "Comments" presented at the Annual Meeting of the Research Committee on the Sociology of Regional and Urban Development, International Sociological Association, 2000, in Amsterdam, The Netherlands.

Shields, R. "Social Spatialisation and the Built Environment: The West Edmonton Mall." *Environment and Planning D: Society and Space* 7 (1989): 147–64.

Simmel, Georg. "Fashion." *American Journal of Sociology* 62 (1957 [1904]): 541–58.

Smith, Cyril Stanley. "Art, Technology, and Science: Notes on Their Historical Interaction." In *Perspectives in the History of Science and Technology,* ed. Duane H. D. Roller, 129–65. Norman: University of Oklahoma Press, 1971.

——. *A Search for Structure: Selected Essays on Science, Art, and History.* Cambridge: MIT Press, 1981.

Smith, Terry. *Making the Modern: Industry, Art, and Design in America.* Chicago: University of Chicago Press, 1993.

Snodin, Michael. *Ornament: A Social History since 1450*. New Haven, Conn.: Yale University Press, 1996.

Soja, Edward. *Postmodern Geographies*. New York: Verso, 1989.

Sparke, Penny, Felice Hodges, Anne Stone, and Emma Dent Coad. *Design Source Book*. Secaucus, N.J.: Chartwell, QED, 1986.

Stagl, Justin. *A History of Curiosity: The Theory of Travel, 1550–1800*. Chur, Switzerland: Harwood, 1995.

Starck, Miriam. "Technical Choices and Social Boundaries in Material Culture Patterning: An Introduction." In *The Archaeology of Social Boundaries*, ed. Miriam Starck, 1–11. Washington, DC: Smithsonian Institution Press, 1998.

Steele, Thomas. *The Hawaiian Shirt: Its Art and History*. New York: Abbeville, 1984.

Steele, Valerie. *Paris Fashion*. New York: Oxford University Press, 1988.

Stewart, Doug. "Eames: The Best Seat in the House." *Smithsonian*, May 1999, 78–86.

Storper, Michael. *The Regional World*. New York: Guilford, 1997.

Strasser, Susan. *Satisfaction Guaranteed: The Making of the American Mass Market*. New York: Pantheon, 1989.

——. *Waste and Want: A Social History of Trash*. New York: Henry Holt, 1999.

Street-Porter, Tim. *Freestyle: The New Architecture and Interior Design from Los Angeles*. New York: Stewart, Tabori, and Chang, 1986.

Surowiecki, James. "Farewell to Mr. Fix-It." *New Yorker*, March 5, 2001, 41.

Szostak, Rick. *Econ-Art*. London: Pluto, 1999.

Taylor, Alex, III. "U.S. Cars Come Back." *Fortune*, Nov. 16, 1992, 52–85.

Thornburg, Barbara. " Sitting on Top of the World." *Los Angeles Times Magazine*, Oct. 11, 1992, 42–50.

Tomkins, Calvin. "The Maverick." *New Yorker*, July 7, 1997, 38–45.

Torres, Vicki. "Bold Fashion Statement: Amid Aerospace Decline, L.A. Garment Industry Emerges as a Regional Economic Force." *Los Angeles Times*, March 12, 1995, D-1.

Toussaint-Samat, Maguelonne. *Histoire technique et morale du vêtement*. Paris: Verdas, 1990.

Tuan, Yi-Fu. "The Significance of the Artifact." *Geographical Review* 70 (1980): 462–72.

United Nations Conference on Trade and Development, *Handbook of International Trade and Development Statistics*. New York: United Nations, 1994.

Underhill, Paco. *Why We Buy: The Science of Shopping*. New York: Simon and Schuster, 1999.

Vanka, Surya. "The Cross-Cultural Meanings of Color." In *Proceedings of the Annual Meetings of the Industrial Designers Society of America*, ed. Paul Nini. San Diego, Calif.: Industrial Designers Society of America, 1998.

Varnedoe, Kirk, and Adam Gopnik. *High and Low*. New York: Museum of Modern Art, 1991.

Veblen, Thorstein. *The Theory of the Leisure Class: An Economic Study of Institutions.* New York: Modern Library, 1934.

Vitjoen, Adrienne. "South Africa/Conscience Raising" *Innovation,* Fall, 1996: 20–22.

Walkowitz, Judith. "Going Public: Shopping, Street Harassment, and Streetwalking in Late Victorian London." *Representations* 62 (spring 1998): 1–30.

Warner, Kee, and Harvey Molotch. "Information in the Marketplace: Media Explanations of the '87 Crash." *Social Problems* 40, no. 2 (May 1993): 167–88.

Westat, Inc. *Draft Final Report: Screening Survey of Industrial Subtitle D Establishments.* Rockville, Md. Environmental Protection Agency Office of Solid Waste, 1987.

Wilkerson, Isabel. "The Man Who Put Steam in Your Iron." *New York Times,* July 11, 1991, 1, 6.

Williams, Raymond. *The Country and the City.* New York: Oxford University Press, 1973.

Williams, Rosalind H. *Dream Worlds: Mass Consumption in Late Nineteenth-Century France.* Berkeley: University of California Press, 1982.

Willis, Paul. "The Motorcycle within the Subcultural Group." *Working Papers in Cultural Studies, University of Birmingham,* no. 2, n.d.

Wilson, Elizabeth. "Fashion and the Postmodern Body." In *Chic Thrills: A Fashion Reader,* ed. Juliet Ash and Elizabeth Wilson, 3–16. Berkeley: University of California Press, 1993.

Wilson, Jay. "U.S. Companies May Be Resting on Dead Laurels." *Marketing News,* Nov. 6, 1989, 21.

Wines, Michael. "The Worker's State Is History, and Fashion Reigns." *New York Times* Nov. 6, 2001, A4.

Wolfe, Tom. *From Bauhaus to Our House.* London: Johnathan Cape, 1982.

Wollen, Peter, ed. *Addressing the Century.* London: Hayward Gallery, 1998.

Woodruff, David, and Elizabeth Lesley. "Surge at Chrysler." *Business Week,* Nov. 9, 1992, 88–96.

Woodyard, Chris. "Surf Wear in Danger of Being Swept Aside by Slouchy, Streetwise Look." *Los Angeles Times,* June 21, 1992, 3.

Yang, Jerry. ""Turn on, Type in and Drop Out." *Forbes ASAP,* Dec. 1, 1997, 51.

Young, Agnes Brooks. *Recurring Cycles of Fashion, 1760–1937.* New York: Harper and Brothers, 1937.

Zacher, Mark, and Brent A. Sutton. *Governing Global Networks: International Regimes for Transportation and Communications.* Cambridge, England: Cambridge University Press, 1996.

Zeisel, Eva. "Acceptance Speech." Read at the annual meeting of the Industrial Design Society of America. Washington, DC, 1997.

——. "The Magic Language of Design." Paper, 2001.

Zelizer, Viviana A. Rotman. *The Social Meaning of Money.* New York: Basic Books, 1994.

Zemtsov, Ilya. *The Private Life of the Soviet Elite*. New York: Crane Russak, 1985.

Zimmerman, Don. "The Practicalities of Rule Use." In *Understanding Everyday Life; Toward the Reconstruction of Sociological Knowledge*, ed. Jack D. Douglas. Chicago: Aldine, 1970.

Zuboff, Shoshana. *In the Age of the Smart Machine*. New York: Basic Books, 1989.

Zukin, Sharon. *The Cultures of Cities*. Cambridge, Mass.: Blackwell, 1995.

INDEX